TRIATHLON ADVENTURES ACROSS AMERICA

Swimming, Biking, Running, and Making Memories Together

TRIATHLON
ADVENTURES
ACROSS AMERICA

Swimming, Biking, Running,
and Making Memories Together

TERRY VANDERWERT

For information about this title or to order additional books
and/or electronic media, contact the publisher:

Terry VanderWert
1084 Ruby Road
The Villages, Florida 32162
SeniorTriathletes.com
seniortriathletes@gmail.com

Cover and interior design by The Book Cover Whisperer:
OpenBookDesign.biz

979-8-9911324-0-4 Paperback
979-8-9911324-2-8 Hardcover
979-8-9911324-1-1 eBook

Printed in the United States of America

FIRST EDITION

To Joy, MY WIFE AND PARTNER IN LIFE AND ADVENTURE. There's no one else with whom I would rather have shared this incredible journey, and no one else who could have supported me so completely. Remaining faithful to your mantra, "Everything, all the time," you embraced every challenge and opportunity. Your unwavering spirit reminds me that no matter what life throws at us, there's always something new to discover and embrace. I hope this book inspires others to do the same with their own adventures.

"She is clothed with strength and dignity, and she laughs without fear of the future."
— *Proverbs 31:25, New Living Translation*

CONTENTS

Preface

I never imagined writing a book, especially one about triathlon. Neither did I expect to write one about my travels with Joy across America through the sport. This changed in June 2023.

On the previous Saturday, I had completed a triathlon in my fiftieth state. Joy and I were staying at our daughter's house, away from our usual routines and schedule. With the extra time, I cracked open *AWOL on the Appalachian*, a book loaned to me by a friend a couple of months earlier. I found it difficult to set down.

This man's story inspired me. It paralleled ours in the physical challenges he faced, the unique places he visited, and the interesting people he met. I realized the value of sharing the triathlon-related experiences of empty-nesters like Joy and me with others who might also enjoy a new adventure.

Over twelve years, Joy and I spent time in each of the fifty states, both at popular tourist spots and in everyday places with regular people, including family and friends. Some of these people shared my love for swimming, biking, and running. Some thought I was a bit crazy; still, through our travels, we gained a new perspective on the real America.

After discussing the idea of this book with friends, family, and members of the Senior Triathletes community, I started writing. As in my first days with triathlon, I climbed a steep learning curve; but, as with triathlon, the adventure of writing our story was rewarding. Reliving our many wonderful experiences produced lots of smiles, a few belly laughs, and more than one lump in my throat.

About This Book

Through our experiences, you will learn about triathlon training and racing.

I chose to self-coach. At first, this was because I didn't think coaches were appropriate for an average triathlete like me. Plus, I enjoyed learning about and testing a wide range of training methods. I have woven these lessons about triathlon training and racing into this story.

Even after I learned how coaches benefit amateur triathletes, I couldn't bring myself to spend money on a coach. While I wanted to finish with respectable times, winning wasn't my top priority.

You will also learn about the many types of triathlons and multisport races. Even within the sprint distance in which I competed, the races varied in size, ranging from local events aimed at raising money for local causes to national championships. The swim, bike, and run courses for these races differed as much as the people and landscapes throughout this country.

Seeing the range of challenges a triathlon can throw at us, someone planning to do their first triathlon will learn the questions to ask in order to prepare. The differences between triathlons may help you choose a race that best fits your training, skills, and comfort level.

For me, each triathlon provided at least one unique experience. I called these "race firsts" in my journal. In many triathlons, I had more than one first-time experience. If you are a first-time or novice triathlete, you can learn from my experiences. If you are more experienced, you may remember the first time you faced a similar situation.

Triathlon has its own language, with special words, acronyms, and abbreviations. Reading the language of triathlon is another way to learn about the sport. I have included a glossary near the back of the book for this purpose.

Still, the language used to describe a triathlon differs between races. For example, "transition" is sometimes used as a noun to describe what other race directors call the "transition area." To economize on words, I have used the shorter version most often.

Family and friends of triathletes will see ways to take part in the sport without ever racing. Volunteering at a triathlon is one way to do this.

Triathlons rely on volunteers, from check-in to beyond the finish line. Joy often volunteered at my races; the T-shirts hanging in her closet are proof. From our story, you will learn about a wide range of potential volunteer assignments: some you might enjoy, and others you may want to avoid.

With that said, this book goes beyond the subject of triathlon. By my early fifties, I had been in each of the fifty states… but not really. My one visit to Delaware was by train between

Baltimore and Philadelphia during a business trip. I never set foot in the state. Similarly, I have seen Alaska several times, but before doing a triathlon there, each time was from the Anchorage airport while waiting for my Asia-bound aircraft to refuel. I have visited many states for business, yet for some, I never strayed far from the road connecting the airport and the company I was visiting—until we experienced it during our triathlon adventure.

Without question, however, Joy and I have now experienced parts of every state in America. Therefore, while this book is not a travelogue, you will learn a lot about the United States.

Throughout our fifty years of marriage, Joy and I have always enjoyed traveling together. Well, maybe not all the time. Travel could sometimes become tense when our competing navigation apps wanted us to go in different directions. This also happened when my GPS tried to take us somewhere Joy thought it made no sense to go according to her reading of a map.

Over the course of our triathlon journey, we lived in three states, each in a different region of the country. Our travels between these homes and triathlons covered much of the country, and we visited some areas multiple times.

While you may find descriptions of parts of America you have visited, I am sure you will find others you never knew existed. We saw amazing landscapes and met interesting people everywhere we went. Hopefully, this book will encourage you to experience the diversity of God's creation and the interesting things humans have done and continue to do while watching over it.

Joy and I often combined triathlon travel with visits to family or friends, several of whom passed away during my twelve years in the sport. An unexpected highlight of this adventure was the additional time we were able to spend with them.

We enjoyed introducing others to triathlon and being with the energetic, fun-loving people of all ages who shared our love for the sport. Sharing the adventure with family and friends made the trips even more meaningful.

How I Collected Information for This Book

Even as a child, I always enjoyed journaling. During one Christmas vacation in the 1960s, my family took a trip from Minnesota to Georgia and Florida; as a preteen, I wrote of our travels. My aunt still clings to the only remaining copy of this report.

Before finishing my first triathlon, I created two documents. One was a Word document entitled "Diary of a Late Middle-Aged Triathlete." This journal contains notes on our travel and race experiences, the people we met, and the lessons Joy and I learned from each event. The second document was an Excel spreadsheet with at least one tab for each triathlon. The spreadsheet included details specific to the race: the date I registered, the cost to register, the swim/bike/run distances, and my times for each of the three legs and the two transitions. For many, but not all, I included screenshots of the swim, bike, and run courses, the race logo, the email confirming my registration, correspondence with the race director, and the rank of my finish compared to those in my age group, my gender, and overall.

I used the Word document through the trip that ended after the triathlon in Washington, State number 26. Beyond this, I recorded the same information in posts on SeniorTriathletes. com, which I started in 2016. I used the Excel spreadsheet throughout the triathlons in all fifty states.

I also saved many of the athlete guides sent by race directors before the triathlon. Most of these documents included maps of the swim, bike, and run courses. Some included details of the swim waves. A few included information useful for triathlon racing.

Writing for a Global Community

Through SeniorTriathletes.com, I have experienced the global appeal of triathlon. My friends include older athletes from around the world who share my interest in the sport. I am writing for all of you, not just my American colleagues.

Standard triathlon distances exist. Still, these often seem like guidelines, especially for local events. For some races, the published distances of the triathlon's three legs mix imperial and metric units—something that would have caused Mrs. Wyman, my favorite high school English teacher, to have picked up her red pen and begun correcting.

I have included the distances of the three triathlon legs published by the race director, with an equivalent in the alternate unit system in parentheses. You will see how much the Sprint triathlon differs between events.

For simplicity, I have included temperatures in degrees Fahrenheit. If you are more familiar with Celsius, just remember the following: For temperatures in the 40s or 50s, it felt cold, at least to me. Temperatures in the 60s or 70s felt cool, yet comfortable. When the temperature was in the 80s or above, I felt hot while racing.

Joy and I hope our adventure inspires you to go on one of your own, either through triathlon or your favorite activity. Maybe it's hiking to hidden waterfalls, kayaking in rivers and lakes, or running a 5k in every state. No matter which activity is right for you, you can benefit from our experience.

TERRY VANDERWERT

"I press on to reach the end of the race and receive the heavenly prize for which God, through Christ Jesus, is calling us."
— *Philippians 3:14, New Living Translation*

2011:
BEGINNING THE ADVENTURE

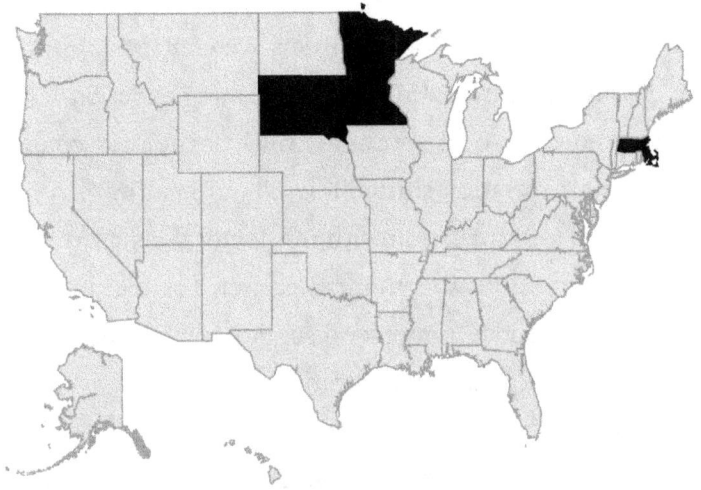

States colored black represent those in which I
completed a triathlon during my first year.

Saturday, September 25, 2010. Six of us—Joy and I, along with our son Ben, and our friends, Jim and Pat Philipsek, with their son Jeff—had spent the day fishing on Cape Cod. Dinner at our house in Chicopee, Massachusetts, that evening included grilled bluefish from our day's catch.

During this time, I was president of an industrial laser and laser machine manufacturing company. The company owned two plants in the United States: one plant in Champlin, a suburb of Minneapolis, Minnesota, and a second in Chicopee, Massachusetts, right beside Springfield. I split my time between the two, traveling both internationally and domestically for the business.

After my first year in this position, Joy and I purchased a house near the Chicopee plant. During most of my time there, Joy joined me, caring for the house and socializing with her Chicopee friends.

Following dinner that Saturday, we chatted around the table on our backyard patio about our fishing experience while relaxing under the cool autumn sky. Over the next couple of hours, our conversation shifted toward our health.

I recalled a conversation with my doctor during my annual physical exam about five months earlier. He had expressed concern with trends in my blood sugar and cholesterol. I was already on blood pressure medication.

The doctor's words echoed in my mind: "These results are nothing that losing 20 pounds won't fix." I realized my face was rounder. My pants were also tighter. However, these facts weren't motivation enough for me to make exercise part of my routine. Neither were they sufficient for me to give up the sweet and salty snacks with which I often rounded out my day.

At first, my doctor's remark caused me to think about losing weight. Of course, I would drop some pounds if I exercised more. I could add to the swimming, biking, and running in which I sometimes engaged, and since I was a Minnesota State High School League certified basketball referee, I thought I might start working some games.

After six months, the only thing that changed was my weight. It had increased. Still, I rarely exercised. There was always tomorrow. Besides, I had time; my next doctor's visit was six months or more away.

Jim's next words that evening would change my life. He told me about the Buffalo, Minnesota triathlon and said we should "do it together next summer."

At that time, my knowledge of triathlon came from glimpses on television of the iconic Ironman World Championships in Hawaii. However, Jim's description of the triathlon in Buffalo intrigued me: a quarter-mile swim, a 12-mile bike ride, and a 5k run.

This seemed doable. I did some swimming, biking, and running. A few years earlier, I had finished a 5k race. All I needed to do was combine the three sports. Winning wouldn't be my priority; my goal was to exercise more often. Plus, the idea of trying something new sounded interesting.

A few days later, I told our daughter, Liza, that I was thinking of doing a triathlon. Without hesitation, she said we should do the Buffalo Triathlon together, as a father-daughter adventure. Secretly, I missed our tradition of Saturday morning breakfasts during her childhood, usually at Pannekoeken Huis. With both of Liza's children now in school, she, too, was ready for a new adventure. It thrilled me to be a part of it.

Then, in December, Joy signed us up for a membership at LA Fitness, which had facilities near our homes in both Minnesota and Massachusetts. Joy knew that the membership would help me both lose weight and prepare for this triathlon. As a stay-at-home mom who, by her own admission, battled weight, Joy had maintained fitness-center memberships for over 30 years, experiencing the value of step aerobics, spinning classes, water aerobics, interval training, and strength training.

She was strong, fit, and full of energy. Her hard work had even led to her achieving the Member of the Month award in April 2005 at the Northwest Athletic Club (now called Life Time) in Maple Grove, Minnesota.

I was out of excuses. My daughter would hold me accountable for my training, and vice-versa; and the Buffalo Triathlon would take place near my home. So, on December 31, 2010, before the race registration's next price increase, Liza and I committed to the Buffalo Triathlon for the following June.

Before I had even completed my first triathlon, Joy convinced me to register for the Maple Grove Sprint triathlon in August. However, I had to finish the one in Buffalo first.

• • • •

MINNESOTA: STATE #1

Minnesota Nickname:
The North Star State

Left to right, before the 2011 Buffalo Triathlon: Jeff Philipsek,
me, my daughter Liza, and Jim Philipsek.

Minnesota Triathlon Details

- Date: June 5, 2011
- Triathlon: 8th Buffalo Triathlon
- Location: Sturges Park, Buffalo, Minnesota

Published distances
- Swim: 0.25 miles (402 meters)
- Bike: 13.3 miles (21.4 kilometers)
- Run: 3.1 miles (5 kilometers)

After registering for this triathlon, I realized how little I knew about preparing for one. Nevertheless, I relished the challenge. I read triathlon-related articles in my spare time. I swam, biked, ran, and did various body weight and core-strengthening exercises six days per week.

From her experience with spinning classes, Joy convinced me to try it for my bike training during the winter months. I gave in, despite my preconceived idea that spinning was "for girls." Once again, I was mistaken. The "girl" who led my 5:30 a.m. classes left me exhausted in the wake of her sprints, climbs, intervals, and endurance segments. I was sweating so much in that hour that I learned to cover the floor around my stationary bike with two to three layers of paper towels to avoid creating a pond beneath me. Not surprisingly, this seemed to keep the bikes around my own unoccupied. Soon, my endurance increased. I began to jog for 10, then 20 minutes after spin class. Rather than the 10 laps I could initially swim in the pool, I now routinely swam 35 or 40 laps without stopping.

Still, after six months of training in swimming, biking, and running, I was not sure I would be able to put everything from my training together to finish the triathlon. So, two weeks before Buffalo, Liza and I did a practice race near our home on Fish Lake in Maple Grove, Minnesota. After completing the course, which was based on the distances of the Buffalo Triathlon, we felt confident we could finish the real one.

Liza made a case for setting a time goal for completion of the race, while I was happy with "just finishing it." After some negotiation, we agreed on a goal of one hour, forty-five minutes. This seemed reasonable after our practice triathlon.

The Tuesday before the event, the race director scheduled an evening practice swim for beginners and those curious about the swim course. By joining the practice swim, we were able to eliminate yet another unknown. Besides, it gave us another chance to swim in one of Minnesota's 10,000 lakes.

The water temperature was in the mid to upper 60s—not surprising since the ice had melted from the lake only a month and a half earlier. In addition to the challenge of the cold water, the wind whipped up waves that forced the race director to cut the practice swim short.

Still, I felt ready. I had trained for swimming in water of this temperature in the lake behind our house, using my triathlon suit and a rash guard swimming shirt. I had the option to rent a wetsuit from a local business with staff on site that evening. Many who had participated in the practice swim rented one of their wetsuits.

Late Friday afternoon, the day before the race, Joy, Liza, and I drove the thirty miles to Gold's Gym in Buffalo to pick up our race T-shirt, timing chip and strap, and race numbers for the bike and run. The packet also included trial-sized packets of gel.

Soon after returning home for the evening, Marilyn Senart, a family friend who would join us the following day, arrived. Liza and I gathered everything we would be taking to our first triathlon. We planned to leave for Buffalo at 5 a.m.

The next morning, Joy, Marilyn, Liza, and I left on schedule. Our two bikes hung on the bike rack attached to the back of our white Chrysler van. As the sun rose during our drive, thousands of acres of rich black earth, lined with rows of corn and soybeans typical of early June, came into view.

We arrived at Sturges Park two hours before the start of the triathlon, in time for the opening of transition at 6 a.m. Leaving behind the muted, sometimes nervous conversation of our drive, we entered the park, now energized by music of Bruce Springsteen, Metallica, AC/DC, and similar bands pumping through a network of tripod-mounted speakers around the registration and transition areas.

Our friends Jim, Pat, and Jeff Philipsek arrived as Liza and I prepared to set up our transition spaces. Jim and Jeff were also competing in the Sprint triathlon, as they had promised last fall. Meanwhile, Liza's husband Scott, son Alex, daughter Kate, and mother-in-law Diana appeared in time to offer some last-minute encouragement.

First held in 2004, the Buffalo Triathlon had become the most popular early season triathlon near the Twin Cities of Minneapolis and St. Paul. Minnesotans were eager to swim, bike, and run outside after the long winter.

With 883 of us set to do the Sprint distance triathlon and over 600 more waiting to do the Olympic distance triathlon, the place felt like a whirlwind that only grew stronger over the course of the morning. Excitement continued to build, in part through a little nervousness about the unknowns we would be facing today. Still, a certain amount of naivete about this triathlon kept my nerves in check.

After checking in, Liza and I went for body marking. For

this, a first for us newbies, a race volunteer used a black marker to write our race number on our left arm, below the shoulder, and our swim wave number on the top of our right hand. They finished body marking by writing our age on our right calf.

We then separated to find our places in transition. For this triathlon, the race staff assigned our spaces by age group. I was given a transition space next to other men ages 55 to 59.

I hung the front of my bike seat on the section of the rack containing my race number. The bike rack was comprised of a sturdy horizontal pole supported by two angled poles at each end, forming a stable A-frame structure. The kickstand on my bike, a feature not found on most bikes at a triathlon, would have made racking my bike unnecessary; but with the bike racked, I could get at the rest of the stuff in my transition space more easily.

Through our reading and practice triathlon, Liza and I had collected the items we wanted to have in our transition areas. Next to my bike lay a green and white striped towel from Joy's Aunt Dee Nelson, folded in half lengthwise and laid out on the ground beside the front wheel of my bike. This green and white square space included everything I would not be taking with me on the swim. This included my running shoes, which I used for both the bike and run. I laid out a pair of sunglasses and a sweat band for the bike leg.

A tan plastic washbasin filled halfway with lake water sat at the front edge of the towel. I would use the water to wash my feet after crossing the sand and grass between the lake and transition. Of course, a second, smaller hand towel sat beside the basin. I would use this to dry my feet before putting on socks and then slipping into my size 13 running shoes.

My shoes used elastic no-tie laces, so at least I wouldn't waste time tying them. The last items on the towel were an extra bottle of Gatorade and a zip lock bag containing a couple of handfuls of gummy bears. I had read somewhere that these sugary treats would top off my fuel supply after the swim.

With everything in its place, I soaked in the sights and sounds leading up to the race. I saw an impressive number of expensive-looking bikes and some strange-looking tear-drop-shaped bike helmets. I eavesdropped on one of the competitors from my age group telling another about the new swimming technique he would be using today.

Fifteen minutes before the pre-race meeting that would lead to the race's start, I went into Buffalo Lake for a short practice swim. This took care of the shock of entering the sub-70-degree water.

Before we knew it, the race was underway. I watched as wave after wave of swimmers took off. Stories on triathlon websites describe the pandemonium that often accompanies 50 swimmers starting together. I had experienced a small taste of this chaos during the practice swim in Buffalo Lake a few days earlier.

What I saw was as expected. I was prepared for contact during the triathlon swim, though I had not been looking forward to it.

Since I started near the edge of the group, I swam my

first strokes unobstructed. This was happening…I was doing a triathlon! *Thank you, Lord,* I thought.

A minute later, my euphoria came to an abrupt end. As my right arm reached forward during a swim stroke, I felt my hand contact something solid. Immediately, the tongue-lashing from the female I'd inadvertently hit began. Apparently, I should have watched where I was going while she and her friend treaded water along the main traffic lane of the course.

The damage had been done. "Sorry", I said as I continued to swim. Still, I wondered why they had stopped to rest in that precise spot. Why hadn't they moved to the side out of courtesy to others?

After completing the swim, I took my sweet time getting from the swim exit to transition. I reached it in time to see a now serious-looking Jim leaving transition with his road bike. He seemed to ignore me as I tried to make light conversation. This wasn't the lighthearted and talkative Jim I knew.

I sat down on the ground, washed each blade of grass and speck of dirt off my feet, put on my socks and shoes, and ate a few gummy snacks. Only now did I feel ready to walk my bike to the place where I could climb onto it and start the bike leg.

As I was making my way to the bike mount line, I realized other racers were proceeding with a much greater sense of urgency than I was. I felt like I was blocking them.

Eventually, I got on my bicycle, now facing a steep hill. Failing to notice the hill before the race, I had left my bike in a high gear, which made the ride out of the park more difficult than necessary. Already, I had learned a couple of important lessons about racing in a triathlon.

I got up the hill and onto the main part of the bike course more slowly than if I had started in a lower gear. I had written the words *pull up* with black marker on my handlebars to remind myself to use the toe cage on my pedals to both pull up and push down during each stroke.

The ride continued south of Buffalo on roads that covered rolling hills, which in turn separated more fields of corn and soybeans sprouting their new growth. Only a few cars and trucks joined us on the course.

My Giant hybrid bicycle sped along the course faster than it had on any of the training rides near my home over the preceding two months. After the race, I learned I had ridden the course at an average speed of over 17 miles per hour. Before today, I had considered averaging 15 miles per hour an accomplishment.

Still, I couldn't believe my eyes as the other bikers zoomed past me. My legs pedaled as fast as they could, especially riding downhill. Compared to others riding hunched over on their bikes, though, my pace looked more like a leisurely stroll with Joy. Something besides the rider was making the difference between our bikes.

For a few minutes near the middle of the course, I rode alongside a teenage girl the age of one of our granddaughters. As we exchanged a few words, I learned that she was also doing her first triathlon.

After the race, I found out that riding beside another biker, other than to pass them, violated the non-drafting rule for this triathlon. Had one of the race officials spotted me, they would have charged me with a drafting violation and added two minutes to my time as a penalty. I was losing count of the number of lessons from this single triathlon.

After returning my bike to its transition space, I headed out on the run course, a flat, paved trail following the shore of Buffalo Lake. The trail headed north toward downtown Buffalo, then, before reaching it, rounded to head west.

I had often run after biking during my training. Today's run proved to be more difficult than I expected. Near the one-mile mark, I slowed to a walk, feet dragging as I continued, bent forward, hands on my waist, to catch my breath. Everything in my body, from my eyes and mouth to my feet, felt heavy. I felt humiliated. From that point until the end of the race, I mixed running and walking. Maybe the effort to maintain a higher speed during the bike leg had taxed my running muscles.

We continued on the paved running trail as it followed the lake shore, turning around at the halfway point to return on the same trail to Sturges Park and the finish line. Now, on the second half of the run, I spotted Liza coming toward the turnaround, her face illuminated with a smile. As we met, we exchanged greetings. Liza's was "Go, Dad!"

I pushed myself to run through the section where Joy and our son-in-law and grandchildren were sitting. As I passed the cheering group, I gave my six-year-old grandson Alex a high-five. I couldn't help but smile after hearing him remark to Joy as I passed, "Boy, is he sweaty."

Not only did Liza and I finish the race, but we both finished in well under the one hour, 45-minute goal. I returned to Earth when I saw the times of others in my age group, including Jim's. My place was 16th of the 20 within my age group.

To endure the most boring treadmill run training, I often listened to audiobooks. One described George Plimpton, a journalist who took part in professional sports such as football, baseball, and boxing so he could better write about the athlete's life. After seeing my results, I imagined how George Plimpton must have felt.

I knew enough about triathlon to finish my first one. I could call myself a triathlete, yet I wasn't the athlete I imagined. Still, tests from my physical exam three months earlier had shown marked improvement in my health metrics.

Joy and I wondered aloud where this first triathlon would lead us. We started talking about possibilities even while sitting on the grassy hill overlooking the amphitheater where the awards ceremony would soon take place.

We missed the road trips we had enjoyed with our children. The weekend getaways to attend our youngest son Ben's college swim team competitions were still fresh in our memories. Through these trips, we had traveled to some off-the-beaten-path places and made new friends. Bathing in the day's excitement, we imagined combining my newfound love for triathlon with our mutual love for road trips. "What if I did a triathlon in every state?" I asked. We looked at each other. "Why not?"

A few days later, we added a timeline, aiming to finish a 50-state goal by age seventy. Why seventy? I believed that much beyond that age, I would not be strong enough to complete a triathlon. I was sure I could complete this goal with the right planning. I needed time, since I worked long hours, traveling between Minnesota and Massachusetts and visiting customers and suppliers both within the country and overseas. Besides, we wanted to spend summer weekends with family and friends at our home on Fish Lake in Minnesota.

If I was to complete this goal, I needed to get on with it. First, I had to find my next triathlon, after the one in Maple Grove in August, in a state other than Minnesota.

SOUTH DAKOTA: STATE #2

South Dakota Nickname:
The Mount Rushmore State

The Missouri River at the Lewis & Clark Recreation Area marina.
Seen on the opposite shore is the state of Nebraska.

South Dakota Triathlon Details

- Date: September 4, 2011
- Triathlon: 4th Triple V Triathlon
- Location: Lewis & Clark Recreation Area, Yankton, South Dakota

Published distances
- Swim: 0.25 miles (402 meters)
- Bike: 14.3 miles (23 kilometers)
- Run: 3.1 miles (5 kilometers)

As I was searching for triathlons in states near our homes in Minnesota and Massachusetts, an e-mail describing the Triple V Triathlon appeared in my inbox. This race, in Yankton, South Dakota, would take place the Sunday of the 2011 Labor Day weekend. With our calendar wide open, and Yankton near enough for a long weekend road trip, I registered for my South Dakota triathlon on June 27th.

After the Buffalo Triathlon, I analyzed my splits: the individual times of the three legs and two transitions. Compared to other triathletes, I spent too long on my transitions. Since overall time to complete a triathlon includes the transition times, I saw a quick way to reduce my time and become faster.

Comparing my times with others in my age group also convinced me I needed a faster bike. I was determined to turn in faster times if I continued racing. Within a month of completing the Buffalo, Minnesota triathlon, I purchased a triathlon bike: a two-toned blue and white Trek SpeedConcept 7.5.

This bike wasn't the top of the line or the most expensive option. Still, the price tag for the bike and accessories, including pedals, carbon-fiber-soled bike shoes that clipped into the pedals, and a bike computer, was more than I had spent on all my bikes combined up to the present. While I debated with myself about spending this amount, Joy said, "I think you should get it." Her nudge was all I needed.

With this bike, I looked a lot more like the other triathletes I had seen in Buffalo. Its blade-like spokes and airfoil-shaped surfaces were designed to make it more aerodynamic. Unlike my other bikes, the brake pads on this one were all covered in an effort to reduce the drag from airflow.

Two features of the bike took some getting used to: 1.) gear shifters located at the end of the two aero bars; and 2.) pedals designed to be used with shoes that clipped into them. While it was not quite like starting over, learning to ride this bike while navigating traffic signs, signals, and turns brought me back to much earlier days of learning to ride.

Within a few days of receiving my tri-bike, I joined a group ride that left from Maple Grove Cycling and rode the course for the Maple Grove Triathlon. The mile-and-a-half ride from our home to the bike shop from which the group would begin the ride required crossing a bridge over I-94. As I made the right turn to get onto the sidewalk that crossed the bridge, I was surprised to see a woman less than 20 feet away, speedwalking toward me.

To avoid riding into her, I grabbed the brake levers, which abruptly stopped my bike. Still inexperienced at unclipping my shoes, I fell to the concrete sidewalk before freeing them from the pedals. While the fall produced a small scratch on my brand-new bike, my pride took the greater hit. It was clear that I needed to get comfortable riding this new bike, and I needed to do so quickly.

Before my second triathlon in Minnesota during the last weekend in August, I rode my new bike several mornings each week, repeating a seven-mile loop on roads around our house. Riding the course's mix of gradual and steep hills helped me gain confidence in handling the bike and riding in the aero position. With more aggressive drivers of motor vehicles than I had expected and a half-dozen controlled intersections, I became more comfortable clipping and unclipping my new biking shoes from the pedals. I also streamlined my transitions, cutting back on gear used. The washbasin and gummy bears stayed at home, and I ran without socks.

The outcome of this race confirmed my belief in the bike's importance and the value of reducing my transition times. Instead of placing in the bottom quartile of my age group, as I had in the Buffalo Triathlon, I placed third of twelve.

On Saturday morning of Labor Day weekend 2011, we began our trip to Yankton, South Dakota. Before packing my bike, I stowed the second-row driver's side passenger seat and the third-row bench in the van's floor. My new bike stood upright behind the front driver's seat of our van, secured against the inside wall using two bungee cords connected to the luggage hook near the second-row door and to a second hook near the rear of the cabin.

Sitting in the second-row passenger seat behind Joy was our granddaughter, Valerie. She had stayed with us the previous week, and it was time to take her back to her home in Hutchinson, Minnesota.

After hugging Valerie, we continued our journey, winding our way through the flat green Minnesota countryside. We passed through the Buffalo Ridge region of southwestern Minnesota, where hundreds of wind turbines captured energy from the wind as it passed unhindered by any hills. Despite the fact that both of us had grown up in south central

Minnesota, neither of us remembered ever being in this part of the state.

From the southwestern corner of Minnesota, we crossed into South Dakota, straight east of Sioux Falls. Upon reaching Interstate 29, we drove south to the Vermilion exit. Our drive past the University of South Dakota on the way to Yankton brought back memories of our son Ben's swim meet here. That's a story for another book.

By mid-afternoon, Joy and I were at our hotel in Yankton. Meanwhile, Ben had made the two-and-a-half-hour drive from his home in Omaha, Nebraska to join us for Sunday's triathlon. He arrived soon after we checked in.

We spent the rest of the afternoon exploring Yankton, then traveled six miles west of town to the Lewis & Clark Recreation Area, located on a mile-wide section of the Missouri River created by Gavins Point Dam. This was where the triathlon swim and run would take place. Across the Missouri River, the longest in the United States, was the state of Nebraska.

We arrived during the time scheduled for picking up the race packet. The race staff gave me a T-shirt and my numbers for the bike and run. After an early dinner, we headed to bed, knowing we would be up early to arrive at the race site when transition opened.

The weather the next morning was perfect for a triathlon. By race time, the temperature hovered around 60 degrees, with a light breeze. The sun shone through clear skies.

With 140 participants, the Triple V Triathlon was much smaller than my first two triathlons. After the body marking, which included a volunteer writing my age on my left calf, I set up my transition space. Compared to my first triathlon, this transition space was lean, with much less clutter to consume time during the two transitions.

After I had finished, I walked around, watching others and soaking in the characteristic energy and excitement leading up to the start of a triathlon. A woman I recognized from the Maple Grove Triathlon a couple of weeks earlier said she had grown up in Yankton. Her parents still lived there.

Before the start of the race, I went for a warm-up swim. This was the first triathlon in which I wore a wetsuit, purchased after my second triathlon in Minnesota a week earlier. In that race, the chill of the cool morning air had caused my teeth to chatter the entire time I waited for my wave to leave the beach. The next day, I drove to REI and bought a triathlon wetsuit.

Today, as I walked into the water, the bottom of the Missouri River surprised me. The floor of most Minnesota lakes is a mix of mud and sand with an occasional outcropping of weeds; traction is never a problem. In contrast, the clay bottom of the Missouri River was slippery, like glare ice. Walking without slipping and falling in the water was a significant challenge, especially at the slight uphill of the exit.

All participants started the swim from the marina's concrete boat launch, 20 to 30 yards from transition. We swam straight toward the opposite shore to an orange buoy, around it, and back to the launch.

About three-quarters of the way into the swim, my swim cap slipped off my head. Rather than litter the river by leaving the cap, I grabbed it with my right hand and swam with it in a clenched fist through the rest of the swim. Because of the slippery bottom, I swam as far as possible toward the shore.

While jogging to transition, I pulled my goggles onto my forehead, then transferred the swim cap to my left hand. In one continuous motion, my right hand reached behind my lower back, grabbed the long string connected to my wetsuit zipper, and pulled it to my waist to unzip the suit. While continuing to jog toward transition, I pulled my wetsuit down from around my shoulders to my waist and removed my arms from the sleeves, leaving my swim cap inside the left sleeve.

Once in transition, I removed my goggles, then finished removing my wetsuit using a technique I had practiced over the past week. After sliding the suit down past my knees to the ground, I jerked each leg upward a few times to pull my feet through the narrow section around my ankles. In less than 30 seconds, the wetsuit lay in a tangled heap on the green and white striped towel in my transition space.

I slipped on my sweatband and sunglasses, then shoved on my bike helmet and snapped the strap ends to secure it to my head. After walking my bike to the bike mount line outside transition, I began my ride through the marina parking lot and past the resort.

At the exit of the Recreation Area, I turned right onto South Dakota Highway 52, heading east toward Yankton. After less than a mile on Highway 52, I followed the course by turning right onto the road over Gavins Point Dam and into the state of Nebraska.

The course continued on the Nebraska side of the Missouri River. At first, we passed groves of trees and one or two riverside restaurants as the road stayed close to the river. However, as the highway diverged from the Missouri, we rode between fields of corn.

The course followed this road to south of downtown Yankton. After crossing back over the Missouri River into South Dakota on Discovery Bridge, we were in Yankton. We continued through town, winding through a residential neighborhood, then past the hospital to rejoin Highway 52. We were now riding west, back to the marina and transition.

Apart from some small hills, the bike course was flat. This ride was my fastest yet, averaging almost 21 miles per hour.

During the last third of the course, I traded positions with a guy with the number 40, his age, written in black marker on his left calf. He passed me, then I passed him. We went back and forth for several miles. He passed me one last time before entering the parking lot for the marina.

I completed this triathlon with the out-and-back run on a flat asphalt biking and running path that followed the shoreline of the Missouri River a few yards from the water's edge.

I finished in the top half for all men, thinking, "That's not bad." However, even though I was the oldest in my 50 through 59 age group, I was not as pleased with my middle-of-the-pack placement within my age group. My new triathlon bike had not been a magic bullet.

Afterward, the 40-year-old guy with whom I had traded leads on the bike course approached me and said, "When I saw your age, I told myself there was no way I was going to let you beat me." I felt flattered that a person almost 20 years my junior saw me as serious competition.

We said goodbye to Ben and began the return to our home in a northwest suburb of Minneapolis. This time, we took a longer route, passing through Watson, Minnesota, on the state's west side.

Watson, known as "The Goose Capital of the World", was then the home of Joy's cousin, Tom Nelson, with whom we got together several times each year.

That evening, we enjoyed our typical dinner with Tom: New York strip steak, spinach salad with bleu cheese dressing, and mashed potatoes. The next morning, we returned to our home, passing through Hector, Minnesota to visit our eldest granddaughter, Veronica.

We had added another state and 767 miles to our triathlon adventure. Only 48 more states to go.

• • • •

MASSACHUSETTS: STATE #3

Massachusetts Nickname:
The Bay State

Elaine Vescio shares a tribute to her triplets before the TDD Triathlon.
Photo courtesy of Elaine Vescio.

Massachusetts Triathlon Details

- Date: September 17, 2011
- Triathlon: 3rd TDD Triathlon
- Location: Douglas State Forest, Douglas, Massachusetts

Published distances
- Swim: 0.25 miles (402 meters)
- Bike: 11 miles (17.7 kilometers)
- Run: 3.2 miles (5.1 kilometers)

Almost one year earlier to the day, Jim had suggested we do the Buffalo Triathlon. Now, I was about to complete my fourth.

On Friday, after a week working in Chicopee, I made the one-hour trip east to Douglas State Forest with Joy. The main reason for this trip was to get the race packet. I also knew we would sleep better having rehearsed the route to the race venue we would be taking the next morning when it was still dark. While at the park, I took advantage of the open-water swim training session offered by the race organizer, Elaine Vescio.

The next morning, we arrived back at the race venue just after sunrise. The temperature was a brisk but sunny 42 degrees. About 30 minutes before the race's start, before a short swim to get used to the water, I wrestled on my wetsuit, helped by Joy, who pulled up its back zipper. With the water at least 20 degrees warmer than the air, the wetsuit kept me warm.

Don and Elaine Vescio, two local racers, had started the TDD Triathlon to honor their triplet sons, Tyrus, Dante, and Daniel Vescio, who had died soon after birth. Today's race would help raise money for the University of Massachusetts Memorial Newborn Intensive Care Unit (NICU) in Worcester, Massachusetts.

Before the triathlon's start, racers, volunteers, and spectators walked onto the beach of Whitin Reservoir to remember the Vescio triplets. During the brief ceremony, Elaine Vescio offered a heartfelt tribute to her three boys, releasing three helium-filled balloons.

The triathlon began with a hail of cheers from the 224 triathletes and spectators as the first swimmer started his race. Exuberant cheers recognized a father towing a green and yellow rubber raft. His son, unable to do a triathlon because of his disability, sat in the raft, beaming as his father pulled him across the water. During the last hundred yards of the rectangular swim course, I reached the pair; as I passed them, I contemplated this father's love for his son. His actions today spoke much louder than words. He was making the most of what life had given him and his family. By all appearances, his thoughts for his son matched—if not exceeded—those he had for himself.

After exiting the water, I jogged across the sugar sand beach to transition: a flat, grassy space set up about 50 yards from the water's edge. After stripping off my wetsuit, I prepared for the bike leg.

Since this would be the last triathlon for me this year, I was using the three-year-old Giant Cypress DX hybrid bike I kept at our Chicopee house. I couldn't justify the cost of shipping my triathlon bike round trip between Minnesota and Massachusetts for a single race. Today's bike was the same model as I had used in my first triathlon—comfortable and in excellent shape. However, it couldn't match the speed of my triathlon bike.

For this triathlon, the race director required us to wear our race bib on both the bike and run legs. The previous evening, I had attached the bib from my race packet to the elastic race number belt. During the swim to bike transition, I planned to wrap the belt around my waist and clip the two ends in one single smooth motion. However, today—the fourth time I had used this race number belt—putting it on did not go as planned.

As I pulled the two ends of the belt toward each other, one end of the elastic strap pulled out of its clip. Without the belt secured, I could not start the bike leg. With no pins to attach the race bib to my triathlon suit, I needed to thread the belt's end through the clip. Only after completing this would I be able to put on the belt that held my race bib.

At home later that day, I secured both ends of the belt using a small safety pin. I was determined that the strap would never again come apart as it had today.

Fixing my race number belt cost me at least two minutes. I wasted valuable time in the swim-to-bike transition, a process I had worked to streamline.

After putting on my sweatband and helmet, I started the bike leg. Most of the bike course followed the rolling roads within Douglas State Forest. A handful of vehicles and a couple of other bikers not taking part in the triathlon joined us on the road that morning. However, the course's hairpin turns, many with accompanying hills, forced us to pay attention.

The repeated hills and valleys of the roads made this course the hilliest I had ridden in my short triathlon experience. Though the bike leg took me longer than I wanted, I completed it with legs that were ready to run.

I finished this triathlon with a run that was fast for me. The out-and-back course covered a mix of grass, dirt trails with tree roots and rocks, and paved roads within the forest. One light-hearted volunteer who passed out water and sports drinks made breezy conversation and shouted out words of encouragement as we made our way toward (and away from) the turnaround at the halfway point.

Joy waited for me near the finish line. As she watched a few of the earliest finishers miss a critical right turn that would lead them to the finish line, she sprang into action as she became the self-appointed volunteer for this part of the racecourse. She darted to where the runners were supposed to turn and stood on the edge of the run course, facing them as they emerged from the tree cover on the dirt trail. In her triathlon volunteer debut, she directed runners to turn at the base of the trail's gradual hill to cross the finish line a short distance ahead.

After I completed the course, I saw that Joy was in the perfect place. I enjoyed watching her guide the rest of the triathletes toward the finish line with her clear, confident instruction.

I finished eighth of 12 in my age group, men ages 55 through 59, and 147th of 224 overall. The fiasco with the race number belt and the slower hybrid bike had contributed to the longer time. I was learning to plan for and adapt to challenges that could arise during a race.

2012:
CONTINUING A SOLID START

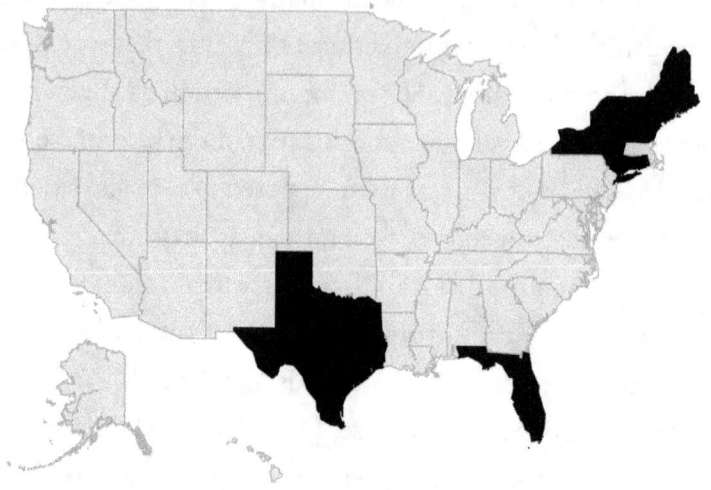

"You woke the bear from his sleep.
You cannot cry when he tangos."
— Hercule Poirot, *A Haunting in Venice*

S eeing improvements in my health and physical fitness, I committed myself to the sport. Some thought I was obsessed with triathlon.

I continued to read books and blog posts on training. Perhaps because of my penchant for testing new workouts, settling on a consistent training regimen proved challenging. Just as I got used to a series of swimming, biking, running, and strength training workouts, a new one that promised better performance would pop up and draw me in. It sometimes felt like trying to tuck an octopus into bed.

Near the end of 2011, I came across an article in which the author recommended writing a post-season review of the past year's training and racing. Using the notes from my first four triathlons in three states, I recorded my answers to the questions in the article and goals for the 2012 season.

In 2012, I added structure to my run training, following a program titled "Run Faster, Run Less." My goal was to become a stronger runner (running was my weakest leg of the triathlon) following the "train your weakness" philosophy.

My reading acquainted me with coaches, though I thought they were for professionals, not someone like me who did triathlons as a hobby. Besides, I was spending enough on triathlon gear and race fees. I couldn't justify adding the cost of a coach.

Thanks to Joy introducing us to a low-sugar diet, both of us began eating healthier foods. By this time, I was twenty pounds lighter. Sure enough, the test results from my first physical exam after starting triathlon training confirmed my doctor's advice.

While traveling domestically or internationally, I continued to train using hotel swimming pools. Most of the major chain hotels in which I stayed also had a fitness center with at least one stationary bike and treadmill. Whenever possible, I ran outside, depending on the air quality, weather, and surrounding neighborhood. To supplement my weight training, especially when weights were not available, I traveled with a Compex muscle stimulator, an electronic device that contracts muscles beneath patches applied to various locations on the body: quads, hamstrings, and upper back muscles, for example.

To make certain I was getting the proper mix of protein, electrolytes, micronutrients, and inflammation-fighting food, I concocted unusual-looking smoothies from protein powder, vegetables, fruits, turmeric, flaxseed oil, and whatever else I found in the refrigerator. It amazed me how good these camo-green (some days tan) drinks could taste after a hard workout.

My training became more consistent as I went to sleep earlier. By the same token, getting up before 5 a.m. to train before work became easier.

My journal documented the following goal for 2012: "To finish Sprint triathlons in six new states (Texas and the five remaining New England states)."

Another goal was to make my triathlon bike available for other races, including those to which we flew. Over the winter, I purchased a Thule RoundTrip Sport hard-sided bike case. I practiced disassembling, packing, and reassembling my bike so I could bring it to any race, whether I was driving or flying.

TEXAS: STATE #4

Texas Nickname:
The Lone Star State

Our weekend group after the No Label Triathlon. Bottom row, left to right:
me, Gordon, Alan. Top row, left to right: Joy, Diana, Carol.

Texas Triathlon Details

- Date: April 28, 2012
- Triathlon: 1st No Label Triathlon
- Location: Morton Ranch Natatorium and
  No Label Brewing Company, Katy, Texas

Published distances
- Swim: 300 meters (328 yards)
- Bike: 14 miles (22.5 kilometers)
- Run: 3.0 miles (4.8 kilometers)

In planning our 2012 triathlon season, Joy and I included Texas on our itinerary. Texas offered the possibility of doing a triathlon earlier in the season compared to the New England states we intended to visit later in the year. Besides, we had two sets of close friends we could meet while in Texas.

Diana Garaghty, a longtime friend from Minnesota, had moved to Katy, Texas, a Houston suburb, a few years earlier. As part of a small group from our church in Minnesota that met in our home each week during the late 80s and early 90s, Diana and her family had been part our lives for over 25 years.

Noticing a website describing the triathlon in Katy, Joy called Diana to check her schedule for that weekend. She was planning to be in town, and insisted we stay at her house. Other friends, Alan and Carol Mercurio, who lived in a suburb of Fort Worth, Texas, said they would meet us in Katy for the weekend.

Joy and I left Minneapolis for Houston International Airport on Thursday evening. The flight to Houston was our first stop on a trip to Massachusetts. I would be working from the Chicopee plant during the next two weeks.

In addition to our regular luggage, we brought along my bike and other triathlon gear. The previous night, I had removed the wheels, pedals, seat post, and handlebars from my bike's frame. Next, I wrapped the frame and handlebars with bubble wrap and foam padding. Following instructions I found in an online video, I secured the pieces in my bike case. The bike would make its first flight as airline luggage.

By the time we collected all our luggage, including the oversized bike case, Alan and Carol had landed. We picked up our rental car, a van capable of carrying the four of us and all our luggage.

The next morning, I reassembled the bike and went for a test ride around Diana's suburban neighborhood. With foam padding and secure straps, the bike had arrived without a scratch and rode just as it had before.

Diana's friend Gordon, Alan, and I spent the rest of the morning following the three ladies, Diana, Carol, and Joy, as they shopped in a nearby mall. After lunch, we drove into Houston, stopping to watch an hour of track and field competition at Baylor University.

Later in the afternoon, Joy and I picked up the race packet at No Label Brewing Company. We finished the afternoon by driving the bike course, surveying it for any potholes, loose gravel, and other obstacles to avoid the next morning during the triathlon.

The No Label Triathlon was my first with two distinct transition areas. Two and a half miles separated the two transitions. The first, between the swim and bike legs, would take place in the parking lot outside the Morton Ranch High School Natatorium. The second, between the bike and run, would occur in a parking lot at the No Label Brewing Company.

On Saturday morning, I awoke at 5:10 a.m. My goal was to leave Diana's house by 5:30 for a race that started at 7 a.m. We left fifteen minutes behind schedule, reaching the Natatorium at 6 a.m., well after most of our competitors had arrived. Finding a place to rack my bike was a challenge. From this, I learned I did not like to arrive late.

After finding a space in transition, I finally racked my bike, laid my green and white striped towel on the ground next to it, and then set my helmet and sunglasses on the towel. My biking shoes stayed clipped into my bike pedals. Since my last triathlon, I had learned that professional triathletes left their shoes clipped into their bike pedals to reduce their transition time. Why shouldn't I do the same?

Following a video I found on the internet, I used a rubber band looped through a safety pin stuck through the strap on the back of my right shoe. I looped the two ends of the rubber band over the locking clamp on the rear-wheel skewer. The rubber band held my shoe in a horizontal orientation. When I got on the bike, I placed my right foot on this shoe and began pedaling, adding my left foot to the top of its shoe. As I started pedaling, the rubber band broke free, staying on the safety pin.

After a few pedal strokes with each of my feet on top of its shoe, I gained enough speed to coast long enough to slip one foot into its shoe and secure the hook and loop strap across its top. With a few extra pedal strokes, I coasted while putting on and securing my other shoe.

I had practiced this routine many times during outdoor rides during the previous fall and this spring, so felt ready to use it in a triathlon.

Following the pre-race meeting, I prepared for my first triathlon swim in an indoor pool. During registration, the race director asked each of us to provide an estimate of our time for completing the 300-meter swim, called the *seed time*. I estimated six minutes. Seed times for each swimmer helped the race director start triathletes with others who would be swimming at the same speed.

Starting in the lane furthest from the natatorium's exit, a new swimmer began every few seconds. We swam to the opposite end, went under the divider to the next lane, and returned to the starting end, where we moved one lane closer to the exit. Repeating these steps, we moved across the width of the pool until we had completed the 300-meter swim.

As I started the swim, the guy in front of me seemed to slow me down. However, I couldn't pass him, so I settled for what felt to be a relaxing swim. I finished in six minutes to the second.

After leaving the pool, I walked outside, careful to avoid slipping on the concrete sidewalk, which was now wet from swimmers who had started earlier. Continuing across a grassy patch, I reached the parking lot, where I dropped my swim goggles and swim cap onto my towel, put on my bike helmet and sunglasses, grabbed my bike from the rack, and headed toward the bike mount line.

Police and volunteers controlled every major intersection and every turn of this flat bike course. With only a slight headwind in one short section near the end of the course, today's ride was fast. My average speed was over 20 miles per hour.

The only obstacle proved to be a caravan of two trucks, each towing a trailer carrying lawn care equipment. Since I was biking faster than the two trucks, I caught them, then slowed to stay behind them. For a moment, I thought of passing. As I crossed the centerline to pass, they turned off the road to the right.

By this point in my racing experience, I had recognized the importance of volunteers for a safe, organized triathlon. From here on in, I would make every effort to thank volunteers and public safety officers as I passed them, especially those controlling intersections with motor vehicle traffic. In most cases, I heard a "You're welcome."

As I was biking to the second transition area, Joy picked up my swim goggles, cap, and the towel I laid on the ground beside my bike. She and our friends drove to the No Label Brewing Company, where she laid out my towel in space number 65, my race number, and set my running shoes and race number belt on top of the towel.

As I coasted toward the dismount line at No Label Brewing, I slipped my feet out of my bike shoes, leaving them clipped into the pedals. After dismounting the bike, I jogged, now barefoot, from the dismount line to the bike rack where Joy had set up my bike-to-run transition space.

My tender, callous-free feet were no match for the surface of crushed rocks along the 30-yard run to the bike rack. "Ouch!" and "Ooh!" passed my lips more than a few times as I crossed the sharp rocks to my second transition space. After racking my bike, I dropped my helmet onto the towel and slipped on my running shoes and race number belt.

The flat run course took us through a neighborhood bordering a row of small older office buildings on the western side of the brewery. Early in the run, I glanced at my GPS watch, realizing I had started out faster than I could sustain. I slowed to my target pace, which I maintained throughout the run.

I kept myself occupied during the run with a lot of self-talk, during which my mind refused my body's request to slow for "just a short walk." My mind won out; I never stopped to walk.

Even though I was in first place in my 55 through 59 age group after the bike, my competitors outran me, leaving me with a third-place finish. Still, seeing my times for each leg brought a smile to my face. My training since the last triathlon appeared to be paying off.

With the race complete, we relaxed together with the other 204 finishers and their guests, sipping on a No Label beer or sports drink and refueling with fruit and protein bars.

We returned to Diana's after the triathlon festivities. My first task was to pack my bike and other triathlon gear for the second leg of our trip to Massachusetts the next morning. I then joined the others as they lounged in and around Diana's pool. That evening, we enjoyed one last dinner together at a local Mexican restaurant. What a fun weekend!

MAINE: STATE #5

Maine Nickname:
The Pine Tree State

One stop on the Casco Bay mail run boat near Portland, Maine.

Maine Triathlon Details

- Date: May 5, 2012
- Triathlon: 10th Polar Bear Triathlon and Duathlon
- Location: Bowdoin College, Brunswick, Maine

Published distances
- Swim: 525 yards (480 meters)
- Bike: 11 miles (17.7 kilometers)
- Run: 3 miles (4.8 kilometers)

The Polar Bear Triathlon and Duathlon was one of Maine's first triathlons of the new year. This also made it popular. Over the past few years, participants had purchased all available slots in this race within an hour of registration opening.

Two weeks earlier, I had learned from a close call with my Connecticut triathlon registration to ask how quickly the race slots filled. It surprised me to learn that some triathlons limit the number of participants and that these entries sell almost immediately. I was ready to sign up for the Polar Bear Triathlon within the first minutes of registration opening.

On Friday afternoon, the day before the triathlon, Joy and I traveled from our Chicopee home to the Maine Running Company in Brunswick to pick up my race packet. We then drove to nearby Bowdoin College, where the race would start and end.

Bowdoin College is a liberal arts school with an idyllic campus. The Bowdoin mascot is the polar bear—the namesake for the Polar Bear Triathlon and Duathlon. The campus includes a competition-sized pool and field house with an inside track. Both the pool and field house were available to us before, during, and after the triathlon.

After checking out parking options for the next morning, we drove the bike course. Before dinner, we checked into our hotel in Brunswick.

Dinner was at J. R. Maxwell & Company on Front Street in historic downtown Bath. After some encouragement, Joy selected the full lobster, complete with bib. Thanks to the waitress, one experienced in extracting the lobster's meat, Joy enjoyed her first lobster.

The Polar Bear event included both a Sprint triathlon, with 10 men in my 55 through 59 age group, and a duathlon. Duathlon comprises a run-bike-run sequence, and is often chosen by those who don't swim or are strong runners.

On Friday evening, amidst drizzling rain and a 50-degree air temperature, the forecast showed rain at the beginning of Saturday's race. Fortunately, the rain passed overnight, and we woke to clear skies. By race time, the clouds had dissipated, the sun was shining, and the roads were dry. Even though it remained chilly, today was a beautiful day for racing.

While setting up my transition space, I laid out the light green biking jacket I kept in the suitcase with my triathlon gear, supplies, and tools. *I might need the jacket today*, I thought.

The swim took place in the college's 16-lane, 25-yard LeRoy Greason Pool. We started in groups of 32, two in each of the 16 pool lanes, based on our expected time to complete the swim we had submitted during registration. The fastest swimmers started first, while those with the longest estimated swim time started last. If competitors accurately estimated their swim times, both swimmers sharing a lane would finish at about the same time.

Before starting, we jumped into the pool and grabbed onto the wall on our side of the swim lane. Our swim started when the start signal sounded.

Once the swim began, a volunteer monitored the progress of the two swimmers from the lane's start end. As we approached the end of our 20th length, the volunteer put a red panel into the water in front of us. This signaled us to exit the pool at the opposite end after completing our 21st length. Once out of the pool, we hurried through the field house to reach transition, which was set up in a grassy space behind the field house.

Wet from the swim, I felt especially chilled as I jogged into the open air. Just before taking my bike out of transition, I put on my biking jacket. It felt too cold to ride without it today.

The bike course left the campus on streets around its northern and then eastern edges. As we continued out of Brunswick through the south end of town, we encountered a few rolling hills. Most roads were smooth, without cracks or potholes, but a half-mile section was undergoing repairs. Thankfully, the race organizer's update days before the race had spoken of this section of the course.

In an e-mail received a few days earlier, I read, "Part of the course will be designated a 'Non-Aero Zone,' which means that you cannot be in aero position on your bike. We make this designation for your safety." I had seen this patch during our drive the previous afternoon, so I was ready to ride with care through this section.

The air was warmer by the end of the bike leg. After racking my bike and taking off my helmet, I stripped off the jacket before heading out on the run.

The three-mile run course covered both paved road and off-road sections. The initial portion followed sidewalks along city streets leading away from the campus. A few blocks further, the course veered onto a damp dirt trail, complete with the usual number of potholes and exposed tree roots. During the last stretch toward the finish line, we crossed a grassy soccer field outside the south end of the field house.

I finished fourth of 10 in my age group, and 113th of the 240 men and women who finished the Sprint triathlon.

While I was racing, Joy once again volunteered. She had enjoyed her experience at the Massachusetts triathlon. Today, her job was to remove the strap containing a timing chip from each racer's left ankle.

Unfortunately, one racer came to the finish line with a nasty brown liquid running down his leg. Joy's imagination, multiplied by her acute sense of smell, forced her to suppress the gag reflex as she unwrapped the timing chip's Velcro strap from this man's ankle. As she later described this torturous experience, I was sure this was the end of her days as a triathlon volunteer.

On our way back to Chicopee late Saturday morning, we passed through Portland, Maine. We took advantage of being in this coastal town to enjoy a seafood lunch at one of the waterside restaurants. Afterward, we caught a ride around Casco Bay on the mail boat, which made stops at several of the bay's islands.

At first, our tour made us feel as if we were in northern Minnesota, with its rocky shores and lighthouses. However, as we proceeded, the differences between the two areas became apparent. The scent of salty sea air and calls of seabirds mixed with the hum of boat motors today contrasted with northern Minnesota, where mournful calls between a pair of loons might occasionally break the area's deafening silence amid the earthy scent of pine and fresh water.

After this relaxing tour, we started our trip back to Chicopee.

But first, we made one more stop: a tour of Allagash Brewing Company. Our experience visiting Allagash would come in handy some years later while waiting for our friends, Jim and Kris Novak, to join us for dinner at Manhattan's American Bar & Grill in a western suburb of Chicago, Illinois. Recognizing the Allagash name on a tap in the bar where we waited, I told the server of our visit to the brewery in Portland. He said that the restaurant owner's wife had grown up in Maine.

The world appeared a little smaller.

VERMONT: STATE #6

Vermont Nickname:
The Green Mountain State

Martins Mill Covered Bridge near Hartland, Vermont.

Vermont Triathlon Details

- Date: May 20, 2012
- Triathlon: 12th Stowe Triathlon
- Location: The Swimming Hole, Stowe, Vermont

Published distances

- Swim: 500 meters (547 yards)
- Bike: 13.7 miles (22 kilometers)
- Run: 5 kilometers (3.1 miles)

During the days before the Vermont triathlon, my left knee started to hurt while running, and my lower back muscles often cramped when swimming. The chiropractor I was seeing in Chicopee wanted me to avoid weight-bearing exercises. Since he attributed my knee pain to tight quadriceps, he also prescribed more thorough stretching in my training.

I suspended my run training and focused on swimming, dabbling in water running in the lake behind our Minnesota house. I expanded my stretching routine to include the quadriceps and stretched more intentionally. Still, the back spasms and knee pain hindered my training.

For the Vermont race, Joy and I left our house in Chicopee, Massachusetts on Saturday morning. We knew we could drive to Stowe in three and a half hours; however, by leaving earlier, we could make three additional stops along the way: Martins Mill Covered Bridge, King Arthur Flour, and Ben & Jerry's Ice Cream.

In our earlier days of living part-time in Massachusetts, I had driven to Montréal for a customer meeting. Before leaving, I found a directory of waypoints, or GPS coordinates, for our portable GPS. The waypoints gave me locations for many covered bridges. During my return from Montréal, I stopped at two of them in Vermont. During today's trip, we visited a third.

After a delightful morning visiting the first two stops and an afternoon of touring Ben & Jerry's ice cream production, which ended in tasting samples of their product, we arrived in Stowe. Following a drive through downtown, we checked into the Town & Country Resort. Our room was within a half-mile of The Swimming Hole, where the triathlon swim would occur.

The Swimming Hole is a non-profit fitness center and pool, founded in 2001 to serve the community in and around Stowe. According to their website, "Small town life has its advantages, but a facility like this isn't usually one of them." The fitness center's red barn-like appearance echoes the locals' belief that "you can fit a lot into a barn."

After driving the bike course, we dined on fish and chips at O'Grady's Pub a few blocks down the street from our motel. Before turning in for the evening, I added air to my bike tires, filled water bottles with drinks for before and during the race, and set out clothing, shoes, and other gear.

The next morning, I rose before dawn. As the sun provided light, I rode my bike to The Swimming Hole, leaving Joy to continue sleeping until closer to race time. With the short commute, I arrived along with the race event staff. Having my pick of spots, however, wouldn't matter for this triathlon.

After the pre-race meeting, each of the 53 competitors took turns swimming the required 10 laps in The Swimming Hole's eight-lane, 25-meter indoor pool. While completing our swim, we shared a lane with another racer who expected to complete the swim in a time similar to ours.

As I approached the end of the ninth lap, a volunteer placed a bright orange sign into the water in front of me. The words "Last Lap" printed on the sign meant I had one more lap to swim. After completing the tenth lap, I pulled myself from the pool. Once I was out, a volunteer wrote my swim time on my left hand using a black marker.

I walked outside, where I joined the other triathletes who had completed their swim and were now preparing for the bike leg. Unlike other triathlons I had completed, this one had us waiting in and around transition until all swimmers had finished.

Once everyone finished their swim and was ready to bike, the race director started a large digital clock at the exit of transition. As the clock ticked toward our swim time, we strapped on our bike helmets and inched our bikes closer to the starting line. Once the clock displayed our swim time, we were free to ride.

The bike course followed public roads, which we shared with cars and trucks as we rode into and through downtown Stowe. The sight of motor vehicles and bikes appearing to race each other was strange. The driver of one slow-moving car honked his horn at me after I passed him along the right side of the road. I guess he didn't appreciate being passed by a bike.

I made it through the traffic with no more incidents and left Stowe at its south end, riding parallel to the Little River. After two miles, we turned right onto the much less congested Moscow Road, now heading west past many small farms.

We kept going on Moscow Road until it ended at a dirt road, then turned around and rode to its intersection with Barrows Road. Except for a steep hill on a section of Barrows Road, the tree-lined course was flat. Continuing north, we passed homes set back into the woods, dairy farms with their corn and hay fields, Stowe High School, and some small businesses. Across open fields, we looked onto wooded mountains, some popular for snow skiing during the winter months. After reaching Luce Hill Road west of Stowe, we turned right and rode back to transition, following Cape Cod Road around the back side of The Swimming Hole.

I knew my swim had taken longer than expected because of the back spasms I was experiencing. I also expected my sore knee to slow my run. As a result, I rode as fast as I could on the bike leg. My bike split was the fastest of those in my 50 through 59 age group, and ninth-fastest among all competitors.

The run followed the Stowe Recreation Path west of The Swimming Hole, passing behind our motel within the first half-mile. We ran to the turnaround of the out-and-back course, past the location where the path crossed the west branch of the Little River for the third time. We then returned on the same path to the finish line.

Because of my sore knee, I found the run harder than other triathlons. It surprised me that the greatest pain occurred in parts of the course with a downhill slope, especially on the footbridges over the river.

I finished third in the men's 50 through 59 age group, eight seconds behind the second-place finisher. Overall, I finished 24th of the 50 finishers of this triathlon.

After collecting my gear, Joy and I returned to the motel. Before packing the van, I stretched my back and legs, then showered.

We had no time for sightseeing on our drive back to Chicopee. Instead, I dropped off my bike and the triathlon gear at our house; then we drove to Bradley Airport in Windsor Locks, Connecticut, for a flight to Minneapolis. We'd return to Massachusetts for the next triathlon in two weeks.

CONNECTICUT: STATE #7

Connecticut Nickname:
The Constitution State

Great Pond in Martin Park, the location for the triathlon swim.

Connecticut Triathlon Details

- Date: June 3, 2012
- Triathlon: 6th TriRidgefield Triathlon
- Location: Martin Park, Ridgefield, Connecticut

Published distances
- Swim: 0.5 miles (805 meters)
- Bike: 13 miles (20.9 kilometers)
- Run: 5 kilometers (3.1 miles)

N ew Year's Day, 2012. We had just finished putting away our food after lunch, and I was sitting dumbfounded at the island in our kitchen. How could this be? Registration for the TriRidgefield Sprint triathlon had just opened that morning. Now, in the early afternoon, all the spots for the race had been filled.

I had counted on completing a triathlon in Connecticut during 2012. The one in Ridgefield was the best fit for our schedule, so I emailed Evan, the race director. Was my understanding correct? Yes, but after Evan and I exchanged e-mails over the next couple of hours, he allowed me to register for TriRidgefield 2012, anyway.

A result of my superior negotiating skills? Nope. Evan's wife, a native of our home state of Minnesota, had convinced him to let me register for the race. In triathlon, as in life, who you know and where you're from matter.

Through this experience, I learned to ask race directors when registration for their triathlon opened and how quickly the race slots filled. This lesson proved beneficial a couple of weeks later, when I registered for the Maine triathlon.

By now, two weeks after the Vermont triathlon, my body had recovered from the back spasms and sore left knee that had plagued me during that race.

We arrived in Chicopee via Bradley International Airport outside Hartford on Friday night. The next afternoon, we drove from Chicopee to Ridgefield to pick up the race packet and drive the bike course.

Once I had collected my race packet at the Ridgefield Bicycle

Company, we drove through the historic part of Ridgefield. This 300-year-old town in the southwest corner of Connecticut has an interesting history. It includes the 1777 Battle of Ridgefield, during which General Benedict Arnold's horse fell after being struck by nine musket balls.

Since the triathlon venue was only an hour-and-a-half's drive from our house in Massachusetts, we returned home later that day. On the way, we stopped for a late lunch of fish and chips and seafood chowder at McGuire's Ale House in Newton, Connecticut. Before retiring for the evening, I packed the car. We planned to leave early the next morning.

On Saturday morning, we awoke at 3 a.m. to leave the house at 3:30. I wanted to be at the race venue when it opened at 5 a.m. We arrived early enough to secure an outside spot on a bike rack near the exit of transition.

Before the triathlon's start, Joy and I walked over to thank Evan and his wife for letting me register for this race. While waiting to meet him, we learned that the race needed a few more volunteers. Would Joy be interested?

Her answer surprised me. She said she would volunteer, as long as this did not involve removing timing chips. She still reacted to the memory of her last volunteer role, the one in Brunswick, Maine. After looking at the options, they agreed that Joy would direct both motor vehicle traffic and racer traffic as bikers and runners exited Martin Park and crossed the highway in front of it.

The triathlon began with a half-mile swim in Great Pond within Martin Park. My wetsuit made the upper-60s water temperature comfortable. Starting from the beach's left side, we swam to an orange pyramid-shaped buoy, turned right, and continued parallel to the beach, toward a second buoy. After a second right turn, we swam back to the sandy shore.

For this triathlon, I employed a new technique for swimming around the two buoys. Those who taught the method said it would reduce the time to swim around small and medium-sized ones. It would also steer us clear of the most crowded swim lanes around the buoys.

Rather than using a normal freestyle stroke, also called front crawl, to swim around the buoy, I used a combination of freestyle and backstroke. As I reached the buoy, ready to make the right turn around it, I raised my left hand over my head to rotate onto my back, staying close to the buoy. After one or two strokes on my back, I raised my right arm over my head to return to my front, then continue to the next buoy or the exit.

The move had become second-nature after practicing it several times in the lake behind our Minnesota home. It reminded me of learning a new dance step: start slow and commit the moves to memory, then, with practice, increase speed while focusing on the quality of each movement. I believe it saved me some time, as I was able to avoid other swimmers who made wider turns around each buoy.

From the beach, a jog of around 50 yards across a grass strip brought us to transition for the bike leg. I left the park for the rectangular bike course, heading west on Haviland Road, away from the early morning sun. The bike course continued on a neighborhood street cut through tall stands of dark green leafy hardwoods on rolling hills.

As I completed the next right turn, dense woods filled both sides of the road as far as I could see. The area felt remote despite being a bedroom community for New York City. At the northernmost part of the course, we turned left to ride south toward downtown Ridgefield. We were within one mile of the New York State line.

We rode a roller-coaster-like series of hills and turns through wooded residential neighborhoods into downtown Ridgefield. After a few more turns, one which took us past a Stop & Shop, we began the northeasterly journey back to Martin Park. Despite the many hills and turns, the course was fast, with my average speed over 20 miles per hour.

As the number of racers on the bike and run courses grew, Joy had more racers to protect. From her position at the entrance to Martin Park along U.S. Highway 7, she worked to keep pedestrians and motor vehicles from crossing in front of bikers and runners.

Joy's heart almost stopped when one pedestrian refused to comply with Joy's call to wait. As the woman jogged across the intersection at the park's entrance, the first biker to return to transition narrowly avoided riding into her. The driver of a motorhome needlessly added to the risk of injury to racers (not to mention Joy's anxiety) by refusing to wait, despite her requests and warning.

Joy also had to contend with racers who seemed bent on riding over their fellow racers. Her message to other incoming bikers was "Stay to the right," to keep them from colliding with runners as they exited the park on the same road.

The first part of the run followed the bike course west of the park. After a short distance, the run course split onto a side street to the left in a loop that rejoined Haviland Road for our final stretch to the finish line. As with the bike course, the run was full of hills, making it challenging.

Meanwhile, at the exit of Martin Park, Joy was so laser-focused on keeping the racers safe that she did not notice me as I passed her on my way out of the park...or as I returned to it.

Though my times in each leg were respectable for me, I finished eighth of 18 in my age group of 55- through 59-year-old men.

Today was the first anniversary of my first triathlon. One year and eight triathlons in seven states later, we were just beginning to recognize what triathlon and our travels across the U.S. would yield.

NEW YORK: STATE #8

New York Nickname:
The Empire State

Kaaterskill Falls in the Catskill Mountains of eastern New York.

New York Triathlon Details

- Date: June 9, 2012
- Triathlon: HITS Hunter Mountain Triathlon
- Location: North-South Lake State Park, Haines Falls, New York

Published distances

- Swim: 750 meters (820 yards)
- Bike: 20 kilometers (12.4 miles)
- Run: 5 kilometers (3.1 miles)

H aines Falls, New York is a two-and-a-half hour drive from our Chicopee, Massachusetts, home. Since transition opened at 5 a.m. and the race started at 7 a.m. on Saturday morning, we traveled to the race venue on Friday and stayed overnight nearby. Arriving on Friday gave us time to explore the mix of water and wooded hills of the Catskill Mountains, a part of eastern New York we had never visited before.

One week before the triathlon, we found another reason to travel to the Catskills on Friday. Dave Kiviat of the HITS Triathlon Series called to ask if he could record an interview in which we would talk about my triathlon goal and how I had selected this race.

Weeks earlier, I had received an e-mail from HITS Triathlon requesting stories from those taking part in this event. I replied, telling them of my goal to do a triathlon in each state of the U.S., a story HITS management found interesting. They thought it might help them promote a series of triathlons across the country.

On Friday afternoon, Joy and I drove to North-South Lake State Park, following the back roads from exit B2 on Interstate 90 in eastern New York. The first stop in the northeastern section of the Catskills, home of the legendary Rip Van Winkle, was Kaaterskill Falls.

While I cannot explain it, I love waterfalls. I think everyone should. I used to take customers from around the world who were visiting our Minnesota plant to northern Minnesota's Gooseberry Falls. Everyone seemed to appreciate them. Joy and I had already visited the waterfalls near our home in Chicopee.

Then, after visiting Hawaii's popular tourist sites during our first few yearly visits to my Aunt Nelda's home in Honolulu, she bought me a book containing guides to hidden waterfalls on the island of Oahu. Over several visits, I hiked to each of them…some more than once.

From Kaaterskill Falls, we drove to the Copper Kettle Motel Cottages in nearby Windham, New York, where I reserved a room for Friday evening. We were happy to support the young couple; they had just purchased the cottages one year earlier.

After storing our luggage in the room, we made our way to the park. Before we picked up my race packet and attended the pre-race meeting, Dave Kiviat filmed our conversation at the bluffs overlooking the Hudson River Valley near Saugerties, New York. Even though I didn't see the video interview, Joy was told by a race spectator the next day that my story appeared in a local newspaper.

The Sprint triathlon was one of five triathlon distances completed over the two-day event. On Saturday, the Super Sprint, Sprint, and Olympic triathlons took place, while the Half and Full Ironman triathlons occurred on Sunday.

Once again, Joy worked as a volunteer. Her first assignment placed her in the transition area during the Sprint distance race. After its completion, they reassigned her to the finish line, a location at which she vowed to never again volunteer. However, today, she hung finisher medals around the necks of those who completed the Olympic-distance triathlon. Another volunteer stooped over to remove the timing chip.

Near the Sprint triathlon's start, the air temperature was a little above 60 degrees. The overcast sky threatened rain.

The almost half-mile swim leg of the Sprint triathlon took place in South Lake. Since this was early June in a region popular with snow skiers, the water was also in the low 60s.

Fifteen minutes before the triathlon, I walked, then dove into the lake to get used to the cold water and inspect the lake bottom. What would I run or walk onto once the start signal sounded?

Many sharp, slippery rocks cover the bottom of South Lake. Stepping on the irregular surface while running into the water could have led to an injury of a foot or ankle. From what I learned during the practice swim, I was able to enter and exit the lake with extra caution.

Thanks to my wetsuit, I stayed warm in the frigid water. Soon after starting the swim, the hand of another swimmer struck my goggles hard enough to let water into the lenses. I swam with goggles half full of water for the rest of the swim.

A light drizzle began as we completed the swim, and the roads were wet and a little slippery as we started the bike leg. This was my first experience racing in rain.

The course included the highest number of hills of any triathlon I had completed thus far. It also included the steepest. As we left the park, we rode up a slight incline before reaching a flat stretch that preceded a downhill section. While riding downhill, I shifted into a high gear, wanting to take advantage of the slope to pick up speed.

As I made the right-angle turn part way down the hill, I found myself staring up to the top of an even steeper one. It caught me off guard, since I had not driven the course; nor did I remember it from the course map. While downshifting, my chain jumped off the front gear, jamming between the large ring and the frame.

I coasted up the hill using the momentum I had built before the turn while simultaneously unclipping my shoes from the pedals. I then got off my bike along the edge of the road. The chain would not budge, so I flipped the bike upside down. In doing so, I succeeded in emptying the sports drink from the bottle strapped between the aero bars.

I noticed the chain was stuck behind an adjusting screw's head. Grabbing the chain, I maneuvered it around the screw head and pulled it loose. As I broke it free, its edge sliced the tips of my index and middle fingers on my right hand. The injury wasn't severe, but my fingertips throbbed as I dozed off to sleep later that night.

I reinstalled the chain and resumed riding, having wasted around one minute. After flipping my bike back to its upright position, I saw the empty bottle between my aero bars. Fortunately, the lower temperature resulted in less sweating, thereby delaying the need for fluids. Still, after this experience, I carried extra hydration in a sealed water bottle. I was still learning what it meant to be prepared in a triathlon.

I relived this experience early the following week as I glanced at the *Minneapolis Star Tribune* laying on a table in the lunchroom at work. It surprised me to see a story not so different from my own experience. The article told of Amber Neben, an Olympic cyclist who had lost her chance at a medal when her chain jammed during a hill climb. She, too, was forced to get off her bike to reinstall the dislodged chain.

The rest of the ride was uneventful as the racers rode the same highway Joy and I had used earlier that morning to travel to the park. Upon reaching the midpoint, we turned around and biked back to transition.

A short distance into the run, a woman caught up to me as we made our way along a wet, muddy trail. As she passed, she commented about her wet shoes. I thought her comment odd. My shoes did not feel wet. Running without socks, I would have noticed wet shoes.

When the drizzle began, Joy had covered my shoes with the towel I normally laid out at my transition space. When I returned from the bike leg, I hadn't noticed the towel covering my shoes. Thanks to Joy's thoughtfulness and her volunteer assignment in transition, my shoes stayed dry. From this experience, I learned to cover my running shoes with a second towel from my triathlon case at any hint of rain.

As I continued the run, a muscle above the front of my left knee tightened. A mix of walking and running kept the pain from growing and the muscle from cramping.

The organizer awarded plaques to the fastest finisher of each year of age based on their age on January first. While I was 59 on race day, I had been 58 on January first. Despite the time to reinstall the bike chain and knee problem during the run, I was the fastest man in my 58-year-old age group.

After the race and before the awards ceremony, Joy and I talked with a couple near our own age from Albany, New York. Afterward, I regretted not getting their contact information, since we would have loved to stay in touch with them. While I remembered the man's name, I could not find him on social media.

From that time on, both Joy and I carried name cards. We were meeting tremendous people, and we wanted to stay in contact.

RHODE ISLAND: STATE #9

Rhode Island Nickname:
The Ocean State

Ida Lewis Yacht Club, Newport, Rhode Island.

Rhode Island Triathlon Details

- Date: September 22, 2012
- Triathlon: 3rd Amica 19.7 Newport Triathlon
- Location: Second Beach and Third Beach, Middletown, Rhode Island

Published distances
- Swim: 0.5 miles (800 meters)
- Bike: 16.1 miles (25.9 kilometers)
- Run: 3.1 miles (5 kilometers)

Joy and I left our house in Chicopee, Massachusetts, at around 3 p.m. on Friday, taking a southern route through Hartford, Connecticut to Newport, Rhode Island. We arrived at the race venue for packet pickup on time, albeit with some difficulty.

Since we had forgotten our portable GPS in Minnesota, we navigated the old-fashioned way, using printed maps. Struggling to find our way to Newport to collect my race packet reminded us that some skills, like this type of navigation, follow the "use it or lose it" principle.

After picking up the race packet, we applied the same map-reading skills to locate our hotel for the evening in Swansea, Massachusetts. To save money, I used points to book a free night at the nearest Holiday Inn.

Our drive to the hotel provided relaxing views of farmland, water, and quaint New England architecture. We never tired of driving through the seaside towns of New England, with their historic colonial homes on streets lined with mature trees, or across bridges with a lighthouse and marina in view. Still, this trip, which should have taken 25 minutes, took forty-five.

By the time we arrived at the hotel, we were more than a little frustrated by the difficulty of reaching both it and the race site, even with the splendid scenery. The reward was a fantastic dinner at Kent's, across the highway from our lodgings. After her positive experience in Maine, Joy decided to order surf-and-turf: a small lobster and a small steak. I selected the fish and chips. Both were excellent.

The next morning, we rose and left the hotel extra early. This time, our route to the race location was more efficient, and we arrived with time to spare.

Like the No Label Triathlon in Katy, Texas, which I had completed earlier this year, the Newport 19.7 used two distinct transition areas. The swim-to-bike transition took place in a parking lot at Third Beach. The bike-to-run transition and finish line would be in a paved section near Second Beach.

After the pre-race meeting near Second Beach, we walked our bikes the half mile to the park next to Third Beach. While waiting for the start of the swim, a light mist covered my goggles.

The half-mile swim in the Atlantic Ocean, my first ocean swim in a triathlon, was in the calm waters of the bay off Third Beach. My wetsuit provided the right amount of insulation to make the swim comfortable. However, beneath the water were sharp rocks that cut my feet in at least two places as I entered. I soon forgot these minor cuts.

The mist continued as we started the bike leg. Soon, water covered my glasses, making them useless. Since I could no longer see through the lenses, I pushed them down on my nose and peered over the top.

Somewhere around five miles into the bike course, I noticed an intermittent hissing sound coming from the front of my bike. With my water-covered glasses pushed down, I couldn't see exactly where the sound was coming from. Soon, I felt a firmness beneath my front tire and realized the hissing sound I had heard was from air leaving the tube. My front tire was flat.

I needed to replace the tube. After making the turn in another ten yards, I planned to pull off the side of the road. I always carried a spare tube and CO_2-powered tool for inflating the new tire in a bag strapped to the bottom of my bike seat. Having practiced changing a tube many times, I felt ready to put this part of my training to use.

As I made the turn, the bike fell from beneath me. The right side of my body crashed onto the asphalt street and grassy shoulder. As I gathered my wits, wide-eyed spectators watched from the opposite side of the street.

After a few seconds, I grabbed my bike to replace the tube. As I did, I noticed blood on my knee and forearm. In the fall, I had suffered a cut on the right side of my leg around the knee and a scrape on my right arm from the wrist to the elbow. My shoulder, which had slammed into the grassy ground next to the road, was painful but otherwise undamaged.

The clock was ticking, so I removed the front wheel's skewer, then pulled the wheel off and set it in front of me. Part way through removing the tire, a member of the volunteer bike maintenance crew came around the corner in his truck. He stopped and asked if I needed help.

Casting any remaining pride and ego aside, I told him I would very much appreciate his help. What perfect timing. While I watched, my Good Samaritan swiftly replaced the tube and reinstalled the chain, which had come off in the fall, so I could continue the race.

Surprising myself, I got back on the bike and flew down several steep hills as if I could make up the lost time. As I jogged into transition to rack my bike, I gave Joy a quick explanation for the blood on my arm and leg.

Unlike the bike course with its many hills, the out-and-back run course was flat. The run was a blur after the excitement of the bike leg. I must have looked pretty battered, though. As I ran toward the turnaround, one runner remarked after seeing my injuries, "You look like I did last week."

Joy was waiting for me at the finish line and led me to the first aid vehicle. A paramedic cleaned my cuts and scrapes, wrapping those on my arm and knee with gauze. We then walked over to check the results. Despite having lost around four and a half minutes with the flat tire and crash, I finished ninth of sixteen in my age group.

While loading the bike into the van, I noticed a half-inch hole in the tire with the new tube poking out like a bubble from a piece of chewing gum. The tire and tube punctures appeared to be from a large piece of glass or sharp rock. Fortunately, the new tube had survived the second part of the ride, still inflated and undamaged.

After leaving Newport, we drove the 140 miles to the Trek bicycle shop in Portsmouth, New Hampshire. Trek Portsmouth was the main sponsor for tomorrow's triathlon, and the location for packet pickup. During the drive, Joy and I spoke of the lessons from today's race.

First, I knew that I would now stop riding at the earliest sign of a leaking or damaged tire. I would be extra cautious when riding on wet roads, especially if I heard water spraying from the tire. My second lesson involved triathlons with two transition areas. At packet pickup, race staff had given us a plastic bag with our race number. After the swim, volunteers used the bags to move items in each racer's swim-to-bike transition space, such as wetsuit, swim cap, and goggles, to the second transition.

I had forgotten to bring the plastic bag to this transition space—something I would be more careful about in future races. After today's triathlon, I had spent several frantic moments digging for my wetsuit and goggles amidst a pile of wetsuits, most of them black like mine.

Fortunately, I found both my wetsuit and goggles. I normally carried extra goggles in my triathlon suitcase, but not an extra wetsuit. I would cherish my wetsuit during tomorrow's frigid swim in the Atlantic Ocean.

• • • •

NEW HAMPSHIRE: STATE #10

New Hampshire Nickname:
The Granite State

The swim start for the 2012 Wallis Sands Triathlon was at Wallis
Sands Beach along US Highway 1-A. The picture is
included with permission from TriME.

New Hampshire Triathlon Details

- Date: September 23, 2012
- Triathlon: 3rd Wallis Sands Triathlon
- Location: Rye Beach at Wallis Sands State Beach,
  Rye, New Hampshire

Published distances
- Swim: 0.33 miles (530 meters)
- Bike: 14.5 miles (23.3 kilometers)
- Run: 5 kilometers (3.1 miles)

U pon arriving at the Trek bicycle shop in Portsmouth, New Hampshire for packet pickup, I took my bike from the back of our rented van and walked it into the store. I asked a technician to replace the damaged tire, inspect the new tube, and check for other crash-related damage to the bike.

Thankfully, the tube was still like new, despite having been used with a punctured tire. The bike had no other damage. We left the bike shop with race packet in hand and a bike ready for tomorrow's triathlon.

After a late lunch of fresh seafood at a small family-owned-and-operated restaurant, we drove the bike course, checking the conditions of the road. The sight of hundreds of cyclists sharing the road with cars and trucks amazed us.

Before checking into our hotel, we made one last stop: a local pharmacy to purchase a tube of liquid bandage to replace the gauze coverings on the cuts and scrapes from my crash earlier today. The gauze would never survive putting on and taking off my wetsuit at tomorrow's triathlon.

Bright red, raw scrapes, each several inches long and still oozing small amounts of reddish liquid, covered my right arm and right knee. Joy applied the liquid bandage to seal these areas. Watching her tend to these scrapes reminded me once again how fortunate I was to have Joy's support. I could have applied the first aid had I been on my own, but I was grateful she was there, and so happy to have her as a travel companion.

My right shoulder was also sore from today's crash. After the New Hampshire triathlon, I seldom swam while my shoulder was healing. Still, my injuries weren't so severe as to prevent me from competing tomorrow.

Three hundred eighty-three men and women showed up the next morning to race in the Wallis Sands Triathlon. The water of the Atlantic Ocean at Rye Beach was cold, in the mid-60s—demanding a wetsuit.

What distinguished this triathlon was the towering waves, which were seven to eight feet high. They appeared even more intimidating after the race director stated that the waves today were the highest seen here all summer. With this combination of water temperature, wind, and waves, it surprised me to see a few hardy souls still preparing to swim without a shirt in only triathlon shorts.

During the pre-race warmup swim, I learned that getting past the cresting waves was almost impossible by way of a frontal attack. Thankfully, the race director had given those of us not experienced with swimming in these conditions advice for getting past the waves and beyond the surf: "Swim under the waves." Following this advice made all the difference. Swimming under a wave before it crashed made it much easier to get into open water.

This lesson reminded me that sometimes, an approach we have used before and gotten comfortable with may not be best. In a way, it's easier when the "tried and true" doesn't work at all, because it forces us to be creative and adopt a different strategy.

Experience is valuable, but sometimes, we need a fresh approach. Willingness to evaluate, then follow the advice of those with more experience is a virtue. This reminded me of the proverb, "Pride goes before destruction, and haughtiness before a fall" (*Proverbs 16:18, New Living Translation*).

Around 50 of us started in each wave, based on gender and age. For this equilateral-triangle-shaped swim course, we swam at an angle away from the beach, under the waves and toward a buoy that held firm in the calmer surf farther from shore. After turning left at the buoy, we swam parallel to the shore toward the second buoy for another left turn. From here, we sighted for the spot from which the swim had started. My return to shore reminded me of body surfing years earlier in the warmer waters of Cancun, Mexico.

The bike leg started and finished on US 1-A, riding between the Atlantic Ocean on the right side and traditional New England seaside houses on the left. Leaving Wallis Sands Beach, the flat, one-loop course comprised a two-mile ride north on US 1-A, continuing as it turned inland toward the south end of Portsmouth.

Where US1-A again turned north, the course split to turn south, curving back to the beach through a section of Rye's neighborhoods. Near mile 10, the course rejoined US 1-A south of Rye Beach for the final four and a half miles back to transition.

For the run, we turned right at the exit of the Rye Beach parking lot, heading north on the coarse gravel shoulder of US 1-A. I started the run with my feet cold from the bike ride. My porous bike shoes allowed air to flow through them. Under normal circumstances, when the air temperature is higher, this kept my feet dry.

Within the first mile, I felt increasing irritation from a small rock between my foot and the insole of my shoe. As the irritation morphed into pain and slowed my run, I stopped to remove the pea-size pebble.

A short distance later, we veered off US 1-A into Odiorne Point State Park, where we reached the midpoint of the run. After turning around, we ran along the same route toward the finish line, which was set up in the Wallis Sands Beach parking lot.

Despite the brief stop to remove the stone from my shoe, I finished the run with an average speed acceptable to me.

One lesson I took from this race is that I should wear socks during the run when the air temperature is cold. My feet were cold after the bike leg. Running with cold, bare feet was uncomfortable. Besides, my imagination conjured up ideas of what might be happening to my feet inside these cold shoes. My feet, not my run, became my focus.

Despite completing the three legs of the triathlon with times that led to podium finishes for my age group in earlier races, I finished thirteenth of 16 in the group of men ages 55 through fifty-nine.

When loading my bike into the van, my right hand brushed the foam pad on the handlebar. The two foam pads were where my forearms rested while riding in the aero position. The liquid on my hand was pinkish red, a mixture of water and blood from my forearm wound, which had leaked into the pad during the ride either yesterday or today.

After returning to Chicopee, I cleaned and bandaged the

scrapes. While these surface wounds would soon heal, the scar down my right forearm still reminds me of these two triathlons.

• • • •

FLORIDA: STATE #11

Florida Nickname:
The Sunshine State

Crabby Bill's Restaurant across the street from Clearwater Beach.

Florida Triathlon Details

- ■ Date: November 11, 2012
- ■ Triathlon: 1st TriRock Clearwater Triathlon
- ■ Location: Pier 60, Clearwater Beach, Clearwater, Florida

Published distances
- • Swim: 550 meters (601 yards)
- • Bike: 13.4 miles (21.6 kilometers)
- • Run: 3.1 miles (5 kilometers)

My journey with Joy to Florida began with a flight from Minnesota to West Palm Beach on Friday, November 2nd. My bike, secured among foam pads and bubble wrap in the Thule hard-sided bike case, traveled with our other luggage.

Our trip to Florida for the triathlon doubled as a vacation to celebrate our 39th wedding anniversary. Following a short drive south on Interstate 95, we reached the Holiday Inn in Highland Beach. This oceanside hotel would serve as our base for a weekend visit with friends and former Minnesota neighbors, Lyle and Diane Swanson, who now lived in nearby Deerfield Beach.

On Monday morning, following a weekend of playing the card game Pinochle and lounging around the hotel pool, Joy and I started our trip to The Villages, an hour's drive northwest of Orlando. On the way, we stopped in Stuart to meet Gary, a friend and customer of the company I managed. After visiting the customer's factory to meet their new management, Joy and I had lunch with Gary at a waterside restaurant.

We spent Monday night with other Minnesota friends, Don and Sue Schreifels, in the house they rented. The next morning, we moved to a house in The Villages. We had rented it for four nights as part of The Villages' Lifestyle visit, a package designed to introduce us to the community.

Through the rest of the week, the mornings included either running by myself or cycling with a group of 60- and 70-year-olds. Afternoons during the week included golfing with Don and Sue at the Turtle Mound Executive Course, taking in a movie at the Lake Sumter Landing theater, riding around in the golf cart that came with the house, and shopping. Each evening, Joy and I danced at one of the Town Squares. It felt like we were dating.

Little did we know that this visit would snowball. The following December, we rented a house and invited our three children and their families to join us in The Villages. Two of them took us up on the offer. Being in Florida also motivated me to restart golfing, at least for a short time, after more than a decade away from the sport.

On Saturday, we drove from The Villages to Clearwater Beach, the location for the next day's triathlon. Before picking up the race packet, we enjoyed a fresh seafood lunch at Crabby Bill's across the street from Pier 60 and the triathlon's transition area. Afterward, we took a short stroll on Clearwater Beach. This would be my first triathlon swim in the Gulf of Mexico.

As we walked across the sugar-like sand mixed with millions of tiny shells, we could understand why tourists identified Clearwater Beach as one of the top beaches in the U.S.. Before leaving the beach for our hotel, we passed several booths belonging to the triathlon's expo. Here, suppliers of triathlon clothing, gear, and nutrition and hydration products hawked their wares.

The next morning, around 150 men and women from 32-two states and five countries gathered to compete in the first-ever TriRock Clearwater Triathlon. A blue sky painted with a few wispy clouds and a cool, comfortable, light breeze flowing off the calm water made this ideal weather for a triathlon.

Before the race's start, we lined up by wave number between barriers reminiscent of the waiting line for an amusement park ride. Each wave included around fifty racers of similar age and gender. Swimmers in the first wave started their race with the sounding of an airhorn. The remaining waves began at five-minute intervals.

Once I had absorbed the initial shock of the 65-degree water, I no longer noticed its coolness. The out-and-back course angled away from the beach and the pier. On the way to the turnaround point, we swam to the left side of several pyramid-shaped buoys meant to keep us on course.

At the midpoint, we swam around the cylindrical buoy and back to shore, again keeping the pyramid buoys to our right. Upon reaching the beach, we ran to the grassy space on the opposite side of the beach into transition.

This race's bike leg included rides up and over three bridges spanning portions of Clearwater Bay. The climb to the crest of each bridge and back down made the course both challenging and, in some parts, fast, with my top speed reaching over 30 miles per hour.

We left Pier 60, passing through the roundabout that led east over the first bridge, Memorial Causeway. A few yards past the bridge's end, we veered right, winding through a residential neighborhood that connected the first bridge to Belleair Bridge.

After crossing our second bridge, we continued to Gulf Boulevard, where we made another right turn. The course followed Gulf Boulevard, crossing over Sand Key Bridge before turning left onto South Gulfview Boulevard. From here, we were less than two miles from transition.

The first part of the run was on the Memorial Causeway Bike Trail. While heading toward the first of two turnarounds on this course, we passed the first rock and roll band along the run course, another distinctive feature of this race.

After one mile, we turned back and headed toward the beach on the same path, passing the band again. At the roundabout across from transition, we continued on the running path alongside South Gulfview Boulevard, the street running parallel to Clearwater Beach. Here, we encountered the next series of bands. Upon reaching the second turnaround, we raced toward the finish line.

This race again showed the competitiveness of older triathletes. Competition for the second, third, and fourth places for the male 55-59 age group was tight; only 19 seconds separated the second and fourth-place finishers.

I finished third in my age group, eight seconds behind the second-place finisher and eleven seconds ahead of the fourth-place finisher.

Before traveling back to Minnesota, we made one more overnight stop in The Villages. We saw Don and Sue again during this visit and danced to a few more songs at Lake Sumter Landing. Afterward, I repacked my bike for the flight home.

2013:
FROM PACIFIC TO ATLANTIC

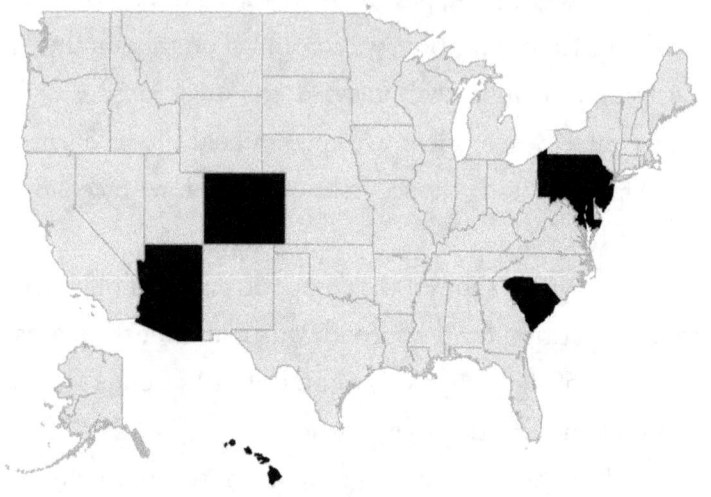

I ended my journal entry from the triathlon in Florida with the following note: *Need to improve the strength of my run.* Running was still my weakest leg.

In planning this year's triathlon season, we set a goal to complete triathlons in the Middle Atlantic states of New Jersey, Maryland, and Pennsylvania, states we could reach by car from Massachusetts in a few hours. I also kept an eye open for triathlons in other states in order to stay on track for the end goal of completing triathlons in all 50 states by 2023.

Another goal for 2013, this one work-related, was to hire a general manager for the Chicopee, Massachusetts plant. After June, Joy and I would no longer be living in Massachusetts for part of the year. This decision was bittersweet. I enjoyed the people in the Chicopee plant and the new products being developed there. Still, deep down, I knew that the business needed a person with stronger product and market knowledge to support the new products.

ARIZONA: STATE #12

Arizona Nickname:
The Grand Canyon State

Hiking to the top of Flatiron in the Superstition Mountains in Apache Junction, Arizona is challenging. Still, the view of downtown Phoenix from here is worth the climb.

Arizona Triathlon Details

- Date: February 9, 2013
- Triathlon: 2nd Tri Catching Cupid Reverse Sprint Triathlon
- Location: Skyline High School, Mesa, Arizona

Published distances

- Run: 3 miles (4.8 kilometers)
- Bike: 12 miles (19.3 kilometers)
- Swim: 400 yards (366 meters)

E scaping the cold and ice of Minnesota in February was reason enough to take part in this triathlon. However, both Joy and I also had aunts, uncles, and cousins who lived in Arizona.

In 2013, these included Joy's Aunt Evelyn Schock, who spent winters in Mesa. Joy's Aunt Dee and Uncle Bob Nelson lived in Vail, south of Tucson, having moved from Minnesota a year earlier. My Aunt Ila Johnson and cousins Julie and Jenny lived in suburban Phoenix. Joy's cousins Bobby Nelson and Steve Schock lived near Tucson. In addition to the triathlon, we planned an aggressive schedule of family visits for our brief stay.

We left Minneapolis on Thursday evening. My triathlon bike traveled with our other luggage inside its hard side case in the aircraft's cargo hold. An uneventful flight landed us in Phoenix on time.

To simplify getting our luggage and my bike case into the rented van, I picked up the van at the offsite rental center while Joy guarded our luggage on the curb outside baggage claim. Once we were together again, we set our GPS for Evelyn's house in Mesa, arriving around midnight.

After breakfast the next morning, Evelyn and Joy played a few hands of the card game Golf. Meanwhile, I unpacked, reassembled, and test-rode my bike. I was ready for the triathlon. We would devote the rest of Friday (and Saturday after the race) to visiting family.

This was my first reverse triathlon. In a reverse triathlon, the order of events is run-bike-swim instead of swim-bike-run for a standard triathlon.

The race began with a young man dressed in a Cupid

costume leading the 93 competitors on a lap around the quarter-mile track of the Skyline High School's outdoor track and field center. Since the triathlon in Florida four months ago, I had been following a new training program for running. This triathlon, the first race of the season, tested this strategy.

My run training had included three different run sessions each week. The first was a six-mile run at a pace that kept my heart rate within its aerobic zone. Two days later, I did five to seven repeats of a quarter-mile to one-mile run at high intensity. I followed each repeat with a recovery period, during which my heart rate dropped to within its aerobic zone. For the third session, known as a brick workout, I ran three miles after a one-hour cycling class.

After one lap on the track, the course continued outside the stadium on sidewalks, then on a running path that wound its way north and east of transition. The loop led back to the transition area set up next to the pool and track. A glance at my watch brought a smile to my face. I realized I had met the time goal for the run I'd set at the start of this year's training. I rode the boost of confidence into the bike leg.

While I was racing, Aunt Evelyn and Joy watched from outside the track, close to transition. Joy described the format and the distances of each leg. Then, Joy listened as Evelyn, who was witnessing a triathlon for the first time, commented on the wide range of ages and sizes of the participants. Evelyn also wondered about the unique-looking bikes. The two of them talked with a few of the participants who dropped out before finishing. Most confessed they had not trained enough for the race.

The bike leg comprised three four-mile loops of a flat, one-mile-square section of public roads surrounding Skyline High School. We rode a mile, turned right, and repeated the sequence for the 12 miles. I never changed gears.

By the third loop of this flat course, I felt bored. I started fidgeting with the cover on the water bottle clamped between the aero bars of my bike. Around mile nine, I drifted off the side of the course into knee-high tall grass. During the few seconds of bouncing over the stones at the base of the grass, I braced for collision with a large rock and falling, or worse yet, cracking my front wheel.

None of these doomsday scenarios played out as I edged my bike back onto the road. The only evidence of this near-disaster was the new streamers: long blades of grass caught in crevices of my bike frame. During the rest of the ride, the streamers fell out. Only the few eyewitnesses to this near-catastrophe knew of my distracted riding.

At the end of the third loop, I entered the parking lot a short distance from transition. While coasting, I slipped my feet out of my bike shoes, leaving them clipped to the pedals. I racked my bike, removed my helmet and glasses, grabbed my goggles, and ran toward the school's outdoor aquatic facility entrance, passing one guy in my age group who had finished his bike leg just ahead of me.

The glory of my fast transition was short-lived as he passed me during the first length of the 25-yard-long pool. Each of us completed the swim by ducking under the lane divider rope upon reaching the end of the pool, swimming to the opposite end, and repeating this sequence. After completing 16 lengths, I was at the stairs leading out of the pool. A few steps later, I crossed the finish line, clean and refreshed.

Four men were competing in my age group: men aged 60 years and older. As I surveyed the results posted by the race director, it seemed ironic that the oldest competitor in the race, a man over 70, had finished first in our age group. Meanwhile, I, the youngest in our group, finished fourth.

The four of us finished well within the top half of the field of young to old competitors. My respect for the mental and physical abilities of older triathletes was still growing.

The Tri Catching Cupid triathlon raised funds for the Arizona Desert Dolphins Synchronized Swim Team. After the race, the Dolphins treated us to a synchronized swimming show. This sport demands strength, endurance, flexibility, grace, and precision. Still, these high school girls made it look easy.

Joy and I enjoyed our time with family on this trip. We would see these aunts and this uncle again. Still, the weekend turned out to be one of our last visits with them before they passed away. Because of this triathlon, we had slipped in one more time with each.

• • • •

HAWAII: STATE #13

Hawaii Nickname:
The Aloha State

Diamondhead Crater from my favorite swimming beach on Waikiki.

Hawaii Triathlon Details

- Date: April 21, 2013
- Triathlon: 12th BOCA Hawaii Lanikai Sprint Triathlon
- Location: Kailua Beach Park, Kailua (Honolulu), Hawaii

Published distances
- Swim: 500 meters (547 yards)
- Bike: 20 kilometers (12.4 miles)
- Run: 5 kilometers (3.1 miles)

For over 10 years, Joy and I had visited my Aunt Nelda in Honolulu, Hawaii, during the peak of the Minnesota winter. This year, we delayed our trip so I could take part in this triathlon.

Still, it seemed like a waste to travel to Hawaii in April, when Minnesota weather often turned springlike, with blossoming flowers and budding trees. This year, however, winter in Minnesota stretched longer than usual. Snow was falling on and off at home throughout our time in Hawaii.

We flew to Honolulu from Minneapolis a little more than one week before the triathlon. The day after arriving, I reassembled my bike, which had accompanied us in the belly of our aircraft, then rode six miles along Kalakaua Avenue to the foothills of Diamondhead. I wanted to be sure the bike worked as expected.

I planned to get in several rides before race day. However, my experience during this ride put an end to those plans. A scarcity of designated bike lanes forced me to ride in heavy traffic comprised of cars driven by tourists unfamiliar with the streets and distracted by the flurry of activity.

Instead of biking, I used the days before the race for extra running and swimming. On my run days, I followed a course from my aunt's condo: south along the Ala Wai Canal, past the Honolulu Zoo, and around Kapiolani Park before returning along the Ala Wai.

For swimming, I walked 10 to 15 minutes west to Waikiki Beach, near the Hale Koa resort, where I swam laps parallel to shore, away from the casual swimmers closer to the beach.

On Saturday afternoon, we picked up my race packet at BOCA Hawaii, in downtown Honolulu between Ala Moana Park and Aloha Tower. The next morning, Nelda, Joy, and I made the half-hour drive to the east side of Oahu to Kailua Beach Park. My triathlon gear, including my bike, fit snugly into the back of Nelda's minivan.

With the sounding of the air horn to signal the start of the triathlon, over 350 competitors ran or walked into Kailua Bay to begin their swim. This was my first triathlon swim in the Pacific Ocean. The 500-meter swim in the calm, clear, warm water of Kailua Bay took me a little over 11 minutes. With the water temperature, wetsuits were neither needed nor allowed, according to USA Triathlon rules.

The single-loop bike course left transition in Kailua Beach Park with a right turn onto a city street, which stayed open to motorized vehicle traffic. After a couple of right turns and one left turn, we were on Kalaheo Avenue, traveling parallel to Kailua Bay Beach.

Two and a half miles further, we crossed a narrow canal, then made a right turn onto Mokapu Road. After crossing Nu'upia Pond, we passed through the gate of Marine Corps Base Hawaii. This was my first time biking on a military base.

Up to this point, the bike course had been flat. That changed as we turned left off Middaugh Street onto Daly Road at Fort Hase Beach. We now faced what I could only call a "nasty" hill. To put this in perspective, this hill caused me to wonder if I would fall over as I inched forward in the lowest gear while giving it my all. The higher cadence of the flat road had given way to a survival cadence.

Near the top of the hill, we reached our turnaround in a base housing neighborhood. Here, a chorus of cheers from members of the families occupying these houses greeted us.

Early in life, we learn the law of gravity: What goes up must come down. Coming down the "nasty" hill required extreme attention and much braking to avoid ending up in Kailua Bay while navigating the right-angle turn near the hill's base. After the excitement this hill provided, the rest of the ride seemed uneventful, following the same flat route I had ridden a few minutes earlier.

Throughout the ride, I used the highest gear in which I could maintain a cadence, or pedal revolution, of 90 revolutions per minute. I had practiced this approach over the past few months after reading about its benefits online. In the end, I achieved the intended results. While I was not always biking as fast as I could, my legs felt strong as I started the run.

To save time in the bike-to-run transition, I used another idea from my reading over the winter. Rather than clipping the race number belt around my waist while standing in my transition space, I connected it while running out of transition. A couple of close finishes taught me the value of saving seconds anywhere possible within the rules.

The single-loop run course left Kailua Beach Park in the opposite direction from the bike course. The difference in the terrain was clear almost immediately. As we entered the secluded Lanikai neighborhood on Kailua Bay, where most of the run would take place, we were faced with a repeating series of hills. As a result, we were running either uphill or downhill, never on flat ground. The payoff was a beautiful view of the twin islands, Moku Nui and Moku Iki.

The final run of six-tenths of a mile was on Kailua Beach. Since the waves washing ashore had compressed the sand, the surface was solid, except for the last few yards. During this last section, soft, deep sand seemed to swallow each step, making the sprint difficult.

As I stepped up to the park floor from the beach to make the final push to the finish line, I saw Joy and Nelda standing next to the path, cheering me on. Their encouragement pushed me to a strong finish.

I finished fourth of the seven in my age group, six minutes behind the guy who finished third. While I was in contention after the swim and bike legs, the three guys in my age group who had finished ahead of me were much stronger runners.

I later asked Aunt Nelda what she had seen, heard, and thought as she watched her first triathlon. Here is what she wrote:

"My first personal experience with a triathlon was when I met my nephew Terry and his wife Joy at the Honolulu airport with an enormous box. Later, as he reassembled his bicycle in my living room, I understood he had come prepared for the triathlon in Kailua, Hawaii.

"On the morning of the triathlon, we arrived very early to set up his transition area. I really didn't know what it all meant until later.

"When Joy and I saw them all swimming, I wondered how they could swim so close together without running into each other. We walked along the beach as they swam, but we couldn't identify Terry. The next time I saw him, he was transitioning onto his bicycle. It impressed me how everything was laid out so that he could grab and go. Then he was off.

"We knew he would travel from Kailua into the Kaneohe Marine Corps base and out again, back to the starting point. Again, I experienced his transition to running shoes. I thought he looked exhausted, and not really ready for the next event.

"Joy and I didn't see him until he came to the finish line. He and all the runners looked so tired. One reason was that the last part of the run was on the beach in soft sand. I've only run about 10 yards in soft sand, and it exhausted me. I thought it was kind of a cruel touch to the end of this last event.

"Other than breathing hard, he was in good shape, which I couldn't say for some others who barely walked across the finish line. Food, drinks, and lively conversation followed. It impressed me to see the camaraderie among participants as they shared their experiences.

"I considered it a privilege to be a spectator that day. I saw my nephew's passion for triathlon."

After the triathlon, we enjoyed the Hawaiian sun for three more days before returning to the mainland. Rather than returning to Minneapolis, Joy and I flew to Hartford, Connecticut, where I would work from the Chicopee plant before doing the next triathlon in a week and a half.

NEW JERSEY: STATE #14

New Jersey Nickname:
The Garden State

Joy and me at Lake Absegami after packet pickup.

New Jersey Triathlon Details

- Date: May 5, 2013
- Triathlon: 6th Bassman Sprint Triathlon
- Location: Bass River State Forest, Tuckerton, New Jersey

Published distances
- Swim: 0.35 miles (560 meters)
- Bike: 11.8 miles (18.9 kilometers)
- Run: 3.1 miles (5 kilometers)

Joy and I left our house in Chicopee, Massachusetts early Saturday morning, eager to visit a part of the Atlantic coast that was new to us. Our destination for the 250-mile trek to the triathlon location was Bass River State Forest, a little over halfway down the Jersey Shore.

When thinking of New Jersey, many of us who grew up in the rural Midwest imagine a sprawling metropolis such as Newark. I had learned differently four decades earlier, during a business trip from Newark to northwestern New Jersey. I remember being surprised by the beautiful wooded areas that dominate that part of the state.

Today's trip from Massachusetts took us through New York City, across the Hudson River, and through the congested asphalt and concrete-covered spaces often associated with New Jersey. By now, the first part of this trip was becoming familiar to us. Twice, Joy and I had used our time on the East Coast to visit Manhattan. During these weekend getaways, we had seen the Radio City Rockettes Christmas Spectacular and other Christmas displays. I had also made work-related day trips to businesses in southern Connecticut and east central New Jersey.

As we continued south, the "asphalt jungle" was replaced with dense stands of oak, pine, and maple trees in suburban neighborhoods. Further south, wooded areas gave way to sections of marshes and wetlands. As we approached Bass River State Forest for packet pickup, we again passed through dense forest, with tall pines dominating the view.

We arrived at the park early Saturday afternoon to pick up my race packet. While there, we took extra time to walk along the beach of Lake Absegami, where I would swim in the triathlon the following morning.

Our next stop was 45 minutes further south: Atlantic City. While neither of us was a fan of casinos or gambling, we wanted to see what had drawn Pat and T, two of Joy's friends from our Chicopee neighborhood, to this city. Twice each year, these two ladies would drive to Atlantic City for gambling and an overnight stay in Pat's timeshare.

We drove along the strip, lined with a mix of casinos: small and large, simple and opulent. With the gusty winds, an air temperature in the mid-50s, and expensive parking, neither of us was interested in an extended stop. Instead, Joy and I took turns walking from a nearby hotel loading dock for a quick look at the famous Atlantic City Boardwalk.

After finishing our drive along the strip, we continued a couple of miles further to Brigantine Beach, where we stopped for lunch at the Pirates Den. Six months earlier, Hurricane Sandy had passed through the region. Despite obvious remnants of Sandy, the beach remained in excellent condition. As we walked along this white sandy beach, we understood its attraction, especially in warmer weather.

After passing through Brigantine, we went to our hotel in Manahawkin for an early dinner and last-minute preparations for the triathlon. I planned to depart the hotel early the next morning in time for the opening of transition. Early in my triathlon journey, I had embraced a philosophy: "The early triathlete gets the best spots in transition."

Bassman featured three triathlon distances: half-Ironman,

Olympic, and Sprint. Other choices were duathlon and aquabike races in half-Ironman and Olympic distances.

The air temperature on race morning was still in the 50s. With the temperature of the Lake Absegami water measuring 65 degrees, the race was wetsuit-legal. While I didn't need any encouragement, the race director suggested triathletes wear a wetsuit during the swim.

The Sprint triathlon began with all 46 of its competitors entering the water. I started too fast, which led to a moment of panic as I became light headed. I'm certain the congestion with which I had been struggling the previous week didn't help.

After slowing my stroke rate, which allowed my heart rate to drop, I was able to continue without difficulty. I finished the swim and made the short run from the exit of Lake Absegami across the beach to transition.

Most triathlons and multisport races have two timing mats in transition—one at each end. This allows timers to isolate the times for the swim, bike, and run plus two transition portions (T1 and T2). In this way, racers entering transition while finishing one leg do not interfere with those leaving it for their next leg.

This triathlon's transition area had a single timing mat at the entrance nearest the lake. As in other races, we left transition for the bike and run legs at the opposite end, where there was no timing mat. Therefore, our bike and run times began as we crossed the single timing mat from the previous leg and included our T1 and T2 times, respectively.

As I crossed the timing mat after the swim, my time for

the bike leg began ticking away. After stripping off my wetsuit and putting on my bike helmet and sunglasses, I walked my bike, with biking shoes clipped into the pedals, to the exit at the opposite end of transition. I mounted the bike where I had been instructed to do so by a race volunteer.

The bike course began with a ride from the Absegami Day Use Area onto local roads south of the park, with Stage Road being the first. After a little less than two miles, we veered left onto Leektown Road. From here, we followed an eight-mile triangular loop with three left turns.

The bike ride could best be described as picturesque, with views of tall stands of pines and oaks interrupted by nearby rivers. The bike course map showed a change in elevation of just over 30 feet.

During the third leg of the triangle, on a section of North Maple Avenue, we passed two large turkey vultures pecking away at a deer carcass. I guess the animal, whose remains lay on the road's gravel shoulder, had wandered into the path of a passing motor vehicle. The pair of vultures seemed unfazed by the many bikers passing within a few feet of them as they continued their cleanup.

This stretch led us to Stage Road, where we turned right to complete the final two miles to transition. After getting off my bike at the dismount line, I walked it across the same timing mat I had crossed after the swim to enter transition. The bike leg was now complete; timing for the run leg had begun.

A dirt hiking trail through stands of tall pine and oak trees served as the first part of the run course. The trail tested our agility—and ankle strength—as we dodged and/or navigated over exposed tree roots and rocks.

Further along in the run, we moved onto paved roads, including one that led us through a section of North Shore Campground, an overnight camping facility. Here, we passed a mix of cheerful, smiling faces along with some expressing bewilderment. The latter group may not have been aware of the triathlon schedule...or even wondered why someone would do such a thing.

I tend to sweat during a triathlon as much as, or maybe more than, anyone. Today, the cool air kept me from breaking a sweat until the very end of the run. Also because of the temperature, my feet felt nothing as I pounded along the trail. I am sure the cool weather helped me meet the run pace goal I had set for my races this season.

To my surprise, I was the top finisher in the 60 through 64 men's age group, and first overall among those 60 and older. With these results, I had now qualified for the USA Triathlon National Championships.

• • • •

MARYLAND: STATE #15

Maryland Nickname:
The Old Line State

The swim for the Maryland triathlon took place in Lake Habeeb
within Rocky Gap State Park.

Maryland Triathlon Details

- Date: June 1, 2013
- Triathlon: 26th Annual Rocky Gap Triathlon
- Location: Rocky Gap State Park,
  Flintstone, Maryland

Published distances

- Swim: 0.25 miles (402 meters)
- Bike: 8 miles (12.9 kilometers)
- Run: 2.5 miles (4 kilometers)

We left our house in Chicopee, Massachusetts on Friday morning, heading in a southwesterly direction. The drive of around 450 miles went through Connecticut and past New York City. Once in Pennsylvania, we traveled through Allentown and Harrisburg, making a stop in the chocolate-themed town of Hershey to tour the Hershey Hotel. We then continued toward the northwest corner of Maryland. During our drive, we came within two miles of the Pennsylvania border.

I had visited the urban and rural areas of eastern Maryland in the past. However, this part of Maryland, in which rugged tree-covered mountains seemed to wrap themselves around us, seemed like another state.

Our route to Cumberland, Maryland, where we would stay the night, included a stop at Rocky Gap State Park to check parts of the swim, bike, and run courses. Before checking into our hotel, we navigated through town to the Cumberland YMCA, for which this triathlon doubled as a fundraiser. After picking up my race packet and dinner at Henny's Bar & Grill across the street from our hotel, I added air to my bike tires, filled water bottles, and laid out shoes and clothing for tomorrow's race.

The next morning, we left our hotel before dawn, in time to get a prime spot for my bike in transition. As the morning progressed, participants of the Sprint and International distance triathlons arrived. The darkness gave way to cloudless sunny skies.

Before the start of the two races, the race director gathered the participants to describe the swim, bike, and run courses.

Following the national anthem, we headed to the beach to prepare for the swim.

The swim was in 243-acre Lake Habeeb. From the beach, we looked across the lake at Evitt's Mountain, named for one of the first European settlers in Allegany County. The water temperature was around 72 degrees, so USA Triathlon rules allowed wetsuits. The swimmers started in four waves, with the Sprint men comprising the first.

The right-angle triangle of the Sprint swim course started from the beach, just to the right of the red *Swim In* arch. As the start signal sounded, we ran or walked into the water and swam along the hypotenuse of the triangle toward an orange buoy. After turning left at the buoy, we sighted toward the red inflatable arch set up on the beach.

The bike course left the park to ascend a short, gradual hill. At the first intersection, we turned left, following the rolling hills of Pleasant Valley Road and climbing 150 feet over the four miles to the turnaround. At the halfway mark, we turned around to ride downhill back to transition.

For the run leg, we left transition, which was set up in a grassy patch, passing the Rocky Gap Casino Resort on Old Hancock Road Northeast. At a little over halfway toward the turnaround point, we turned right onto Gorge Road Northeast, now heading toward Rocky Gap Dam. Halfway across the dam, we turned around.

During the last mile of the run, it surprised me to see a man with the number 70-something written on his right calf pass me. For this race, the number meant he was in his seventies.

I crossed the finish line after running the last few hundred yards on a grassy path. My time placed me third of seven in the age group of 60 through 64 men and 29th overall.

While cooling down after the race, I walked over to talk with Jim Chapman, the man in his 70s who had passed me during the run. His ability impressed me. How did he train for running? Could I apply it to my run training?

Our wives jokingly commiserated, describing themselves as "triathlon widows" while Jim and I talked about the run training, strength training, and stretching he credited for his performance. Over the next 30 minutes, Jim described how he normally started the training season with a couple of months of easy runs three times per week to build a fitness base. Only after this phase would he increase the intensity of his training. Progressing in this way had reduced the risk of injury, allowing him to run faster.

Jim then used hill repeats and intervals between runs of 10 to 20 minutes to warm up and cool down. The hill repeats and intervals increased his running strength and endurance. I was already using intervals in my run training program. He suggested I add a few different squats to strengthen my hips and larger leg muscles.

Within the next week, Jim emailed me a summary of his run training plan, including details of the stretching and strength training he used. He also described his approach to fueling and hydrating for training and racing.

This experience with Jim confirmed that men and women beyond age 70—the age at which I once believed life (or at least sports competition) to be over—were doing incredible things in triathlon. It also showed the camaraderie, the support within the sport through which athletes of all ages and abilities could selflessly share what they had learned.

Once I had showered and changed clothes at the park, Joy and I headed northeast toward Quakertown, Pennsylvania. Tomorrow, I planned to do a Sprint triathlon outside this town.

PENNSYLVANIA: STATE #16

Pennsylvania Nickname:
The Keystone State

Before the Maryland triathlon, we toured the Hershey Hotel during our
east-to-west voyage across Pennsylvania.

Pennsylvania Triathlon Details

- Date: June 2, 2013
- Triathlon: 11th Independence Triathlon
- Location: Lake Nockamixon State Park,
  Quakertown, Pennsylvania

Published distances
- Swim: 0.25 miles (402 meters)
- Bike: 10 miles (16 kilometers)
- Run: 2 miles (3.2 kilometers)

Quakertown is located a little less than 50 miles north of Philadelphia. We learned of the town's historical importance during our ten-mile trip east from our hotel to Lake Nockamixon State Park to pick up my race packet.

Our drive took us past Liberty Hall, the first permanent residence in Quakertown. Liberty Hall was also the resting point for the Liberty Bell during the evening of September 23, 1777. After that one night, Jacob Mickley continued to move this symbol of the American Revolution to its permanent hiding spot in Allentown, Pennsylvania. I now understood why "independence" had been included in the triathlon's name.

Covering 5,000 acres in Bucks County, Lake Nockamixon State Park is a recreational playground nestled amidst rolling hills. After our arrival, we searched along the main roads for any sign of the triathlon. As we passed the Marina Visitors Center and several picnic areas, we asked a few people if they knew of it. No one did.

After a few tense moments, we found the people handing out race packets for this triathlon. The race staff also shared valuable information for parking during the race.

Following their advice the next morning made parking, then setup of my transition space, a peaceful experience. While I was taking care of last-minute preparations, Joy set up her lawn chair under the shade of a tall tree alongside the wife and father-in-law of another racer. From this vantage point, they could watch the activity in and around transition.

As with the Massachusetts triathlon, the race began with a father towing his son in a rubber raft along the swim course.

Meanwhile, the rest of the over 400 competitors waited for the start of the race. As I watched the raft move further from shore, I wondered if a connection between these displays of a parent's love for a child and the sport of triathlon existed.

Piles of multi-faceted rocks the size of a mini basketball covered the shoreline of this part of Lake Nockamixon. Getting over and past the rocks, with their razor edges and pointed corners, required extra care to avoid injury. For this reason, before the start of each wave, those assigned to it walked with caution past the rocks into the waist-deep water. At this depth, smaller, blunt-edged chips of the larger rocks along the shore covered the lake bottom.

As the father swam further from shore, the race director signaled those assigned to the first of four waves to walk into the water. At the sounding of an air horn, this group began their swim. As the swimmers in the first wave ventured farther from shore, the race director called those in the second wave to the starting line. He repeated this for the third wave, then the fourth and final one in which I swam with other triathletes aged 40 and over. When the start signal sounded, I lunged forward, buried my face in the water, and threw my right arm forward as I brought my lower body to the surface to begin my swim.

Transition was set up on a flat grassy space just up the hill from the lake. To protect our feet from the sharp rocks at the exit of the swim, the race staff placed non-slip rubber mats in the water. The mats continued up the grassy hill to help us avoid slipping while running up the hill.

While I raced, Joy and her two new friends took in the

activity within transition. They watched as some swimmers wandered aimlessly, trying to remember where they had racked their bikes. Others arrived at their transition space and wrestled off their wetsuits. A couple fell over as they lost their balance.

Later, they watched as bikers returned, some using a spectacular flying dismount to get off their bike. Many of them ran their bikes to their transition space with a single hand on the bike seat, then slipped on running shoes and headed back out of transition, all within seconds.

The bike route left the park, turning onto a state highway on which we rode for three miles to the first of two U-turns. With only a few slight hills, the flat course helped me keep an average speed of a little over 18 miles per hour.

We rode back on the opposite side of the highway, over the same small hills. However, instead of turning into the park, we passed the entrance, continuing one mile to a second U-turn. After making the turn, we rode back to the park entrance and to transition.

The flat out-and-back run course paralleled the shore of Lake Nockamixon on an asphalt trail covered by canopies of tall deciduous trees, including oak, maple, and poplar.

During the first half of the run, a young lady who I guessed to be in her late twenties strode past me. As she did, she let out a fart that seemed out of character. I looked at her, expecting to hear "oops" or "sorry" or something similar. Hearing and seeing no reaction, the middle-schooler still living in me released a soft chuckle.

The single turnaround for the course involved running a

loop encircling a flagpole on the peninsula next to the lake's marina. Minutes later, I crossed the finish line, completing a race in under one hour for the first time.

My time—59 minutes, 59 seconds—placed me second in my age group and 132nd of the 441 finishers of the Sprint triathlon.

With only a Sprint triathlon today, we attended the awards ceremony and returned to the hotel before breakfast was finished. After a shower, we were ready to begin our trip back to our Chicopee home. Tomorrow was a workday.

Still, we sacrificed some time on our return trip to explore a region of Pennsylvania that was new to us. Rather than take the most direct route through the northern part of greater New York City, we headed north toward Scranton, Pennsylvania, following smaller state roads.

The route passed through charming small towns in and around the spectacular Pocono Mountains. Driving through it reminded us of the Black Forest region of Germany, where we had made connections with Joy's German relatives a few years back.

After merging onto I-84, we continued through southeastern New York State into southwestern Connecticut. At one point, we drove within five miles of the bike course for the Connecticut triathlon in Ridgefield. The last leg of this trip followed the route we had used a year earlier when traveling from Ridgefield, through Hartford, and on to Chicopee.

COLORADO: STATE #17

Colorado Nickname:
The Centennial State

Enjoying ice cream and conversation with my parents.

Colorado Triathlon Details

- Date: September 8, 2013
- Triathlon: 1st Inverness Triathlon
- Location: Colorado Athletic Club, Englewood, Colorado

Published distances

- Swim: 525 meters (574 yards)
- Bike: 12 miles (19.3 kilometers)
- Run: 3 miles (4.8 kilometers)

My parents needed to experience a triathlon and see why I enjoyed the sport. While I had played basketball and baseball in high school, I hadn't, as far as they knew, competed in any sports since then. It surprised them to hear me describe a significant goal—visiting the 50 U.S states—in a sport they knew little about while I worked long hours and traveled around the world. I wanted to find a triathlon that both fit our schedules and was near their home in the south Denver suburb of Parker. The Inverness Triathlon in nearby Englewood satisfied these conditions.

To make the most of our road trip from Minnesota to Colorado, we included extra days for visiting family in South Dakota and Nebraska as well as friends in Colorado Springs. We began the six-day, six-state trip on Wednesday morning, heading first to Rapid City, South Dakota. My triathlon gear and bike sat protected inside the van behind its two front seats.

We wanted to visit Joy's Aunt Evelyn and cousin Boni. One goal in seeing Evelyn was to make good on our promise to treat her to breakfast or lunch as a thank-you for her hospitality when we stayed with her in February for the Arizona triathlon.

On Thursday morning, after breakfast with Evelyn, we drove to Colorado Springs, home of our friends Steve and Lori Erickson. We had first met them in the late 1980s when we lived in the same neighborhood of Inver Grove Heights, Minnesota. Joy and Lori ran for state legislative offices soon after meeting. Our friendship as couples grew from here. It wasn't until later that we realized why: We all viewed life as an adventure to be experienced, not just observed. Steve said that his mother once told him, "You need to mature, but you should never grow up." While living in Alabama for Steve's job, their adventures had involved sailing. Both Steve and Lori described sailing as "hours of boredom followed by moments of sheer, exhilarating panic." Steve and Lori were now continuing their adventure, exploring the United States via motorhome camping. As they camped in different parts of the country, they visited family and friends. We were doing the same, only through triathlon.

In the afternoon, we toured the Broadmoor Hotel and other areas of Colorado Springs we hadn't seen during earlier visits. On Friday morning, we finished the first half of our trip with the hour-and-a-half drive from Colorado Springs to my parents' house.

Mid-Friday afternoon, I took my bike for a ride around my parents' neighborhood. Within a few blocks, the seat had dropped a foot and was now resting on the frame. While I could still ride the bike, my legs did not extend as far as they could with the seat at its correct height. As a result, it required greater effort to ride at my normal pace.

After returning to their house, I rechecked the seat post clamp using the torque wrench I kept in my triathlon suitcase. The wrench confirmed that I had tightened the clamp to the specified torque. Not wanting to overtighten the clamp and risk cracking the bike's carbon fiber frame, I called the Trek bike shop in Parker for ideas on how to solve the problem. We agreed that I would bring the bike into the shop on Saturday morning.

In my experience, almost everyone working at bike shops is eager to help those visiting their store. The guys at Treads, the local Trek dealer, were no exception. Over the next two hours, my bike sat on a trainer near the middle of the showroom floor while two technicians huddled around it to solve the mystery of the sinking seat.

As they tried each new idea, I climbed onto my bike and rode it long enough to determine if the seat would stay at the correct height. After a handful of failed attempts, they landed on what appeared to be a solution.

With a grit-filled, sticky substance smeared around the seat post, the seat remained at the desired height throughout the test ride. The technicians believed the added friction between the seat post and clamp provided by the gritty material would keep the post from sliding down. I believed they had solved the problem, but still didn't understand what had changed since the last time I had ridden the bike.

After all that time and effort, they refused payment. Still, I purchased a tube of the gritty material in case I needed more later. I left the bike shop feeling ready for the triathlon and confident in my bike.

Early the next morning, I drove to the Colorado Athletic Club in nearby Englewood, where the triathlon would take place. Joy came a half-hour later with my parents. Steve and Lori had traveled from Colorado Springs to witness their first triathlon.

The Inverness Triathlon, my first at an altitude of over one mile, included individual and relay Sprint triathlon and aquabike events. In the relay version of the Sprint triathlon, one member of the three-person relay team swam, then the second one did the bike leg. A third team member completed the run.

The aquabike included the swim and bike distances of the triathlon with only a short walk or jog to the finish line from transition. Two team members shared in completing the two legs of the aquabike relay, one for swimming and another for biking. Individuals who couldn't or didn't want to run the triathlon distance chose this event.

Before starting the triathlon, the race director asked all swimmers to gather at the starting end of the six-lane outdoor pool. The pool deck and space behind it at the other end remained clear for the swimmers exiting to transition. A couple of rows of chairs sat behind the exit end of the pool deck. Joy, my parents, Steve, and Lori watched from there.

After everyone who planned to swim arrived at the pool, the race director instructed us to form groups of five according to our estimated time to complete the 525-meter swim. The next few minutes felt like triathlon's version of speed dating. After meeting more racers than normal, I joined four other swimmers whose swim pace was near mine.

One guy swimming in my group told me he was competing in the individual aquabike race. He had chosen this event because of a chronic knee problem that kept him from running.

The swim that kicked off the triathlon and aquabike races required completing 21 lengths of the 25-meter pool. The odd number of lengths meant we would exit the pool after completing our swim at the end opposite from where we had entered.

The race director had reserved one lane for individuals who expected to complete the swim in seven minutes, 30 seconds or less. They swam alone in this lane. I think the race director believed these racers were the ones with the greatest likelihood of winning the entire race. I'm sure he didn't want their swim time to suffer by being paired with a slower swimmer.

The remaining five lanes were for the rest of us. The slowest swimmers, with the longest expected swim time, started in the first wave. Five swimmers whose expected times were similar stood at the end of each of the five lanes. One of the five started every 10 seconds in what is called a time-trial start.

From the exit of the pool, we walked or jogged the short distance to transition, which was set up in the parking lot outside the fence around the pool. Once all five swimmers of a group had completed the course, another group of five repeated this sequence until all swimmers had finished their swim.

The bike course left the Colorado Athletic Club, heading north on Inverness Parkway. After connecting with Inverness Drive East, the course followed this city street along the western edge of Centennial Airport to the airport's north end. Motorized traffic on this early Sunday morning was almost nonexistent as we rode past modern office buildings and an occasional green space or pond. Over the first two and a half miles, we descended 120 feet. From here, the course ascended 180 feet over the next eight miles.

After riding the half-mile along the northern tip of the airport, we turned south. For much of the rest of the ride, we followed the airport's eastern edge, now on even quieter streets among office buildings.

As we rode toward the southern end of the airport, we made side trips to two separate airport gates. Instead of entering the airport property, we turned around using a loop in the front of each gate. We continued past the airport and beyond the south end of the Athletic Club. Two right turns later, we were back at transition.

As I proceeded further along the bike course, I saw that the gritty material applied at the bike shop was not holding the seat up. By the time I finished the bike leg, the seat had dropped the entire height it had fallen during Friday afternoon's ride. At least it had taken longer to do so today.

With the seat lower, each pedal stroke generated less power than it had with the seat at its correct height. As a result, I took longer to finish the course. What should I have done differently? The guys at the bike shop in Parker did everything they knew to do.

My focus on running over the summer meant most of my cycling training had taken place on a stationary bike at LA Fitness. Still, I should have ridden the bike on the course around our neighborhood before leaving for Colorado. Had I noticed the problem earlier, there might have been time to really fix it.

The single-loop run course started on a walking and running trail in a small park behind the fitness center. Upon completion of a single loop of this trail, we moved onto a city sidewalk that led away from the fitness center, parallel to its rear side, then back to the fitness center. Reaching the driveway leading into the fitness center's parking lot, we all sprinted across the finish line.

Even though the run course was flat, I mixed running and walking for this race. I expected the run to be a challenge with the difference in altitude between our Minnesota and Massachusetts homes and Denver, and I had learned during previous visits to my parents' home that running at higher altitude was more difficult for me.

Despite the problem with my bike seat and the challenges of running at the mile-high altitude, I finished 50th of 200 overall and second within my age group of men 60 through 64.

Triathlon is not the most exciting spectator sport. The swim, and perhaps the flurry of activity in transition during a race, are the exceptions. Despite this, my parents stayed for the entire race. Seeing their stoic looks in a picture taken during the event caused me to wonder how much they enjoyed watching this triathlon. Still, they never said a thing to make me think they had not appreciated their time with us.

After the awards ceremony, we said goodbye to my parents and to Steve and Lori, then started our two-day journey to Minneapolis. We spent the first night in Omaha, Nebraska, with our son Ben, daughter-in-law Lindsey, and granddaughter Mari.

Later the following week, I took my bike to Maple Grove Cycling, the store where I had purchased it. As I explained the problem, the technician told me of a recall on the seat post clamp, which Trek had announced over the past few days. As I inspected the latest bikes and helmets, he installed the redesigned clamp. I never again used the grit-filled material.

• • • •

SOUTH CAROLINA: STATE #18

South Carolina Nickname:
The Palmetto State

Sand volleyball at Coligny Beach on Hilton Head Island.

South Carolina Triathlon Details

- Date: October 12, 2013
- Triathlon: 22nd On-On Tri Hilton Head Triathlon
- Location: Coligny Beach, Hilton Head Island, South Carolina

Published distances
- Swim: 500 meters (547 yards)
- Bike: 12.4 miles (20 kilometers)
- Run: 3.1 miles (5 kilometers)

Sitting together one evening in early November 2012, Joy and I imagined the 2013 triathlon season. Joy wanted to visit South Carolina's Hilton Head Island after friends had said how much they enjoyed their time there.

At about the same time, the race management company for the On-On Tri Hilton Head Sprint Triathlon opened registration for the 2013 race. Upon learning that this triathlon coincided with the week of our 40th wedding anniversary, we decided this would be the year to visit South Carolina and Hilton Head.

Joy and I departed Minneapolis on Thursday, October 10th, eleven months after registering for the South Carolina triathlon. Over the long weekend, I would compete in the race, and we would celebrate a milestone wedding anniversary.

We reached Savannah at noon after taking an early-morning flight with a layover in Atlanta. After picking up our rental car, we drove to the Savannah Visitors Center to join the Old Town Trolley Tour of historic Savannah.

The tour through this historic city passed along streets lined with oak trees draped in Spanish moss. According to the guide, Henry Ford had considered using the moss to fill car seats. The material was—and still is—abundant, cost-effective, and renewable. What he did not know at first was that many tiny insects, some that bite, like to make the moss their home.

The tour continued past stately mansions, cobblestone squares, historic cemeteries, and a section of the Savannah River. Throughout the tour, our guide mentioned movies filmed in Savannah such as *Forrest Gump*, *The Lady and the Tramp*, and *The Longest Yard*.

About three-quarters of the way through the tour, we hopped off the trolley for lunch at Paula Deen's restaurant, Lady & Sons. The buffet-style lunch included Southern staples of grits, fried okra, and peach cobbler. We added other items more commonly found on our Minnesota table, including green beans and fried chicken.

After finishing the tour, we left Savannah, driving north to Hilton Head Island and crossing from Georgia into South Carolina just outside Savannah. The 40-mile trek to our hotel, The Beach House Holiday Inn at Coligny Beach, took a little over one hour.

We followed a short walk on the beach with a swordfish dinner at Steamers. Before retiring for the night, we relaxed in the hotel's outdoor hot tub.

After lunch on Friday, Joy dropped me at Road Fish Bike Shop to pick up my rented bike, a Trek Madone 3.1. Months earlier, I had secured a rental on this bike for the triathlon. Three things favored renting a bike for this race. First, at $50 for a 24-hour rental, renting was less expensive than bringing my bike as airline luggage for $150 each way. Earlier, I asked Delta Airlines to sponsor me in triathlon by giving me free bike shipment. Regrettably, they declined what I considered a reasonable offer.

Second, renting a bike near the race site was more convenient, especially given the short time we had for this trip.

Renting avoided the hassle of unpacking and reassembling my bike after arriving at the race venue, then disassembling and repacking it after the race.

Besides, traveling with my bike, secured inside its hard-sided case, meant we needed to rent a larger, more expensive vehicle than the mid-size sedan I had reserved. Saving money on the car rental was a third factor in favor of renting a bike.

Still, I wanted a bike that fit my six-foot three-inch frame and wouldn't slow me down in the triathlon. Since my second triathlon, I had raced using a triathlon-specific Trek SpeedConcept. The one exception had been the triathlon in Massachusetts. However, no bike shop on Hilton Head Island rented a tri-bike. The closest rental option was a road bike, without aero bars.

Staff at the bike shop exchanged their pedals with my own from my triathlon bike. In this way, I could use my cycling shoes. They also adjusted the seat height. After a quick test ride and a second seat adjustment, I started back to the hotel.

The ride to our hotel reminded me why I had become reluctant to ride on city streets. While approaching a parking lot exit, a school bus barreled across the sidewalk into the street, either oblivious to me or unconcerned for my safety. Had I not braked hard enough to lift the back wheel off the sidewalk, the bus would've struck me.

Packet pickup for this triathlon occurred later in the afternoon. Remembering the close call with the school bus earlier in the afternoon, I walked instead of rode the few blocks to Go Tri Sports. As I crossed a bridge on the walking trail, I noticed a three-foot-long alligator in the water below. I could not recall ever having been so close to one in the wild.

No problem, I thought. Our swim tomorrow was in the gator-free ocean, not a local lake or pond where these critters live.

The next morning, while it was still dark, I walked with the rented bike and my swim gear, including wetsuit, to transition setup in a parking lot across South Forest Beach Drive. Today's commute was even shorter than it had been for the Vermont triathlon.

Before the race's start, over 100 competitors walked from transition back across the street onto Coligny Beach. Once we had regrouped on the beach, the race director gave us instructions for the swim.

Before starting, we walked up the beach 550 yards, the distance of the swim, to the starting line. Once there, we waded into the water to between chest and neck deep and waited for the starting signal.

With the sound of an airhorn, the entire group of triathletes began swimming parallel to the beach until they reached the location marking the end of the swim. The waves were small today, making it easy to swim in a straight line and stay on course.

After exiting the water, we ran what seemed like a hundred yards across the beach and through the hotel parking lot, passing by a window of the room where Joy and I were staying. We continued across South Forest Beach Drive into transition.

After removing my wetsuit, I grabbed the rented bike and jogged to the line designated for mounting. Hopping onto the bike, I slipped my feet into my shoes, already clipped into the pedals.

The bike course was three four-mile loops of a flat, tree-lined section of local streets. The triangular course left transition, which was near the Coligny Circle roundabout at the intersection of Pope Road and South Forest Beach Drive. After a little more than a mile, South Forest Beach Drive split into two roads. We stayed to the right to ride back to Pope Road, where we made another right turn. Then, at the Coligny Circle roundabout, we took the first exit back onto South Forest Drive for the second and third loops.

The rental Trek bike worked well, confirming my decision to rent a bike for this triathlon. My bike pace today matched what I would have expected with my triathlon bike.

The run course comprised a shortened single loop of the bike course. "Flat and fast" is often used to describe courses like this one. The flatness of today's course set a new bar for the purity of this definition. This was not surprising, since sea-level waterways and ponds occupy 40 percent of this small coastal island.

The flat course no doubt helped me to a first-place finish in my age group, which we celebrated during the awards ceremony under the Holiday Inn Tiki Hut. This was the icing on the cake of an otherwise marvelous trip. Our experience on Hilton Head Island had lived up to the reviews from Joy's friends and our expectations.

2014:
SETTLING IN

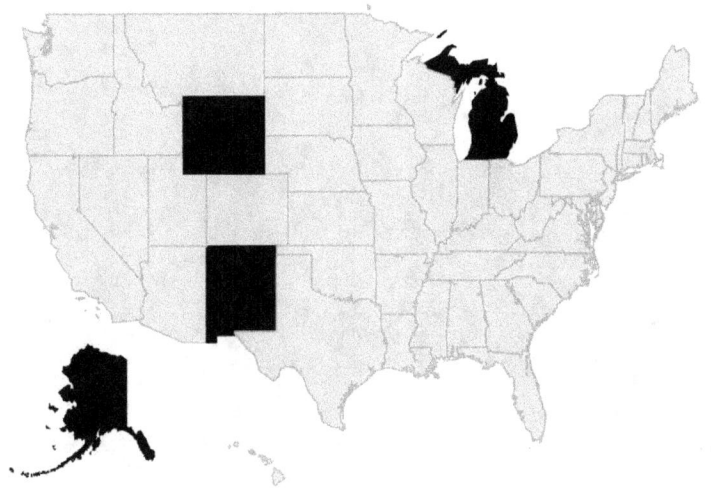

Now into this journey through three years,
Though still learning, had quelled all my fears
Of training and racing in swim, bike, and run.
Besides, I had learned triathlon is fun.

With races complete in states one through eighteen,
I was settling in to do ones in between
Some close, some far.
One by air, others by car.

During this year, we ventured further from home
Each race gave us fresh places to roam.
The triathlons were another excuse to see
Family and friends with whom we wanted to be.

• • • •

WYOMING: STATE #19

Wyoming Nickname:
The Equality State

Gillette, Wyoming is also called the Energy Capital of the Nation.

Wyoming Triathlon Details

- Date: May 3, 2014
- Triathlon: 11th Razor City Splash & Dash Triathlon
- Location: Campbell County Aquatic Center, Gillette, Wyoming

Published distances
- Swim: 900 yards (823 meters)
- Bike: 12 miles (19.3 kilometers)
- Run: 5 kilometers (3.1 miles)

While attending the Arizona triathlon more than a year earlier, Joy's Aunt Evelyn found she enjoyed watching triathlons. Then, when we had seen her the previous September on our way to the Colorado triathlon, she had mentioned wanting to attend another race. We decided that a triathlon in Gillette, Wyoming, a two-hour drive west of her summer home in Rapid City, South Dakota, would be a great way to get Evelyn to another race.

Joy and I left our Minnesota home on Thursday evening, spending the night in Mitchell, South Dakota, home of the world-famous Corn Palace, a site we had visited a few years earlier. We rose early the next morning, reaching Rapid City in time for lunch with Evelyn.

While we had planned for her to join us on the rest of the trip to Gillette, she wasn't feeling well enough to travel. After lunch, we said farewell to Evelyn and her daughter Boni, promising to return the next day with a full report on the triathlon.

After checking into our motel, we drove around Gillette before picking up my race packet. Sitting at an elevation of 4,600 feet in the high plains of northeastern Wyoming, Gillette is the State's third-largest city.

We learned that in 1891, Edward Gillette, engineer and surveyor for the Chicago, Burlington and Quincy Railroad, recommended the route of the railroad, which passed through what was then called Donkey Town. City founders changed its name to honor Gillette.

Today, Gillette's most common nickname is "Energy Capital of the Nation." The name comes from the city's location in a region boasting plentiful reserves of coal, oil, and coalbed methane gas.

Meanwhile, the Razor City Splash & Dash Triathlon gets its name from another of the city's nicknames, "Razor City." Legend has it that the nickname came from linking Edward Gillette to the razor blade company bearing his surname.

After a stop at the Campbell County Aquatics Center to get my race packet, Joy and I ate an early dinner at the Prime Rib restaurant.

The next morning, we rose early to reach the Aquatics Center just as the triathlon's transition area was being opened to participants. We arrived a few minutes ahead of the race staff.

Transition was located in a grassy space outside the exit of the pool on the southeastern corner of the Aquatics Center. After setting up my space, I chatted with the race director. During the conversation, I shared with him my goal of completing a triathlon in each of the 50 states by age seventy. As more racers arrived, the conversation shifted. Before long, race volunteers were summoning us into the Aquatics Center for the triathlon's swim leg.

Passing the check-in desk, it surprised me to see an Olympic-size pool in the recreation center of a city the size of Gillette. Later, I learned that it was the only pool of this size in the entire state of Wyoming.

For today's triathlon, Aquatics Center employees had reconfigured the 50-meter pool to a 25-yard pool with 20 lanes—more than enough for all swimmers to start the race together. Before starting the race, we arranged ourselves in groups of five, all of whom expected to complete the swim in a similar time. Once we had formed our group, the five of us got into the pool. For this race, my group included four young women.

Each of us needed to supply a person to count our laps. The race director instructed our lap counter to place a red board into the water as we approached the end of the pool before beginning our last lap. Joy ticked off one more volunteer performance by counting my laps.

Once the air horn sounded to start the triathlon, one of the five swimmers started every five seconds. The five swimmers would remain in this lane for the entire swim. Despite some lane congestion, I completed the swim almost three minutes faster than my estimated time. I found this highly encouraging.

With her volunteer duties complete after my swim, Joy hung out with other volunteers and spectators, most of whom were from Gillette and the surrounding area. Joy was struck by their warmth, especially the effort locals made to be sure she felt welcomed. "Sweethearts" summed up her impression of them.

From the map of the bike course, our route looked a lot like a capital letter T, with the starting point near the bottom of the vertical section. We left transition outside the Aquatic Center and exited the parking lot at its northeastern corner, turning left onto East Warlow Drive.

After riding a couple of blocks, we turned right onto Hannum Road, now at the base of the T. From this point until we returned to this spot near the end of the bike leg, motor vehicle traffic was light as we rode with pastureland on both sides.

Our ride included two turnarounds on Northern Drive, one at each end of the top horizontal section of the T. What was missing from the simple description of the course as a flat letter T were the four steep climbs and descents with rolling hills between. The hills made this short ride more challenging, though still quite fast.

Somewhere around mile three, on a flat section of Northern Drive, I noticed pronghorn deer in the field alongside the course. Biking with deer next to the course was another triathlon first. With a tall fence separating us from the deer, I never worried that they would run onto the course.

The flat run course took us through a peaceful residential neighborhood of Gillette. The course left from the eastern side of the Aquatics Center parking lot, looped around streets to the south, and, further along, southwest of the Center before returning to the parking lot and finish line.

I finished 26th of the 71 participants in this triathlon. Since I was the only participant over 60 years of age, I earned a first-place age group prize. When calling me to claim the prize, the race director added a few words to describe our mission to cover the USA through triathlon.

After the awards ceremony, Grant Egger, a reporter for the *Gillette News Record*, told Joy and me that he was writing a story covering the Splash & Dash Triathlon. He asked to interview us, to which we happily agreed. A few days later, Mr. Egger emailed me a copy of the newspaper article pictured below.

We left Gillette at 12:15 p.m. for our first stop, Rapid City. We planned to make good on our promise to update

Evelyn on our trip and the triathlon. As an experienced triathlon spectator, she asked all the right questions. After catching her up over sweets and a cup of coffee, we said our farewells and headed toward Minnesota.

Three months later, Evelyn passed away. We truly appreciated the time we had spent with her on this and earlier trips as well as our shared interest in triathlons.

Extreme fitness, extreme fun

By GRANT EGGER

NEWS RECORD WRITER
gegger@gillettenewsrecord.net

The water was fine, the tires were filled and the running shoes looked good.

About 100 people took part in this year's Razor City Splash and Dash Triathlon on Saturday, swimming, biking and running their way to some well-earned medals. The event — put on by the Campbell County Parks and Recreation Department — involved a 900-yard swim at the Aquatic Center, a 15-mile bike ride and a 5-kilometer run,

Among the faces in the crowd were Adrian Gerrits and Wendy Lloyd, both of Gillette. Gerrits had the overall top time of 1 hour, 3 minutes and 12 seconds. Lloyd was the top female, crossing the finish line with a time of 1:16:27.

Teams also participated. Taking home the trophy in the corporate category was North Platte Physical Therapy.

Also in the middle of the action was 62-year-old Terry Vanderwert. The Maple Grove, Minnesota, resident easily traveled the furthest to compete, but also has an interesting story behind why he did.

He's trying to compete in triathlons in as many states as he can.

He's been doing this for only four years.

"My wife and I try to couple the triathlons with visits to people we know in the area," Vanderwert said, his wife Joy by his side. "We've been out to Hawaii, she has an aunt in Arizona, we've got friends in Texas. So this is state No. 19."

The couple has family in Rapid City, which made for a quick trip to Gillette. And South Dakota had already been knocked off the list when Vanderwert completed a race in Yankton, where his son from Omaha, Nebraska, was able to come up. Next up is Alaska in the first week of June.

Vanderwert finished the Gillette triathlon in 1:26:35. He and Joy were happy to be a part of it, and pleased with how the event was run.

"We loved it," Joy said.

"I enjoyed it very much," he said. "It was a great course. The hills on the bike were very challenging, but they were fun. The pool was fantastic. I don't think I've ever seen such a large pool."

"It was beautiful," Joy added. "But the warmth of the people. I'd like to mention that. They are sweethearts."

"It was just very relaxed," Vanderwert said. "It was fun."

Gillette News Record article from the
2014 Razor City Splash & Dash Triathlon.

ALASKA: STATE #20

Alaska Nickname:
The Last Frontier

Mt. McKinley from the Princess Wilderness Lodge restaurant patio.

Alaska Triathlon Details

- Date: June 1, 2014
- Triathlon: 21st Annual Eagle River Triathlon
- Location: Chugiak High School, Chugiak, Alaska

Published distances
- Swim: 500 yards (457 meters)
- Bike: 12.6 miles (20.3 kilometers)
- Run: 3.1 miles (5 kilometers)

During the summer of 2012, almost a year after embarking on our triathlon adventure, Joy and I attended the wedding of her cousin Linda Pieschel's son. During one reception speech, we learned that the bride and groom, Michael and Erika, were moving to Anchorage, Alaska, where he would serve with the United States Air Force at Joint Base Elmendorf-Richardson.

Upon hearing this, Joy and I turned to each other and together whispered, "Alaska." Later that evening, we shared with the newlyweds our plan to visit Alaska within the next four years. We imagined that even though they agreed, they believed we would never follow through. Little did they realize we had started laying plans for the Alaska triathlon during our drive home from their wedding reception.

About two years later, Joy and I arrived in Anchorage two days before the Eagle River Triathlon. We intended to cram a lot into our week-long stay in Alaska, so we used these days to tour Anchorage. Sampling the local cuisine, especially its seafood, was a must. We dined at Seward's Folly Bar & Grill, Gwennie's, and Bridge, a seafood restaurant recommended by several locals.

On the day before the triathlon, we connected with Michael and Erika at Glacier Brewhouse in downtown Anchorage. By now, they had welcomed their adorable son.

After lunch, we picked up the race packet at Chugiak High School, headquarters for the Eagle River Triathlon. To reach it, we drove 25 miles northeast of downtown Anchorage, just off Alaska Highway 1, also known as Glenn Highway.

We then picked up the Scott road bike I had rented from Chain Reaction Cycles. As with the South Carolina triathlon, I brought my pedals and biking shoes to use with this bike.

While still new to triathlon, I had never considered Alaska a hotspot for the sport. Alaska residents embraced this event. The Eagle River Triathlon was a popular race that had been held every year since 1993 (with the exception of 2003).

When I arrived the next morning at the Chugiak High School parking lot for transition, I realized I had missed important information about this event. Had I read the triathlon's Facebook page, I would have known that the race organizer did not provide racks for holding bicycles in transition for this race. Most racers had brought their own means of supporting their bikes. Some racers were using purchased stands, while other bikes stood upright in homemade racks.

Since transition covered a large area considering the number of participants, I stood my road bike upside down, balanced on a tripod: two points at each end of the bike's handlebars and the third on the bike seat. I protected these points from scuffing against the pavement of the parking lot by placing one of the green and white striped towels from my triathlon case between the asphalt and bike.

Had I brought my triathlon bike, I would have laid it on the pavement since it cannot stand upside-down in the same way. Other racers left plenty of space around my bike, no doubt afraid that it would tip over, knocking their bike down.

After getting past that minor hurdle, Joy and I chatted with other triathletes before the start of the triathlon. One of these was a young lady and her parents. We learned she and her husband were living in Fairbanks. However, her parents were visiting from Hutchinson, Minnesota, a farming community about an hour's drive west of our Minnesota home. That was interesting.

However, as we continued talking with her, we learned she had grown up outside Hutchinson and swam in high school with our daughter-in-law, Lindsey. Suddenly, the world felt smaller. Over 3,000 miles from home, we had not only met someone who knew a family member, but I had raced alongside her.

The swim leg took place in the Chugiak High School swimming pool. The 500-yard swim comprised 10 laps, or 20 lengths, of the 25-yard pool, all within the same lane, with one swimmer per lane.

We started in the order of our bib number, with around 100 of us completing the swim every hour. This approach spread the start time for the entire field of 364 triathletes over almost four hours.

The outside temperature at the start of my race was just under 50 degrees. By the time I completed the swim and was heading out onto the bike course, a light drizzle was falling. With this combination of temperature and rain, I felt cold during the ride. I also rode more cautiously, since the roads appeared slippery.

The course left transition in the Chugiak High School parking lot, turning north following Birchwood Lane for almost four miles to the first turnaround. After turning around, we returned on the same road, continuing past the entrance to transition to a second turnaround, about two and a half miles past the school. From this second turnaround, we rode back to transition.

The rented bike I was using today did not fit me as well as the Trek bike I had ridden in South Carolina, and my time to complete this leg of the triathlon showed it. I made a mental note to pay closer attention to fit when renting a bike next time.

The run followed a single-loop, out-and-back course. Its first section followed a paved trail that left transition heading east. After passing under Alaska Highway 1, we turned left to follow another paved trail that paralleled the highway. We ran between the highway and tall pine trees toward the halfway mark. As we approached the turnaround, we made a loop among the trees to point ourselves toward the finish line. From here, we returned to transition and the red inflatable *Finish Line* arch.

Many racers were still on the course when I completed the triathlon. Some had even waited to start their swim. Since I needed to return the rented bike to avoid another day's charge for it, we left the school, returned the bike, and went back to the hotel for a warm shower and dry clothes. When we returned to Chugiak High School, the race staff had left.

However, later that day, I checked the timing company's website, where I learned I had finished third in the men 60 through 64 age group. For this finish, I earned a ceramic plaque, which I picked up from the same store where I rented the bike.

From the same website, I noticed that the young woman who swam in high school with our daughter-in-law had done even better. She was the fastest female finisher of this year's Eagle River Triathlon.

While it had rained on race day, the weather during the following week was perfect. We put over 1,000 miles on the rental car, first driving north to Fairbanks and passing Chugiak High School on the left. En route, we spent one night in Talkeetna; from there, we took an air tour of Mt. McKinley and the surrounding mountains and glaciers.

Our destination for the next night was scheduled to be Fairbanks, but this leg of the trip did not go as planned. Somewhere near two-thirds of the way to Fairbanks, we heard a *thump-thump-thump* sound from the front of our rental car. From the way the car handled, I knew the noise was not coming from a flat tire.

I pulled off at the nearest rest area, got out of the car, and walked around it. Satisfied that the tires were all still inflated, I got down on the ground to look under the car. It surprised me to see the sagging engine cowling—a molded black plastic covering underneath the engine compartment. The front part of the cowling was no longer connected to the body. Apparently, air flowing beneath the car as we drove down the road had caused the cowling to oscillate and periodically bounce off the highway.

I called the rental car company to explain the problem. Could I trade it in for a replacement in Fairbanks? No. My only option was to return the vehicle to Anchorage Airport, the same place I had picked it up.

Our return to Anchorage therefore included a second stop in Talkeetna—this time to purchase a roll of duct tape. I used the tape to secure the cowling to the body, as was necessary for a safe drive to Anchorage.

At Anchorage Airport, I completed the paperwork for our replacement car, and we resumed our journey to Fairbanks. By the time we reached the Princess Lodge near Denali National Park and Preserve, we had driven over 500 miles in one day.

Ready for a break, we snagged a room at the Lodge. Before heading to bed, we sat on the patio outside the nearest restaurant and ate dinner with a view of Mt. McKinley through a cloudless blue sky. While seated at our table, Joy shared her picture of Mt. McKinley on social media. Within minutes, we learned from her friends' comments that such a clear view of the mountain was rare. The hassle with the car had produced an unexpected reward.

During our driving tour of Fairbanks the next day, we saw an advertisement for North Pole, a Christmas-themed town around 15 miles southeast of Fairbanks. As we continued driving to North Pole, then back to Fairbanks, we kept our eyes open for a restaurant that served moose meat. Finding one would satisfy Joy's curious desire to sample moose.

After two nights in Fairbanks, we returned to Anchorage, continuing south to the Kenai Peninsula and Seward, where we stayed for two days. For one full day, we joined Kenai Fjord Tours to visit Resurrection Bay.

The tour treated us to close-up views of glaciers and the occasional breaking away of a small chunk of ice, called calving. From the boat, we also saw a variety of birds, sea lions, and humpback and killer whales.

Throughout our stay, we experienced the long periods of sunlight typical of June in Alaska. I never tired of waking in the middle of the night to peek outside. It never grew darker than Minnesota dusk. Thank goodness for the thick, room-darkening curtains.

Though we never did have the chance to taste moose meat, our visit to Alaska left us with a wonderful impression of this beautiful state and its people.

• • • •

MICHIGAN: STATE #21

Michigan Nickname:
The Great Lake State

Drizzle began during my warmup swim in Lake Antoine.

Michigan Triathlon Details

- Date: June 29, 2014
- Triathlon: 4th Annual Northern Lights YMCA UP Northwoods Triathlon
- Location: Lake Antoine County Park, Iron Mountain, Michigan

Published distances

- Swim: 500 meters (547 yards)
- Bike: 17 miles (27.4 kilometers)
- Run: 3.1 miles (5 kilometers)

The Michigan triathlon took place in a section of the state known as the U-P, short for Upper Peninsula. Michigan's U-P is situated north of the main part of the state, separated by the Straits of Mackinac. The Great Lakes of Superior, Michigan, and Huron all border the U-P.

Iron Mountain, the location for this triathlon, stands on the west side of Lake Michigan. Because of this, our travel was much quicker than if the race had been held in a city east of Lake Michigan.

Still, we took a roundabout path to Iron Mountain to visit Joy's cousin Linda and her husband Tom Pieschl in Ironwood, Michigan. After a relaxed drive along the southern end of Lake Superior in northern Wisconsin, we crossed the border into Ironwood. Late Friday afternoon, we reached Tom and Linda's home.

In Alaska two weeks earlier, we had already met their new grandson. They were now planning their own visit to Alaska to meet the newest addition to their family.

After breakfast in Ironwood the next morning, Tom and Linda took us to some of their favorite sites. Stops included Copper Peak, home of the world's largest manmade ski jump. At Black River Harbor, swarms of black flies chased us back into our vehicle, just as Tom had forewarned.

Later that morning, after bidding farewell to Tom and Linda, we made the southeasterly journey to Iron Mountain, continuing to soak in the laid-back feeling of the region. After a late lunch and a drive through this town of just over 7,000 residents, we checked into our hotel. Before picking up the race packet at Lake Antoine Park later in the afternoon, we drove the bike course, something we often did before a triathlon.

On race morning, 35 triathletes gathered at Lake Antoine Park for the Northern Lights YMCA UP Northwoods Sprint Triathlon. The temperature of 748-acre Lake Antoine's water, where the swim would take place, was in the low 70s. The air was even cooler.

After setting up my triathlon space, I put on my wetsuit. Before doing so, I strapped on my belt with the bib bearing my race number, something I had not done before in a race. The race director told us to wear our race number during both the bike and run legs. Putting on the race number under my wetsuit would save the few seconds in transition before climbing onto the bike.

Around 15 minutes before the triathlon began, I walked into Lake Antoine to examine the bottom and adjust to the water. Since the water was clear, I could see the sandy silt base, perfect for visitors to the surrounding park, campsites, and cabins. As I came out of the water, a light mist was falling, causing some spectators to open their umbrellas.

My wave of ten swimmers was the first to begin. With a fast start, I found myself alone, sure I was leading the wave. I told myself, "I might be the first swimmer out of the water." My thoughts went to the previous months of swim training and the obvious payoff. I imagined entering a new level in my triathlon racing.

Right around that time, a young woman on a stand-up paddleboard woke me from my dream. From her position above me, she yelled down to tell me I was off course. Instead of keeping "the buoys on my left," I was swimming on their left side. Returning to reality, I rejoined the wave, realizing I wasn't leading it. I thought, *triathlon sure keeps me humble.*

When I first began in triathlon, I was humbled, sometimes humiliated, by anything I did not know or had not completely learned. Training and racing continued to remind me of my physical limits.

While they were not something I wanted all the time, I now realized that humbling experiences were no longer something I despised. After all, I managed a business in which we developed products based on technologies I often did not fully understand. I found that humility helped me approach people in a way that created trust. Reminders in the context of triathlon grounded me to be a more effective manager.

The drizzle ended by the time I had finished my swim. The roads showed only a hint of the rain as we headed onto the bike course.

We exited the eastern edge of Lake Antoine Park and turned right to ride past houses and cabins on a series of narrow roads hugging the shoreline of the circular lake. The bike course followed the circumference of Lake Antoine, merging onto Lake Antoine Road, which led to the entrance to the park.

Rather than follow Lake Antoine Road as it turned into the park, we continued straight onto Upper Pine Creek Drive and the first hills of the course. Somewhere within the next two to three miles, two young deer crossed the road in front of me—another new experience in a race. While I never rode close enough to collide with the curious animals, I did slow down. Had something caused the deer to cross back over, the situation could have changed in an instant. Better safe than sorry.

Two miles farther, the road made a right turn, and the bike course became even more hilly. The next right turn brought us onto the shoulder of U.S. Highway 2. We rode here for a little more than one mile before exiting onto Lake Antoine Road. We were now on the final stretch back to transition.

The first part of the run course took place on gravel roads within the campground of Lake Antoine Park. Several campers, some in lawn chairs set up next to the road, were sipping their morning coffee between cheers for the triathletes.

The course continued out of the park to the south, following the same road around Lake Antoine we had biked earlier. At the course's halfway point, we looped around a cone and headed back to the finish line.

With a faster bike split than the other man in my 60 through 64 age group, I finished ahead of him and near the middle of the pack overall.

Since we were expecting family at our home for dinner that evening, we left almost immediately after the race. Following a shower at the hotel, we set out on the six-hour trek across Wisconsin to our Maple Grove, Minnesota home.

NEW MEXICO: STATE #22

New Mexico Nickname:
Land of Enchantment

Rock, paper, scissors sculpture in the Santa Fe Art District.

New Mexico Triathlon Details

- Date: September 20, 2014
- Triathlon: 7th Annual City of Santa Fe Triathlon
- Location: Genoveva Chavez Community Center, Santa Fe, New Mexico

Published distances
- Run: 5 kilometers (3.1 miles)
- Bike: 12 miles (19.3 kilometers)
- Swim: 400 meters (437 yards)

During a call with friends Steve and Lori Erickson in early July, Joy and I decided that this was the year to do a triathlon in New Mexico. As they had done so many times before, our friends invited us to their cabin in the Sangre de Cristo Mountains in south central Colorado.

We had visited them the previous year at their Colorado Springs home before the Colorado triathlon. Then, they had driven to Englewood to watch the triathlon with Joy and my parents. Still, we had never been to their cabin.

This time was different. Our calendar was clear for the period around the City of Santa Fe Triathlon. Joy and I wanted to visit both Santa Fe and our friends' cabin, which was located halfway between Santa Fe and my parent's house south of Denver.

We began the journey of around 2,500 miles on the Wednesday before the triathlon. Later that afternoon, we arrived at the home of our son Ben, daughter-in-law Lindsey, and their daughter, Mari, in Omaha, Nebraska.

The next morning, we resumed our trip to Santa Fe, following U.S. highways to avoid the interstates and their dense truck traffic. Driving the U.S. highways turned out to be a tremendous choice. The route was a hundred miles shorter, and the traffic much lighter. On top of this, we found traveling through the smaller towns more entertaining.

We arrived at our hotel in Santa Fe in the dark. After dinner at a chain restaurant next to the hotel, we crawled into bed for a welcome sleep.

The next morning, we drove to the historic Santa Fe Plaza, where we hopped on a bus for a guided tour of the city. The tour took us past the Loretto Chapel with its mysterious staircase. Legend has it that the spiral staircase was the result of special prayer nuns in the church recited for nine consecutive days. On the ninth day, a carpenter appeared. Using only a hammer and a carpenter's square, the unknown man built what is called the Miraculous Staircase using wooden pegs. Another part of the mystery is that the wood the carpenter used to construct the staircase was not native to the region. After finishing the project, the man disappeared without asking for payment.

Our tour then continued through the arts district of Santa Fe and into the surrounding areas of the city. After lunch on the plaza at the Thunderbird Bar & Grill, where I had dined during a work-related trip several years earlier, we walked back to explore the Loretto Chapel and exhibits within the arts district.

Later in the afternoon, we popped over to the Genoveva Chavez Community Center, the headquarters for the triathlon. I picked up the race packet, adding this race's T-shirt to my growing collection.

Steve and Lori arrived at the hotel as we returned from packet pickup, ready for authentic New Mexican cuisine. While spicy dishes are not my usual pre-race meal choice, I couldn't pass them up while in New Mexico.

Between the time I registered for this triathlon and race day, I learned something surprising about Santa Fe. One day at work, I mentioned my plan for the New Mexico triathlon to a colleague. He asked if I knew the altitude of Santa Fe; I replied that I did not.

He informed me that Santa Fe was 7,250 feet above sea

level. I had traveled to Santa Fe several times for business, never realizing that its elevation was 50 percent higher than that of a more famous high-altitude city, Denver, also known as the "Mile-high City."

The 2014 City of Santa Fe Triathlon was a reverse triathlon, the second run-bike-swim triathlon in which I had raced. I had completed my first reverse triathlon a year and a half earlier in Mesa, Arizona.

Today was my first time wearing a black and green braided bracelet, color-coordinated with my triathlon suit. The bracelet was handmade by our eight-year-old granddaughter, Kate, especially for this triathlon.

Race morning brought still, clear skies and an air temperature in the low 60s. Before the start of the triathlon, we walked south of the Community Center, past the lot where our van was parked, and onto Rodeo Road. This was where the race would begin.

Both the downhill slope of this road and peer pressure caused me to start faster than I intended: seven and a half miles per hour, according to my GPS watch. The result was a lot of walking later in the run.

The single-loop course continued on Rodeo Road for around one mile. Just before reaching the bridge that crossed a dry riverbed, we turned south onto a paved trail that followed the river's edge. Upon reaching a footbridge, we crossed the arroyo near the backside of the Santa Fe Place Mall, proceeding on the trail behind the mall to our turnaround. From there, we began the return on the running path back to Rodeo Road. This time, we crossed over Rodeo Road and followed this running path.

We passed behind Sam's Club and in front of a Santa Fe Fire Department station before reaching the back of the Community Center. The last section of the run went along a delivery road behind and around the east side of the Center. We arrived at transition, which was set up in a parking space next to the pool on the Community Center's south side.

The out-and-back bike course departed from the rear of the Community Center, merging onto Richards Avenue. After two left turns within the first one-third mile, we rode south on Richards Avenue, away from the city center. As we continued further south over Interstate 25, traffic became lighter, then almost nonexistent. The course became hillier, and we rode down the steepest hills.

After almost three miles, we passed Santa Fe Community College and turned right onto Avenida Del Sur. We were now riding on residential neighborhood streets lined with earth-tone adobe-style houses. Soon after passing the Institute of American Indian Arts, we reached the six-mile mark and the turnaround.

Our return to transition followed the same streets we had ridden minutes earlier. Now, riding up one of the steeper hills, I felt lightheaded. I was sure I would need to walk my bike to the top of this hill. However, as I slowed, the feeling went away, and I continued. Further along the second half of the course, I even passed a few racers.

The swim leg took place in the eight-lane, 50-meter indoor

pool of the Community Center. At each end of the pool, we ducked under the lane divider to cross into the adjacent lane, then swam to the opposite end.

The swim is my favorite leg of the reverse triathlon. Though it may not be ideal for the pool water, swimming after running and biking tends to wash away sweat and dust from the first two legs. I exited the pool refreshed.

I finished third of three in my age group. Today, this earned me a place on the podium and a medal, a square wooden medallion with laser-engraved triathlon logo and name.

After the race and awards ceremony, we followed Steve and Lori as they drove their Jeep to their cabin. Our home for the next four days would be the Malcolm Forbes Wagon Wheel Creek Estates, a few miles northeast of Fort Garland, Colorado.

Getting to the cabin from the main highway involved an eight-mile, 20-minute trek up a rugged, winding gravel road. While climbing to 10,000 feet, we spotted over a dozen cattle and an equal number of mule deer. Steve told me the homeowner's association generated income by allowing nearby ranchers to graze cattle on the property.

We spent three of the next four days at the cabin, gazing south and west across countless miles from atop the mountain. For our remaining day, we drove to the Great Sand Dunes National Park and Preserve. Before reaching the park to explore the large sand dunes up close, we stopped for a hike to Zapata Falls. I love hiking to waterfalls. Their music relaxes every part of me.

Ending our stay with Steve and Lori, we hugged, then began the three-hour drive north for an overnight stay with my parents. The next night, we made a second stop at our son Ben's home during the 10-day trip.

2015:
CROSSING THE MIDPOINT

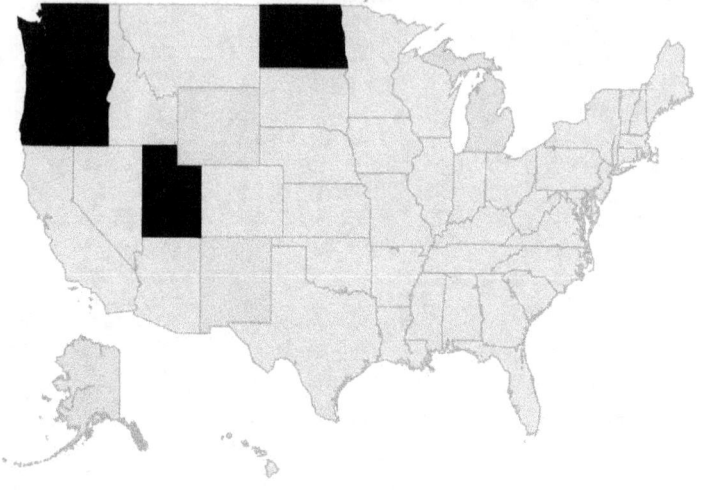

We set two goals for 2015.

Completing a triathlon in North Dakota was the first. North Dakota was one of the U.S. states with the fewest triathlons. One of the three triathlons in North Dakota scheduled for 2015 involved kayaking and mountain biking rather than swimming and road biking. I had little interest in mountain bike training.

What would I do if they quit holding the only regular Sprint triathlon in North Dakota after this year? I could create my own triathlon somewhere in the state based on standard Sprint distances. Still, the easiest thing to eliminate any concern was to sign up for the Bismarck Triathlon, which I did in February.

A second goal was to complete triathlons in the Pacific

Northwest. During our stay at their cabin after the New Mexico triathlon, Steve and Lori had invited us to join them along the Oregon Coast the following autumn. While they ultimately could not make the trip for reasons we understood, Joy and I proceeded with our plans.

Later in 2015, on Halloween, I completed my first half-marathon in St. Paul, Minnesota, a goal prompted by thoughts of eventually doing longer-distance triathlons.

NORTH DAKOTA: STATE #23

North Dakota Nickname:
The Peace Garden State

Transition area before the start of the Bismarck Triathlon.

North Dakota Triathlon Details

- Date: July 18, 2015
- Triathlon: 11th Bismarck Triathlon
- Location: Harmon Lake Park, Mandan, North Dakota

Published distances

- Swim: 500 meters (547 yards)
- Bike: 20 kilometers (12.4 miles)
- Run: 5 kilometers (3.1 miles)

While registering for this triathlon, I learned I could save on the fee if I shared with Facebook friends my plan to compete. After sharing the post, Tom Lipp, a friend and colleague from the early 2000s, wrote to say he had completed the Bismarck Triathlon a year earlier. Tom was now training for Ironman Wisconsin.

Around 10 a.m. on Friday, we set out from home for the next day's Bismarck Triathlon. The GPS coordinates for our destination were Epic Sports in Bismarck for race packet pickup.

Driving to Bismarck from our Minnesota home was as easy a trip as one can make: Start the audiobook, get on Interstate 94 going west, and continue driving for just under six hours. Around halfway along our route, we passed through the Red River Valley, one of the flattest landscapes and most fertile agricultural areas in the U.S., and, for that matter, the world.

Still, I couldn't shake my concern about the temperatures I was expecting during the race. The average high temperature during the week before the triathlon had been 100 degrees, and I was not a fan of running in extreme heat.

Bismarck is the twin city of Mandan, North Dakota, the location of Harmon Park and the Bismarck Triathlon. The Missouri River divides the two, with Bismarck to the east and Mandan to the west.

After collecting my packet and the race T-shirt, we checked into our hotel for the evening. Since Harmon Park was 20 miles from the hotel, we skipped the pre-race visit to drive the bike course. Instead, we headed downtown, taking a side trip to visit the North Dakota State Capitol building.

Following a short walk around the renovated downtown, we stopped at Blarney Stone Pub, a restaurant recommended by the hotel desk clerk. Dinner tonight included authentic Irish food: creamed cabbage and corned beef for Joy, and fish and chips for me.

The Bismarck Triathlon, including Sprint, Sprint relay, and Olympic-distance triathlons, started at 10 a.m., the latest of all my races so far. Transition opened at 8:30 a.m., a time when most triathlons have already begun. Despite momentary misgivings for not visiting the race site yesterday when our GPS directions came into question, we made it to Harmon Park with plenty of time to spare.

Rather than the hot, still air I had been expecting, the temperature this morning was a chilly 60 degrees. On top of this, the wind was howling, averaging 25 miles per hour and gusting to forty. With no trees within the park or hills surrounding the bike course, the wind rocked our van as it blew by unhindered.

As the race start time approached, volunteers assigned to place the buoys in Harmon Lake for both the Sprint and Olympic distance swims realized they were fighting a losing battle. Wind overpowered anchors, causing the buoys to drift. On top of this, volunteers in kayaks (which would provide a rest stop along the course for swimmers needing a break) spent all their time paddling to stay near the course. With the wind today, they could not provide the level of support for swimmers intended by the race director.

Moments before the start of the race, the race director made the decision to change the swim course, designating a new one that would run parallel to shore. The race director then deemed the revised course, which one swimmer later reported to be 250 meters according to data on his GPS watch, safe for the conditions of the day. And the race director was right; everyone finished the swim.

For the bike leg, the numbers on my bike computer told the story. My average speed was 14 miles per hour, while my maximum speed was 37 miles per hour. While biking uphill, into the wind, my pace was between nine and 11 miles per hour. I avoided the aero position during most of the ride, fearing being blown off the road.

During the first two miles, the gusting wind resisted every stroke of the pedal. The real fun, however, began after turning right.

For the next four miles, the wind pushed from the side, forcing me to lean left and adjust to its gusts. The scary ride continued after turning around, except now I leaned to the right, still into the west wind.

After turning for the final two miles, the wind, now at my back, pushed me. I reached my maximum speed while riding downhill during this last section.

In general, I prefer that the run course not include a hill right out of transition. My legs are already struggling to adapt to running after biking; but today, I was not getting my wish. The run started uphill on the same road within the park used for the bike course. With the wind today, the bike ride was tough, and my legs were more tired than normal. Yet as I left transition and started on the hill, I saw Joy's smiling face and heard her encouraging words. Whenever she was not volunteering or engaged in deep conversation with another spectator-and-newest-best-friend, Joy could be found near the beginning or end of the racecourse. It amazed me how much stronger I felt with her cheering me onward.

The out-and-back run course shared the first one and a half miles of the bike course, again passing the campground within Harmon Park and the much-appreciated cheers from campers-turned-spectators. As on the bike leg, we faced strong headwinds during the first half of the run. After the turnaround, the wind pushed us toward the finish line.

I ended the race with the second-best time of the five participants in my age group of 60-and-over men. My 1:27:41 time was nothing to brag about, but I finished with no injuries.

Following the race, we went back to the hotel for a shower. Before we had left for the triathlon this morning, the woman at the front desk had extended our checkout to 2 p.m. so I could clean up and change clothes after the triathlon. We left the hotel at a little before 1:15 p.m. and returned home.

• • • •

UTAH: STATE #24

Utah Nickname:
The Beehive State

The Utah State Capitol in Salt Lake City.

Utah Triathlon Details

- Date: September 7, 2015
- Triathlon: 7th Annual South Davis Labor Day Triathlon
- Location: South Davis Recreation Center, Bountiful, Utah

Published distances
- Swim: 350 yards (320 meters)
- Bike: 12 miles (19.3 kilometers)
- Run: 3 miles (4.8 kilometers)

The South Davis Labor Day Triathlon in Bountiful, Utah resembled many triathlons put on by local fitness and community centers. These races give members a deadline upon which to focus their training. Besides, the cost to register is easy to justify when you consider the race swag, including T-shirts and other giveaways.

To make the long trip from Minnesota to Utah easier to justify, Joy and I combined this triathlon with others in Oregon and Washington. During this almost two-week, 5,396-mile road trip, I planned to compete in triathlons in three states within seven days.

On our way to Bountiful from Minnesota, we stopped overnight in Omaha, Nebraska to stay with our son Ben, daughter-in-law Lindsey, and now two granddaughters, Mari and Anna Joy. The next day, we made the long drive to Salt Lake City's northern suburbs.

We arrived a couple of days before the triathlon to visit some of Salt Lake City's unique places. On Saturday, we first toured the Latter-Day Saints Conference Center, then listened to an organ recital at the Mormon Tabernacle.

The purpose of our next stop within the complex was to search family records at the Family Search Center at the Joseph Smith Memorial. Here, I learned about my paternal grandmother, Vera, who died when my dad was 13 years old, and her parents. Meanwhile, in tracing her roots, Joy learned that she comes from French and English royalty—something of which she still reminds me.

After sitting for three hours, we drove west to the Great Salt Lake to walk along the beach. I took a short stroll into the salty water, remembering a time around 55 years earlier when my siblings and I swam in the Great Salt Lake during a summer vacation.

I was fortunate to grow up in a home with parents who enjoyed traveling to different places within the United States and Canada. We even drove from San Diego, California across the border into Mexico when I was six years old. I still remember the strawberry soda and pickled jalapeños.

During summers, between the last cultivation of our corn and soybean fields and harvest, our family often traveled to northern Minnesota or to the western states for two weeks. It was during these trips west that I fell in love with the Grand Teton Mountains and Yellowstone National Park. During one of these adventures, we had traveled through Utah, where we floated in the Great Salt Lake and learned about the extra buoyancy the salty water provided.

After lunch on Sunday, Joy and I drove part of the bike course using the map provided by the race director. We could not drive the entire course since several miles of it used a shared biking, walking, and running trail near the Legacy Nature Preserve. Neither did I ride the trail portion of the course, a decision I would question the next day.

This Labor Day Triathlon, organized by the South Davis Recreation Center, was my first triathlon on a weekday. It was also my first race on a national holiday.

Participants in the Sprint triathlon could choose to do the three legs on their own or as part of a relay team. Others competed in the shorter novice individual triathlon.

Before the start, swimmers gathered on the deck of the center's 14-lane indoor pool. Individuals in the Sprint triathlon, and those doing the swim leg of the relay, lined up according to their expected swim time. Starting with the fastest, one swimmer jumped into the first lane every few seconds to begin their swim. Upon finishing the first length, we passed under the lane divider and swam back to the starting end in the second lane. After going under the divider into the third lane, we swam the third length.

For the Sprint distance race, we repeated this serpentine path across all 14 lanes of the 25-yard pool. Those competing in the novice distance triathlon started after those in the Sprint triathlon. Their swim ended after six lengths of the pool.

After completing the 350-yard swim, I climbed up from the pool onto the deck and walked through the doorway at the building's end onto the outdoor sidewalk leading to transition and our bikes. Transition took place in a parking lot belonging to the Bountiful city park behind the fitness center. Those of us competing in the individual event put on our helmets, grabbed our bikes, and walked them past the timing mat and bike-mount line before climbing on.

Once inside transition, swimmers competing in the Sprint relay removed their timing chip strap, handing it to the team member responsible for the bike leg. Having put on their helmet during the swim, each biker was free to leave transition after attaching the timing strap around his or her left ankle.

I had raced at more than a mile elevation in Colorado and New Mexico. Bountiful, at 4,300 feet, is still high enough for individuals from the middle plains of the U.S. to feel the effects of altitude during biking and running.

From transition, we made our way to the Legacy Nature Preserve trail through a series of right-angle turns. This led us through the first neighborhood, past modest, single-story, single-family homes. We continued under Interstate 15, past a golf course, and then through more neighborhoods like the first one. Just before reaching the preserve trail, we passed several small businesses.

The next section of the bike course used a walking, running, and biking trail that curved to follow the edge of the Legacy Nature Preserve and a divided four-lane state highway. The trail remained open to bikers, runners, and walkers not taking part in the triathlon. However, with swimmers starting one at a time, the bikers spread out. Between the tall uncut grass and the occasional tree and cluster of scrub bushes lining the trail, the curves in the path, and the space between bikers, I often felt like I was the only rider on the trail.

From the map I had used during yesterday's drive, I knew that mile nine of the bike course left the trail and returned to the neighborhood streets. As the time I expected to exit the trail came and went, a voice inside chided, "You should have ridden this stretch of the course yesterday." The further I rode, the louder the voice became. Without other bikers nearby, I began to question if I had missed the turn.

I remembered hearing of triathletes, including professionals, who had lost races by missing a turn on the course. This happened despite race directors' best efforts to mark all turns.

By now, I knew to use the racecourse maps and instructions provided before the race to become familiar with the course. We often drove the bike course before the triathlon for this reason. Ironically, familiarity with the course often proves more significant in races with fewer participants, since the gap between racers can be larger.

I resisted the negative voice, telling myself to trust the race director to have marked the course or to provide a volunteer to keep us on course. Sure enough, a few blocks ahead, I spotted the sought-after volunteer. After a quick turn, I rode another block on the trail before crossing the parking lot and riding back to the neighborhood streets toward transition.

After leaving transition, the run course headed one block west to the street that passed in front of the South Davis Recreation Center. Following the first right turn, the rectangular course continued on sidewalks in the neighborhood north of the Center.

I felt the effects of altitude to the greatest extent during the run. Fortunately, dozens of supporters lined the course. Smiling faces shouted out words of encouragement over the sound of ringing cowbells. Music along the course arranged by the race organizers provided a much-needed distraction to my breathing as I worked toward the finish line.

I finished fourth of eight in my age group, and within the top half of the 350 people completing the Sprint triathlon.

After leaving the race, I showered at the hotel before our next long drive. We packed the rest of our luggage into the back of the van and headed toward the next destination: Bend, Oregon. While we weren't sure how far we would want to drive today, we knew we wanted to visit Crater Lake National Park south of Bend. We were confident we could find a hotel along the way.

OREGON: STATE #25

Oregon Nickname:
The Beaver State

Scene from the bike leg of the Best in the West Sprint Triathlon.
Photo courtesy of Best in the West Triathlon Festival.

Oregon Triathlon Details

- Date: September 12, 2015
- Triathlon: 5th Annual Best in the West Triathlon Festival
- Location: Lewis Creek County Park, Foster Lake, Sweet Home, Oregon

Published distances
- Swim: 500 meters (547 yards)
- Bike: 12 miles (19.3 kilometers)
- Run: 5 kilometers (3.1 miles)

Our route to Bend took us through northern Utah, across the corner of southwestern Idaho, and into the eastern edge of central Oregon. As we crossed from Idaho into Oregon, we passed acres of barren soil. We recognized a few large yellow onions that lay near the end of the just-harvested fields. These were the first onion fields we remembered seeing.

While tempted to stop and walk out into a field to see if we could identify the type of onion, we resisted. Besides, there was no place to stop along the narrow two-lane road. After passing through this area of eastern Oregon, onion fields gave way to grasslands and desert-like landscapes.

Late Monday evening, four days before the next triathlon on Saturday, we arrived in Bend, Oregon. The next morning, we started our tour of western Oregon with a drive south to Crater Lake National Park.

We spent most of our time in the park touring the crater rim, stopping to read the information placards. After completing our drive around the crater, we headed to the park's southern entrance. On the way, we witnessed smoke from the fires that were sweeping through the forests of northern California and southern Oregon that August. Some small fires were still burning within the park.

As we continued toward the southern end of Oregon, our route passed through Fort Klamath and Grants Pass, Oregon into the northwest corner of California. Skirting the eastern edge of Crescent City, we connected with Highway 101, also known as the Oregon Coast Highway. During the next three days, we made our way along the entire length of the Oregon coast on this highway, passing for a short time into the southern end of Washington State.

We could eat, sleep, and stop whenever and wherever we wanted. Our one deadline was to be in Sweet Home on Friday afternoon for the triathlon's packet pickup. We took our time, stopping and lingering at places that caught our attention. When we felt tired, we chose a hotel. During the three nights, we stayed in Brookings, Florence, and Seaside, all along the Oregon coast.

Our journey along the Oregon Coast Highway provided many awe-inspiring moments as we soaked in the stunning inland and coastal landscapes and structures. We made the most of our proximity to the Pacific Ocean by indulging in the local seafood for lunch and dinner.

The most memorable seafood meal was during our overnight stop in Florence. During dinner at the Waterfront Depot Restaurant, we feasted on crab-encrusted halibut filet with a sweet chili sauce. We had learned of our love for halibut during a trip to nearby Seattle, Washington, a decade earlier. After returning home from this trip, we found the Waterfront Depot recipe online. While we have not perfected the recipe, we have made several attempts, creating a tasty runner-up.

Following lunch at Mo's on Thursday afternoon, we walked on the beach outside the restaurant to get a closer look at the harbor seals and sea lions in the bay. We found locals fishing for salmon, while others were loading pieces of whole chicken inside metal cages as bait. While we stood around with questioning looks on our faces, a couple of retired teachers gave Joy a lesson on crabbing. Once again, I watched her effortlessly engage strangers who soon began acting like long-lost friends. I had often studied her to see how she does this. Some of her ease rubbed off onto me over the course of our marriage, but still, I had a long way to go to be comfortable without feeling as if I were interrogating someone I had just met.

By Friday afternoon, we arrived in the Willamette Valley, a part of Oregon known for its vineyards and wine production. Before stopping to pick up the race packet, we stopped in Sweet Home for lunch and an oil change for our van.

While setting the appointment for the oil change, we learned we were in the "Grass Seed Capital of the World," Linn County. The region's cool, damp winters and warm, arid summers create the perfect conditions for cultivating grass seed varieties, including Kentucky Bluegrass, tailored to cooler seasons.

Headquarters for the Best in the West Triathlon Festival was Lewis Creek County Park, a few miles east of Sweet Home. The park is home to Foster Lake, a reservoir created by a dam along the South Santiam River.

We intended to set up our campsite for the night within the park after I picked up my race packet. While registering for the triathlon, I read that race volunteers could camp within Lewis Creek County Park for free. Joy decided she would volunteer for the race, since she enjoyed volunteering at triathlons. Free camping at the park would be a bonus.

While driving from Utah to Oregon on Monday, we purchased a two-person tent for Friday night's campout. Camping offered two benefits. First, it saved the cost of a hotel. Also, by camping at the race venue, we avoided rising before dawn to arrive at the race site for the opening of transition.

Evergreen trees covered the perimeter of the park, while parking spaces, a restroom facility, and a large green space for transition filled the space in the center. This park had everything needed for tent camping.

Still, with unseasonably high humidity and a temperature close to 90 degrees, camping lost some of its attraction. We were too accustomed to air conditioning to sleep in these conditions. The longer we stayed at the park, the less appealing camping became.

Upon mentioning our change of heart toward camping to the volunteers at packet pickup, one of them said we would not find a vacant hotel room in Sweet Home this weekend. Still, while in Sweet Home for dinner, we checked with several motels. Thanks to a last-minute cancellation at the third one, a clean, air-conditioned room became ours for the night.

The Best in the West Triathlon Festival, managed by Best in the West Events, spanned two days. Saturday included Sprint and half-Ironman distances of the triathlon and duathlon races. Each multisport race had a relay option. For the relay, two or three people shared the race's two or three legs.

On Sunday, college men and women competed in the Olympic-distance race. Others took part in the Olympic-distance triathlon or duathlon, either on their own or as part of the men's, women's, or co-ed relay teams.

Sunday also included events for children and those wanting to experience racing in a triathlon. Kids could compete in either a short or long-course swim and run. Children and adults could test triathlon with a "try-a-tri" distance. Each leg of this event was half the length of the Sprint triathlon.

On Saturday morning, we arrived at the park at 5:30 a.m. for the opening of transition. Joy volunteered at the registration table, providing race packets for those who hadn't checked in on Friday.

Saturday's event began with the half-Ironman triathlon swim. With Foster Lake's water temperature below 78 degrees, this race was wetsuit-legal according to USA Triathlon rules. Sprint distance racers started after all the half-Ironman racers had finished the swim and were on their bikes.

With a shotgun blast, we swam away from the beach toward the first orange buoy on this rectangular course. After the second left turn, we swam toward the shore. Upon reaching the beach, we jogged across the sand and a few dozen of yards of grass into transition.

The flat bike course left transition in a direction away from the lake with a turn onto North River Road, which runs along the northern edge of Foster Lake. After riding two and a half miles, I glanced left at the western end of the lake and Foster Dam. Here, we encountered the only notable hill on the course, a drop of a hundred feet over a quarter-mile.

Three and a half miles farther, I reached the turnaround on a residential street in Sweet Home's northeast corner. After turning around, I finished my bike leg, following the same route back to transition.

The first part of the run course crossed a grassy patch and

a wooden footbridge. Beyond this, we ran on paved roads and trails in the park. The rolling hills, with climbs of 50 to 70 feet, provided enough of a challenge to make the race interesting. However, the shade beneath the evergreen trees lining the path led to a pleasant finish to the triathlon.

After completing my race, Joy and I rushed back to the motel for a shower. Our goal was to complete the five-hour drive to Bremerton, Washington by late afternoon, in time for packet pickup for the next day's triathlon. After clearing out of our motel room, we returned to the park for the awards ceremony for both the half-Ironman and Sprint distance races.

I finished third of three in my age group of men ages 60 through 64. With this finish, I earned an award assembled from a pony-sized black horseshoe. Glued to the apex of the shoe was a bronzed five-pointed star bearing the triathlon's name. A tan braided rope encircled the shoe.

I had now completed triathlons in exactly half of the United States. Tomorrow, I would start the second half.

WASHINGTON: STATE #26

Washington Nickname:
The Evergreen State

A section of the Tri Turtle Tri T-shirt with registrants' names.
My name is at the top of the turtle's right flipper.

Washington Triathlon Details

- Date: September 13, 2015
- Triathlon: 10th Annual Tri Turtle Tri SprintPlus Triathlon
- Location: Wildcat Lake County Park, Bremerton, Washington

Published distances
- Swim: 0.5 mile (805 meters)
- Bike: 15.6 miles (25.1 kilometers)
- Run: 3.4 miles (5.5 kilometers)

Generally speaking, race directors set the tone for a triathlon. They are also responsible for its success and longevity. After registering for this triathlon, I saw why Tri Turtle Tri had continued over the past decade. Lisa Ballou, race director, was the reason.

Some, like Lisa with her "Lisa B, your Tri Turtle" email signature, inspire you to be part of the event they are managing. Lisa's enthusiasm and fun-loving spirit were contagious.

So was her commitment to those who benefit from this event. Since its first year, Tri Turtle Tri has donated part of its proceeds to local fitness and wellness programs. This triathlon funded a free community-wide "Family Fun Run" that encouraged families to get more fit, together.

For this, its third year, Tri Turtle Tri partnered with Tri Turtle Wellness to award a college scholarship to a graduate of Klahowya Secondary School. To apply, students submitted an essay related to triathlon. Applicants wrote about the meaning of the Kitsap Tri Babes' motto: "The miracle is not that I finished, the miracle is that I had the courage to start."

Lisa's emails also encouraged both seasoned and novice triathletes. Take, for example, this one describing the swim course, sent a few days before the triathlon: "The ½ mile swim will travel in a clockwise triangle. Volunteers will be positioned on surfboards almost every 100 yards along the course. Swimmers can stop and rest at these markers. In addition, there will be swim volunteers in the water with flotation noodles to aid swimmers needing personal assistance." Lisa started with a summary of the swim course, then added words to encourage any less-confident swimmers. She communicated a clear, yet important message: "Volunteers are everywhere to help, so relax and enjoy your swim during the triathlon."

After the Best in the West Triathlon awards ceremony, Joy and I plotted a course for Wildcat Lake Park in Kitsap County, northwest of downtown Bremerton, Washington.

As we passed through downtown Bremerton, we looked down from the bridge to see the Puget Sound Naval Shipyard on the Sinclair Inlet of Puget Sound. A few minutes later and with time to spare, we arrived at Wildcat Park to collect my race packet. We were less than 10 miles from the eastern edge of Olympic National Park.

Being in the Seattle area brought back fond memories of our visit to the city about a decade earlier. During that trip, we visited the famous Pike Place Market. After making sure we saw the iconic fish-throwing, we wandered through the market, sampling some delicious treats along the way.

At one stand that specialized in Middle Eastern food, we sampled *toum*, a garlic spread with the consistency of mayonnaise. After tasting a sample, Joy told the vendor, "This tastes exactly like what I get at my favorite Lebanese restaurant, Port of Beirut in West St. Paul, Minnesota."

The man replied, "It should. My uncle owns that restaurant, and he's the one who taught me how to make it."

On the morning of the triathlon, just under 300 triathletes gathered in Wildcat Park to swim, bike, and run in and around

Wildcat Lake. Distances for the individual legs of this triathlon were longer than those of the typical Sprint triathlon (the reason for "SprintPlus" in the event's name).

The temperature of the water in Wildcat Lake today was below 78 degrees. According to USA Triathlon rules, we could wear our wetsuits. The cool drizzle this morning made the wetsuit even more desirable.

I began the half-mile swim, thinking it followed a clockwise triangular path. I understood we'd make two right turns before exiting the lake at the same spot we had entered. After making the second turn for the swim back to shore, I set a trajectory for the place from which we had started. As I neared the beach, I realized the actual exit was 10 to 20 yards left of the start. I adjusted my course, but still wasted several seconds, maybe close to half a minute.

Two mistakes of mine led to this mishap. First, I ignored the swim exit on the racecourse map. I also missed the part of the pre-race meeting during which Lisa pointed out where swimmers would exit. Had I paid attention, I could have picked out a tall tree behind the exit to use for sighting. This reminded me once again of the importance of knowing the racecourse beforehand.

From the exit, I climbed a steep hill to reach the flat section leading to transition. I jogged the rest of the way, dodging (but sometimes stepping on) sharp rocks protruding from the ground.

On the bike, we rode local roads west of Wildcat County Park. Sparse traffic gave us freedom to enjoy the evergreen trees, deciduous shrubs, and ground cover, interrupted by a gravel driveway for a home or small business every once in a while.

A short distance before reaching the turnaround, we exited the main road to the right. This road looped around to rejoin the main road a half mile southwest of where we left it. We were within three miles of Hood Canal, a fjord that makes up part of Puget Sound.

While tall, straight pines still dominated the scenery, the landscape reminded me of the northern part of Minnesota, with its splotches of bogs and wetlands within the stands of cypress trees.

After rejoining the main road, we continued on to transition. Even though the course featured an elevation gain of almost 900 feet, it had not seemed hilly. Three reasons contributed to this. Other than a steep hill at the start and finish, elevation changes were gradual. Second, with little vehicle traffic on this Sunday morning, the forests and wetlands provided a distraction. Then there was the third reason.

Near the end of my ride, the rain became the main reason for not noticing the hills. As the drizzle continued throughout the race, more water collected on the road. My focus shifted from the scenery to my front tire. A hissing sound from the front of my bike brought back the unpleasant memory of a similar sound, one I had heard during the Rhode Island triathlon in the minutes before I fell as a result of a flat tire. Focused on the sound and remembering the pain of the crash, I grew convinced my front tire was losing air. With water collecting on my safety glasses, I could not get a clear look to check my suspicion.

When I could no longer stand not knowing if a crash was imminent, I stopped along the edge of the road. After dismounting, I inspected each tire by squeezing it between my index finger and thumb. Thankfully, both tires felt inflated, though they were dripping water. I relaxed and finished the bike leg.

After racking my bike, I left transition and headed off toward the entrance to the park for a counterclockwise run along the roads cut through the woods surrounding Wildcat Lake. The tree-lined run course followed the left side of the local road, traveling against the negligible Sunday morning traffic. The course included a continuous series of hills, most gradual but with a couple of challenging ones. Reaching the last hill's peak, I turned left and sprinted to the finish line.

For most triathlons, the race company gave us the T-shirt during packet pickup, either the day before or the day of the race. With Tri Turtle Tri, a volunteer handed the T-shirt to each of us after crossing the finish line. An illustration of a sea turtle, the triathlon's logo, appeared on its front. Names of race registrants filled the turtle shape. I found my name at the top of the turtle's right flipper.

I had finished fifth of eight in the men's 55 through 64 age group, and in the top third of all finishers.

After thanking Lisa for a well-run triathlon, Joy and I went back to our hotel to shower and finish packing for the next leg of our trip. As we had done with previous triathlons, we made the most of our Seattle location by visiting family.

Our first stop was at Anthony's HomePort and Oyster Bar in the Seattle suburb of Des Moines. Joy's cousin Karyn Nelson and her son Eli joined us for a delicious seafood lunch. We finished around mid-afternoon and made a short trek to nearby Kent, where we would stay the night before resuming our journey home the next day.

Coeur d'Alene, Idaho was our first overnight stop during the four-day return to Minnesota from Seattle. We made two more stops: one in Bismarck, North Dakota, and a second in Watson, Minnesota to visit Joy's cousin, Tom. We finished the trip with a brief stop at our eldest granddaughter Veronica's home in Hector, Minnesota.

2016:
FILLING IN THE MIDWEST

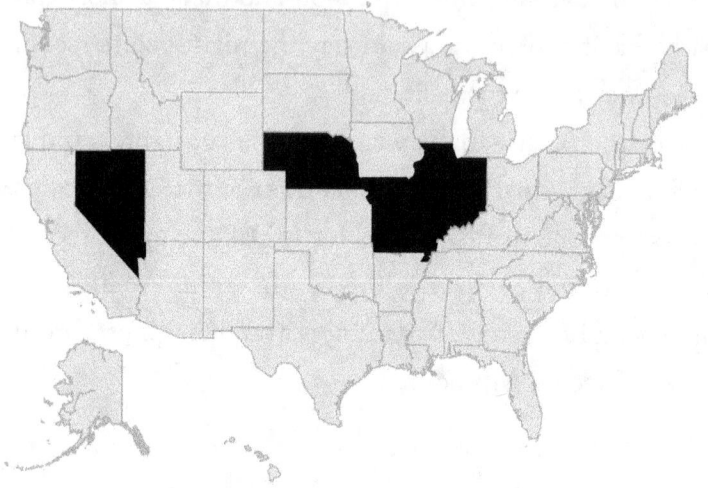

My daughter Liza was the first to encourage me to share my triathlon experiences with other older triathletes. Early in the year, I had taken an online course through American Writer & Artists, Inc. (AWAI) on developing a website. The result was SeniorTriathletes.com.

One of the first tasks in building the website was to define its audience and mission. The mission I set for the website, one that I have continued, was to provide information and inspiration for triathletes and similar multi-sport endurance athletes ages 50 and over.

As I added to the site, I spoke with other older triathletes. Their remarkable achievements amazed me. I enjoyed hearing each story: how they started in triathlon, their approach to training, and the sport's impact on their life. My hope was to tell these stories in a way that would cause other older adults to become more active, preferably through triathlon. I was sure the health improvements I had found through the sport could be duplicated by others.

Visitors to the website began asking for help with their triathlon training. To add related content, I tested and documented the results of my own. I also interviewed more senior triathletes, several of whom also coached older athletes.

My goal for this year was to complete triathlons in states in the central part of the U.S. I also wanted to help my father adapt to his new life concurrently with my participation in a triathlon in Nevada.

• • • •

NEVADA: STATE #27

Nevada Nickname:
The Silver State

Preparing for the swim in Lake Mead at the Nevada triathlon.

Nevada Triathlon Details

- Date: April 16, 2016
- Triathlon: 16th Rage Triathlon
- Location: Boulder Beach, Lake Mead Recreation Area, Boulder City, Nevada

Published distances
- Swim: 750 meters (820 yards)
- Bike: 12.4 miles (20 kilometers)
- Run: 5 kilometers (3.1 miles)

When I had raced in three states (Utah, Oregon, and Washington) within a seven-day period, Joy and I found the chance to drive to parts of the northwestern U.S. we hadn't visited before. Combining three races into one trip seven months earlier had given us the ability to share the long distances and driving time.

Combining two or more triathlons on one long trip was not always possible. Neither was it always the best choice; this was certainly true for my first triathlon of 2016. Joy and I traveled 3,659 miles through 12 states in six days to compete in a Sprint triathlon lasting an hour and 39 minutes. Some might say we were crazy.

This time, we had a reason. My mother had passed away the previous June, six months short of her 65th wedding anniversary with my father. Dad now lived alone in his home in Parker, Colorado. He was lonely, and I wanted to see him. Our plan when I registered for the Rage Triathlon on November 2, 2015 was for my dad to join Joy and me on the trip to Boulder City. Apparently, he had enjoyed his time at the Colorado triathlon.

However, in March, Dad fell, injuring one of his legs. Even though he was recovering, he would be in pain while sitting in our van for hours at a time as we drove to Nevada. Before we left Minnesota for Colorado, Dad informed us he would not be making the trip with us. We would keep part of our original plan, though: We would stop at his home on the way to Nevada. We also planned to visit him on the return trip, after the Nevada triathlon.

Joy and I left Minnesota at noon on Tuesday, April 12th

for our first stop, an overnight stay with our son Ben and his family in Omaha, Nebraska. With perfect weather, we spent the late afternoon across the street from their house, cherishing the giggles of our two granddaughters as we pushed them on the park's swing sets.

The next morning, we continued our journey to my dad's house, arriving late Wednesday afternoon. During dinner at one of my dad's favorite restaurants, Texas Roadhouse, my dad relayed the forecast for snow along Interstate 70 west of Denver during the weekend we were planning to return to Denver for our second night's stay with him.

In November, while planning the 2016 triathlon season, I had assumed there would be no problem traveling through the Rocky Mountains of Colorado in April, during early spring. I later learned that April has Colorado's second-highest average snowfall. It did not look promising for a second visit to Denver during this trip.

After breakfast the next morning, I read of a winter storm warning for a major part of Utah. The warning covered the city where we hoped to sleep that evening. We got through the area affected by the storm, seeing only a few snowflakes, but the rain on the leading edge of the storm reinforced Joy's dislike for mountains—especially driving in them.

Late Friday afternoon, we arrived in Las Vegas in time to pick up my race packet and T-shirt at Trek Bicycle in the southeastern suburb of Henderson. From here, we continued to our hotel in Boulder City.

While I added my numbers to my bike and race number belt and topped off the air in my bike's tires, Joy scoured a printed list of nearby restaurants she had found in our hotel room. She decided we would eat at Evan's Old Town Grille after reading a glowing handwritten endorsement of the restaurant left by a previous guest.

We found Evan's, a quaint diner-style restaurant in the historic part of Boulder City, to be a popular spot for both residents and tourists. Our tasty and budget-friendly dinner choices confirmed the note Joy had read.

Back at the hotel, we settled in for a restless night's sleep. The wind howled loudly as the night passed. As its wail grew, so did my restlessness. Visions of being blown off the road during the bike leg, or, worse yet, of the race being canceled filled my thoughts. I was still remembering several white-knuckle moments on the bike at the triathlon in North Dakota the previous year.

As I crawled out of bed to silence my alarm, I grabbed my phone to check the weather app. It confirmed what I heard from the bed: a wind advisory and "high winds with gusts past 40 miles per hour."

After a commute of less than 10 minutes, we pulled into the Lake Mead National Recreation Area for the Rage Triathlon, my first triathlon in a national park. Once we had arrived in the lot next to transition, I glanced at my phone, weather app still open, to see 55 degrees displayed.

Transition occupied a section of road leading to the beach.

This was another first for me. Participants lined their bikes along the two edges of this corridor on a first-come, first-served basis. *Swim In* and *Run Out* were posted nearest the Lake Mead end, while *Bike Out* was at the opposite end. Picking out my transition spot after the swim and bike proved more challenging with this layout.

For most triathlons, organizers set up rows of bike racks, both perpendicular to and on both sides of a pathway through the center of transition. Before the race, I usually count the number of rows from the *Swim In* entrance to the row with my bike, remembering the correct side of the center aisle so I can quickly grab it for the bike leg. Today's layout required a different approach to finding my transition space after the swim and bike.

As race time grew closer, the wind was still whipping up waves on Lake Mead. They were strong enough for the race director to adjust the swim course mere minutes before the start of the triathlon.

Triathletes started the open water swim in waves based upon race distance, gender, and age group. The event included triathlons of Sprint and Olympic distances, including relays of both. Those in the Olympic distance triathlon waves started first.

My wave of 90 comprised men aged 40 and over, plus Clydesdales. Just before our group started, the race director told us to enter the water. Because of its clarity, I could see small sharp rocks and shells lining its bottom. After the race, I found three cuts on my feet.

My swim today included two challenges common in

triathlon open-water swims. Early in the swim, one guy decided he was going to pass me, no matter what. His path took him over the top of me. A second man seemed unable to swim in a straight line. With his zigging and zagging, this swimmer kept moving in front of me. After he made one extra-wide zag, I got in front of him.

The out-and-back bike course left the parking lot next to transition, turned right onto Lakeshore Road, and continued on roads within the Recreation Center. The hills throughout the course went almost unnoticed as I fought against the wind.

My average speed was a little over 15 miles per hour. However, I reached a top speed of 36 m.p.h. while going down one hill with the wind at my back. Just as I had done in the triathlon in North Dakota, I avoided riding in the aero position, fearing being blown off the road. I seldom rode in high winds during my training, and lacked the confidence to do so today.

The first part of the out-and-back run course followed Boulder Beach Front Road, then passed through Boulder Beach Picnic Area. At the far edge of the picnic grounds, we connected with a paved multipurpose running and walking trail that took us to the turnaround.

The entire run course was flat and protected from the wind by hills. I started slowly, giving my legs time to adjust to running. As they began to feel lighter, I ramped up my pace. I finished strong, with a time I considered good for me.

I finished first in the men's 60 through 64 age group, and 67th among 157 men of all ages. It impressed me to see a man with only one arm standing on the podium while receiving an award for his age group. I also appreciated seeing the man who had finished first in my age group at the triathlon in Mesa, Arizona.

While Joy and I sat at a picnic table eating food provided by the race director, I met a young man with whom I had shared the run course during the triathlon. Timothy Alejo, then a candidate for a Doctor of Physical Therapy degree at A. T. Still University (ATSU) in Las Vegas, told us about his studies in AquaStretch™ therapy. We learned that this type of therapy holds promise for seniors, especially those who had spent a lot of time sitting and now want to increase their mobility. A great pleasure of the sport of triathlon was meeting the interesting and knowledgeable people who shared our passion for wellness and fitness.

While I was racing, the winter storm was dumping some of the 30 to 60 inches of snow on Interstate 70, west of Denver. Snow closed the highway for several hours over the course of 48 hours. Returning by the same route we had used to get to Nevada would have required us to delay our return by two days. This wouldn't work. Home and work obligations forced us to return, which we began following a southern route.

After crossing Hoover Dam a few minutes from Lake Mead, we were in Arizona. We crossed Arizona into New Mexico, stopping for the night in Tucumcari. The next day, we continued through New Mexico and passed through Texas, Oklahoma, Kansas, and Missouri before grabbing a hotel room in Des Moines, Iowa.

While this route was much longer, it didn't matter. I was

with my best friend, Joy. When we took a break from talking or commenting on the sights—and, in some areas, the smells—of the places we passed, we listened to one of the audiobooks we had brought for the trip. The one we enjoyed the most was *The Wright Brothers* by David McCullough.

MISSOURI: STATE #28

Missouri Nickname:
The Show Me State

Ben and me in our transition space before the TriZou Triathlon.

Missouri Triathlon Details

- Date: May 1, 2016
- Triathlon: 8th Annual TriZou Triathlon
- Location: University of Missouri at Columbia, Columbia, Missouri

Published distances
- Swim: 0.25 miles (402 meters)
- Bike: 14 miles (22.5 kilometers)
- Run: 5 kilometers (3.1 miles)

was living proof that triathlon was an enjoyable way to improve one's health. Besides, I wanted to inspire others, especially the inactive members of my family, to get or stay fit and make better food choices. I sensed progress when, in 2014, our daughter Liza and her husband Scott, and our youngest son Ben and his wife Lindsey completed the Maple Grove Triathlon with me during a weekend celebration of a milestone birthday for Joy.

Then, while sitting on our patio one afternoon during the summer of 2015, Lindsey announced that she and Ben wanted to do a second triathlon with me. Since they lived in a suburb of Omaha, Nebraska, the most obvious choice was a triathlon near them. Another possibility was one in central Missouri, where Lindsey's mother, Joan, and husband, John Neuner, lived. Joy and I wanted to visit them, so I also searched for races near their home.

I found the TriZou Triathlon on my go-to website for triathlon races, RunningintheUSA.com. This triathlon would take place at the University of Missouri at Columbia on May 1st.

Mizzou, the university's nickname, is a one-and-a-half-hour drive north of Lindsey's mom's home. Also, my uncle Wayne lived 20 minutes from Mizzou. Joy shared our plan with Wayne through social media. He invited us to spend the night before the triathlon with him, his wife Anita, and son Ethan. Travel for the triathlon gave us a chance to reconnect with them.

On November 7, 2015, I registered Ben, Lindsey, and myself for TriZou. The event included options for Sprint and Super Sprint triathlon distances and a duathlon based on the Sprint triathlon distances. Both the Sprint triathlon and the duathlon included a relay option.

Lindsey's cousin Jeff, also from Omaha, and I chose the Sprint distance; Ben and Lindsey chose the Super Sprint.

Joy and I left our Minnesota home for central Missouri around 1 p.m. on Thursday, April 28th. A little over nine hours later, we arrived at John and Joan's place south of Jefferson City, passing by the Missouri state capitol building as we approached our destination.

Their home was situated on a farm nestled among the thick woods covering the foothills of the Ozark Mountains. In some places, rolling hills give way to flatter woods and lush fields with grazing cattle and grasses for feeding livestock. The only noises outside the house came from birds and rustling leaves. Stress drained away as we took in the sights and sounds.

During this season, however, the calm was short-lived. Within hours, my eyes were itching and my nose was running, a reminder that spring weather and allergy-causing tree pollen came earlier here than in Minnesota.

On Friday, Ben, Lindsey, and our two granddaughters, Mari and Anna, joined us. We lounged inside the house, chatting about topics as diverse as canning vegetables and the latest news. John and Joan treated us to real Southern hospitality, the kind you know when experienced.

We left the house long enough to tour the pasture and private fishing pond, with John driving one of his four wheelers. Joan taught us how to identify poison ivy using the rhyme "leaves of three, let them be."

On Saturday afternoon, Ben, Joy, and I traveled to Mizzou to pick up our race packets with T-shirts and race numbers. Over the past few days, Anna had developed an ear infection that kept her and Lindsey from sleeping. We agreed with Lindsey that she should skip the triathlon and care for Anna.

After picking up the race packets, we walked over to Stankowski Field where transition was set up along the track. This would be my first triathlon with transition on a university track-and-field facility.

Next to the track was the Mizzou Aquatic Center, where the pool swim for the triathlon would occur. The *Swim In* and *Run Out* signs were posted near the Aquatic Center's end of the oval track. *Bike In* and *Bike Out* were on the opposite end.

We then set out to drive the bike course, which, when studying the map, looked a little like a parallelogram. We gave up after a few minutes, as I realized my skill in reading the map provided by the race director needed honing. Later, during the triathlon, I would confirm that we had only driven a short distance on the actual course.

We made our way to my Uncle Wayne's house, where we would stay that night. That evening, Wayne and Anita treated us to more Missouri hospitality with homemade pizza (with crispy, thin crust—Joy's and my favorite) and Missouri wines. Between bites and sips, the six of us laughed while attempting to solve several of our country's problems.

Even though triathlon is only a hobby, I often acted as if decisions associated with it held life-altering significance.

Tonight, I wrestled with the following question: *Where should I rack my bike on the track?*

The phrase *open rack* accurately described transition for TriZou. This meant transition spaces were available on a first-come, first-served basis and were not pre-assigned by race number. During the night, while tossing, turning, and analyzing various options for the best location to rack my bike, I got the answer. The best spots were those nearest to the *Bike Out* gate. In this way, I could minimize the walking or jogging distance with my bike to reach the bike mount line.

My tossing and turning came from more than thinking through where to rack my bike, though. The antihistamine, taken before bed to relieve my itching eyes, added to the restless sleep.

I aimed to arrive at the race site for the 5 a.m. opening of transition to secure a prized space. Ben, Joy, and I rose at 4:30 while it was still dark, careful to leave Wayne's house without disturbing our hosts.

With a few minutes' delay in packing our van in the dark and extra time to track down coffee, we reached our destination at 5:10. We found many bikes already on the rack; transition had opened early. With this many racers arriving so soon, I felt anticipation and excitement around the track.

Ben and I set up our transition spaces next to each other, a quarter of the way around the red rubberized asphalt track. Jeff arrived a few minutes later, forced to set up his transition space a few yards further along the track from the *Bike Out* exit.

While we were laying out our transition spaces and walking

to the pool, Joy was dozing upright in the front passenger seat of our van, which we had parked outside the black metal security fence surrounding the track.

TriZou, which included my first swim in a Division One university pool, had earned its reputation as "The Largest Pool Swim Triathlon in the Midwest." Over 600 triathletes and duathletes would be using this pool today.

The 400-meter swim for the Sprint triathlon comprised eight lengths of the 50-meter pool in what this race director called a "snake-style" pattern. With each rhythmic tweet of the starter's whistle, another swimmer jumped into the pool and took off toward the opposite end. Upon touching the end, he or she would duck under the lane divider to enter the next lane, swimming back to the starting end. We repeated this sequence for the eight lengths. Those in the Super Sprint triathlon swam two lengths.

As I swam, Lindsey recorded my race using her phone camera. I had often wished I could see my stroke, but never asked someone to video it. After the triathlon, I watched her recording. I noticed that my right arm reached its full extension during each stroke, but my left arm only unfolded part way. I made a mental note to work on extending both arms, starting with my next swim session.

As I began the bike leg, my bike computer displayed the temperature: 64 degrees. Following the indoor swim, this felt comfortable. For the Sprint distance, we covered a seven-mile loop twice. Super Sprint participants rode the course once.

The race director had described the course as "technical"

because of its many turns. Our first turn after leaving transition took us onto Tiger Avenue. During the first few blocks of the course, we rode past the Veterans Administration (VA) hospital, then turned onto Stadium Boulevard. Once on Stadium, we rode past the Hearnes Center, the university's basketball arena, and other campus buildings. As we left the campus, buildings gave way to acres of green space to our right. The first of two steep inclines began soon after turning onto Old Highway 63 and continued for most of the ride until the next turn. Following this turn, we left the green space to ride behind Walmart and other businesses south of Mizzou.

We faced the second hill along Providence Road near the end of the first and second loops. Fortunately, a decline before the hill allowed us to gain speed before starting the climb. As we ascended, we passed the Missouri University Research Reactor (MURR). MURR is home to the most powerful university research reactor in the United States. Its products include radioactive materials for medicine and materials testing.

These hills, with several right-angle turns, made me feel like I was at home, riding along the seven-mile course in the streets around our house in Minnesota. My bike computer seemed to agree, as it reported speeds similar to those I had attained during training rides.

Before beginning the second loop, and again near its end, we passed the Mizzou Tigers football stadium. After completing the second loop, we passed through a tunnel under Stadium Boulevard to reach transition.

After hanging my bike from the rack by its saddle, I slipped off my helmet and bent over to slip on my running shoes. As I stood up, the world around me blurred. The background came into focus a moment later as I held my position. *Maybe I just stood up too fast*, I thought. *That was a fluke.*

As it turned out, it was not a fluke. A half-mile into the run, I felt disoriented again. As before, stopping caused the world to stop spinning. For the rest of the run, I mixed jogging with walking.

The run course continued within the campus, passing by more dormitory and classroom buildings. The only hill on this otherwise flat course was at the bridge that took us up and over College Avenue.

Walking gave me more time to notice the surprising number of spectators cheering other racers and holding signs with the message *LIVE LIKE JOSH.* Sipping on a sports drink after crossing the finish line, I asked others what this message meant. Within seconds, I found a young man with the answer. I learned that Josh Seidel and several family members, all Mizzou alumni, had competed in TriZou each year. Sadly, Josh had died in 2013 as a result of an accident at the business he owned. After his death, a group of his high school and college friends established the Josh Seidel Memorial Foundation. The foundation's mission is to carry on Josh's legacy by awarding scholarships and helping schools and other organizations.

A few weeks after TriZou, I spoke with Josh's mother, Terri, who had done the swim leg of TriZou as part of a relay team with her two daughters. I published her story on SeniorTriathletes. com, the website I had started earlier in the year.

I finished fifth of nine in my age group, and 311th of 483 participants. From the energy in the air that morning, I had expected a lot of competition in this triathlon, which it delivered. While I had lost time during the run, I still would have finished near the middle of my age group of 60- through 64-year-old men with a typical run time.

After the race, I felt fine. I imagined the dizziness had been caused by my body's reaction to either the pollen or the antihistamine. Liza, now a registered nurse, believed the antihistamine was the root of the problem.

Even in my fifth year of triathlon, I was still learning. Over the past four years, training during pollen season had always taken place indoors. I generally avoided antihistamines, only taking one as a last resort.

That changed right before TriZou. I was not ready to race with allergy symptoms. I made a mental note to avoid committing to a spring triathlon during which the tree pollen count would be high.

Joy and I started our drive home after lunch with Ben and his family. Rain fell throughout the trip, but traffic was light and the roads were clear. Traveling on U.S. Highway 63, we saw of mix of dense patches of trees and hilly farmland with small fields of corn, soybeans, or hay. These were interrupted every few miles by small towns that supported local farmers.

Farther north, near Pella, Iowa, the landscape flattened, and the trees thinned to expose a seemingly endless patchwork of fields. Pella hosts an annual festival called Tulip Time. Because of my Dutch heritage, we had often considered attending Tulip

Time. This time, we were one weekend too early. Still, since we were close, we made a detour to drive through Pella, a decision that did not disappoint. As we passed through downtown, thousands of tulips highlighted the preparation underway for the following weekend's celebration.

NEBRASKA: STATE #29

Nebraska Nickname:
The Cornhusker State

For this triathlon, we racked our bikes in transition the day before the race.

Nebraska Triathlon Details

- Date: August 14, 2016
- Triathlon: 35th Annual USA Triathlon Age Group National Championships
- Location: Levi Carter Park, Omaha, Nebraska

Published distances

- Swim: 750 meters (820 yards)
- Bike: 20 kilometers (12.4 miles)
- Run: 5 kilometers (3.1 miles)

While we were together in Missouri for the TriZou Triathlon, Lindsey had mentioned that Omaha would be hosting this year's USA Triathlon Age Group National Championships (AGNC). This seemed like the right time to complete a triathlon in Nebraska. Competing in the AGNC also meant racing with the best amateur triathletes in the USA.

The Age Group National Championships, managed by USA Triathlon every year since 1982, took place over two days. On Saturday, over 2,170 men and women competed in the Olympic-distance triathlon. The next day, 1,250 triathletes gathered for the Sprint distance race. With such a high number of competitors, this would be my largest triathlon so far.

During packet pickup on Saturday, I and other competitors in the Sprint triathlon racked our bikes in transition, leaving them overnight. This would limit the chaos on race morning that could result from so many people moving their bikes into transition.

The water temperature in Carter Lake today was 82 degrees, well above the maximum of 78 degrees at which USAT rules allow use of a wetsuit. So, after setting up my transition space, I grabbed my swim cap and goggles, leaving my wetsuit next to my bike, and left transition.

Halfway between the exit of transition and Carter Lake, I paused near the yellow Fellowship of Christian Athletes (FCA) banner planted in the ground. Before the race, several dozen participants and a few spectators gathered for Bible reading and prayer. A middle-aged man, a leader of FCA, started by reading verses 23 and 24 from the fourth chapter of John's Gospel.

"But a time is coming, and even now has arrived, when the true worshipers will worship the Father in spirit and truth; for such people the Father seeks to be His worshipers. God is spirit, and those who worship Him must worship in spirit and truth" (John 4:23-24, *New American Standard Bible)*. Commenting on the verses, the leader reminded us that our performance and attitude on the triathlon course represented another way for us to worship God. He closed with a prayer for all triathletes, volunteers, and spectators.

As we neared the start time, the air temperature was 69 degrees. With 85 percent relative humidity and no breeze, the air felt sticky—warmer than expected for this temperature.

While walking to the dock where the swim would start, I noticed a guy asking a volunteer doing body marking to write something on his chest. I couldn't hear what he was saying; however, while waiting beside the lake, I could read the marking. It included *$1*.

Russ Jones, age 61 according to another body marking, told me he had raced in the first triathlon ever held in the U.S.. On September 25, 1974, 46 men and women competed in the Mission Bay Triathlon in San Diego, California. This race included a six-mile run, five-mile bike, and 500-yard swim. The marking on his chest memorialized the $1 entry fee for this race.

After today's triathlon, I checked the internet for information on Russ Jones. It surprised me to learn that beyond competing in the first-ever triathlon, Russ had also won both the second and third Mission Bay Triathlons, in 1975 and 1976.

Today, Russ was racing what he called "retro." He wore

shorts, but no shirt. For the bike leg, he said he would ride his vintage Raleigh ten-speed bike.

At a quarter to eight, all 160 entrants in my swim wave (males aged 60 years and older) walked or jumped into horseshoe shaped Carter Lake, next to the park and Omaha's Eppley Airfield. We were told to start the swim with one hand on the dock. However, with the large number of us in this age group, the line extended far beyond the end of the dock.

With the start signal sounding, we were off. Despite the large number of swimmers, it surprised me to see the water so calm. By now, I had completed many open-water triathlon swims. Most included a period of chaos, with other swimmers bumping into or trying to swim over the top of me. All I noticed today was an occasional fingertip touching my foot as a swimmer drafted behind me.

The bike course, which followed city streets to the north and west of the park, was flat, except for two modest hills. Less than one mile into the bike course, Russ Jones and his beautiful baby blue 1970s Raleigh bike passed me on my carbon-fiber triathlon model. After I passed Russ once, he passed me again. I never saw him again until we met on the run course.

After I got off my bike, I jogged with it to my transition space. A few of my fellow racers tripped while crossing a bumpy section within transition. I was prepared for the bumps. While walking the path from my bike's location within transition to the bike mount and dismount line on Saturday, I had stumbled across a couple of bumps. Rehearsing the paths into and out of transition was now a part of my pre-race ritual.

The out-and-back run course, all south of transition toward downtown Omaha, was flat and wide open to the sun. Cheering volunteers and spectators encouraged runners along its entire length. During the first half, a man serenaded us with guitar music, and a cheerleading squad from a local high school or college entertained the group near the turnaround.

The 74 percent relative humidity, still air, and clear, sunny skies all contributed to a tough run—which, for me, meant much walking mixed with jogging. My actual pace was far from my goal. I knew each step walked was putting me further down the list of finishers. Still, as I resumed running, my heart rate spiked, and I couldn't seem to get enough air. Maybe I had pushed too hard on the bike? Or had my training not been consistent enough?

Learning from the printouts of competitors' times that I finished 55th of 61 in the men's 60 through 64 age group produced a mixed bag of emotions. My low finish bothered me. It reminded me that I was not a superstar athlete, even as my peers were accomplishing impressive things in triathlon. Still, I was competing, and one state closer to completing a triathlon in each state.

Surveying the crowd, it pleased me to witness the camaraderie among athletes and the many older triathletes. I saw Jim Chapman, whom I had met a few years earlier at the Rocky Gap Triathlon in Maryland. Jim had qualified for the ITU World Championships in his age group of 75- through 79-year-old men.

While cooling my upper body using towels soaked in ice

water and resting my legs in an ice bath, I spoke with a man from Michigan who appeared close to my own age, plus or minus a couple of years. Now in his second year of triathlon, he shared how his training had helped him to lose the 50 pounds he had gained after giving up running following an Achilles tendon injury a few years earlier.

Back home, I analyzed the demographics of the two triathlons. It intrigued me to see that 42 percent of the male and female participants in the Sprint distance were 50 years and older. Over one third of the longer Olympic-distance race participants were 50 years and over. With competitors' ages spanning 15 to 84, the percentage over age 50 demonstrated how important older athletes are to triathlon.

ILLINOIS: STATE #30

Illinois Nickname:
Land of Lincoln

Our trip to the Illinois triathlon took us on a section of the iconic Route 66.

Illinois Triathlon Details

- Date: September 11, 2016
- Triathlon: 7th Annual Litchfield Triathlou Triathlon
- Location: Lake Lou Yaeger Beach, Litchfield, Illinois

Published distances
- Swim: 0.25 miles (402 meters)
- Bike: 13 miles (20.9 kilometers)
- Run: 3.1 miles (5 kilometers)

Litchfield is a farming community located 40 miles south of the Abraham Lincoln Presidential Library in Springfield, Illinois. Driving past corn and soybean fields into this town of just over 6,000 residents brought back a flurry of childhood memories.

My family, in which I was the eldest of four children, had lived on a farm outside the south-central Minnesota farming community of Trimont. I still remember crying my eyes out while watching *The Alamo* one Saturday afternoon at the single-screen theater a block from the store where my dad and mom were shopping for next week's groceries.

In those days, almost everything we needed could be found within a few miles of our home. Today, this once-vibrant community of about 600 residents struggles to survive. Its population is a fraction of what it was during my early childhood.

As we exited I-55 for Litchfield, we noticed a sign pointing in the opposite direction toward Gillespie, Illinois. Since Joy's maternal grandfather's last name was Gillespie, we couldn't help but see what we might learn by driving only 10 miles southwest. Since Joy did not know of any relatives in this town, we could only speculate about family connections based on the names of businesses shared by Joy's aunt and uncles.

After this detour, Joy and I returned to Litchfield and our hotel near the western edge of town. After checking in, we drove into Litchfield's town center for dinner at a diner-style restaurant. Here, we saw the fruit of Litchfield residents' labor to keep their town strong. We felt a welcoming sense of community as they invited visitors to enjoy events like the Litchfield Triathlou Triathlon.

The next morning, Joy and I woke before sunrise and reached the race site for the 6 a.m. opening of transition. I still liked to arrive early to claim a prized position within transition, either at or near the end of a rack. With my transition space thus secured, I found it easier to recognize my bike after completing the swim. Racking my bike on or close to the end helped reduce my transition times, even if only by seconds.

In my earlier days of triathlon, some pre-race rituals seemed obsessive, even to me. However, arriving early and checking my transition space in the minutes before the race always made the triathlon a little less stressful. Even if I couldn't arrive early, I despised showing up at the last minute and scrambling to find a space in transition, a scene I often witnessed.

I learned to check my transition space a few times before the start of each race. Sometimes, I found my running shoes, bike helmet, or other gear, which I had laid out earlier in my preferred pattern, now scattered in different places as other racers set up their spaces next to mine.

Today, I was glad I had made one last check. Minutes before transition closed for the start of the race, I walked past my transition space, thinking, *where is my bike?* After a moment of panic, I realized that someone—a latecomer—had racked their bike in my original position, moving my bike two positions down the rack.

I had arrived early this morning to grab a space next to the center aisle through transition. It didn't bother me too much that another racer had moved my bike, as it was still hanging close to the end of the rack, but still, I expected more consideration from triathletes.

Without this last-minute check, my bike would have appeared missing as I arrived from the swim, causing a moment of panic and wasted time as I searched for it. My pre-race routine averted this mini-crisis.

As we approached the start, the weather was, to quote one of my favorite movie characters, Mary Poppins, "practically perfect." The temperature was in the high 60s, with only modest humidity. The sun shone through calm, clear skies, and the temperature of Lake Lou Yaeger was a comfortable 78 degrees.

At this water temperature, the race was wetsuit-legal according to USA Triathlon rules. Still, I made the short swim without it. I had not yet tried sliding my tight-fitting wetsuit over my new, somewhat bulky Garmin triathlon watch. I followed the triathlon mantra: "Don't try anything new on race day."

With 65 triathletes in each swim wave, the risk of collisions, being hit, or being swum over was significant. As I came from behind to pass a swimmer doing the breaststroke, I felt the person's right foot punch me in the chest. At that moment, I imagined what it would feel like to let a well thrown, chest high pass from an NFL quarterback slip through my fingers. While the kick did not injure me, it got my attention. After today, I would add to my pre-race checklist: keep a wide distance from anyone doing the breaststroke.

The bike course left transition and the park with a gradual climb. At the entrance, we turned right and followed flat paved roads between soybean fields, cornfields, and the occasional grove of trees near small farm homes. A few sharp curves kept the ride interesting. Throughout the course, I saw places, especially at sharp bends in the road and at turns, where the race staff had swept loose sand and gravel from the roads to keep the bike course safe.

The race website described the run course as having "plenty of flats, and a couple hills throughout." We started the run by descending a concrete stairway—a triathlon first for me. Upon reaching the bottom, we entered the road and the main part of the course.

I remained vigilant in my search for the flat sections, ever hopeful I would find one. Further along, I wondered if the person who had written "plenty of flats" had ever run the course. I would have written "plenty of hills."

After finishing the race, I spoke with a young woman who, I learned during the awards ceremony, was the overall winner. I felt vindicated to know she shared my feelings about the hill-covered run course.

The triathlon name, Triathlou, is a play on words based upon its location, Lake Lou Yaeger Beach. However, the race director didn't stop there. The medal placed around the neck of each finisher included the lake's name near the base of an image of one of the most important pre-race facilities: the loo, also known as the porta-potty.

I finished first of three in my age group of men ages 60 through 64, and 46th of 104 overall. With this finish, I received a pair of sunglasses, the age-group award for this race.

While I enjoyed snacks and drinks afterward, a local sponsor massaged and stretched my leg muscles. After the massage, one of the race staff diagnosed and fixed a problem with my bike cadence sensor.

Joy and I then talked with Paul Guthrie, who had finished his first triathlon in second place in my age group. I found it remarkable that he had done this despite having one artificial knee and two artificial hips, which limited his ability to train for the run. He also rode an older hybrid bike with an incurable problem in shifting between certain gears.

Paul described his goal, which was similar to mine: to hunt turkeys in each of the 50 states. He already held a world record for bow hunting turkey in Guatemala. While we talked about bikes, another guy around my age said he had completed the 56-mile bike leg of a half-Ironman triathlon using his mountain bike. He emphasized the accessibility of doing a triathlon on a budget.

We left for a week in Chicago, happy to have met these two active older athletes with a lifetime of interesting experiences and inspiring stories.

• • • •

INDIANA: STATE #31

Indiana Nickname:
The Hoosier State

Entrance to Potato Creek State Park, the day before the triathlon.

Indiana Triathlon Details

- Date: September 17, 2016
- Triathlon: 7th Annual Tri the Creek Triathlon
- Location: Potato Creek State Park, North Liberty, Indiana

Published distances
- Swim: 500 meters (547 yards)
- Bike: 11 miles (17.7 kilometers)
- Run: 3.1 miles (5 kilometers)

knew this day would be interesting as soon as I stepped outside our hotel in Plymouth, Indiana. Rain was pouring down hard enough for me to run across the parking lot to our van, suitcase in hand, to avoid being soaked. This wasn't my first triathlon with rain; however, the rain this morning was the hardest I had ever experienced before a race.

In February, I had signed up for triathlons on consecutive weekends: one in Illinois, and this one. The two triathlons functioned as bookends for a week at a trade show at McCormick Place in downtown Chicago. Despite the notorious Chicago traffic, the triathlon venue was an easy two-and-a-half-hour drive southeast of Chicago.

Tri The Creek, the name of the triathlon, came from its location at Potato Creek State Park. The entire racecourse was contained within the boundaries of this 3,840-acre park three miles east of North Liberty, Indiana. According to the Indiana Department of Natural Resources website, the park's name comes from the potato-like roots found on area creekbanks. Native Americans who lived alongside early European settlers harvested the roots.

Today, the park contains a mix of woods, prairie, and wetlands, a haven for birds and other wildlife. On the eastern edge of the park is Horsemen's Campground, where horses and their riders can relax on miles of trails amidst diverse flora.

At the opposite end of the park, near Worster Lake, where the triathlon swim would occur, we found a traditional campground. As Joy and I drove the bike course, exploring the park on Friday evening before the next day's triathlon, we counted dozens of families arriving with their campers and trailers for a late-season weekend of camping.

For this triathlon, the organizer had reserved packet pickup for race morning. While it had not been my goal, I arrived first in line to get my race packet. Besides forcing Joy to rise earlier than she liked, the early start allowed even more time for the gear in my transition space to be soaked by the ongoing rain.

Because of the weather, I racked my bike with plastic bags over my shoes, which I left clipped into the bike pedals. The rest of the gear, including bike helmet, biking glasses, and running shoes, stayed with me in the van. Joy and I waited inside until near the start of the race.

As the time for closing the transition approached, I delivered my bike helmet, glasses, and running shoes to that location. Despite the fact that the rain was easing, it was still pouring hard enough to drench everything in my transition space that had not been covered.

I set my bike helmet top down on the aero bars and stuffed my clear safety glasses inside before covering it with a plastic bag. I pushed the bag onto the helmet, hoping to prevent it from being blown away by the wind.

Next, I laid a towel on the ground next to my bike with my running shoes on top of the towel. I would use this to wipe sand and small rocks from my feet before hopping on my bike and putting on my running shoes. Because of the rain, I put down a second towel, folded to be as thick as possible, on top of my running shoes with the goal of keeping them dry for the run.

For this event, the Sprint-distance triathlon was one of four races. The other triathlon distances were Olympic, Super Sprint, and "Super Kaya-Tri", which included a two-mile kayak instead of a swim. This was my first triathlon with a kayaking option.

As the clock neared the race's start time, rain persisted, albeit lighter. The temperature of the calm air was a comfortable 67 degrees. The water temperature in Worster Lake was 72 degrees, so racers could use a wetsuit if they chose. I left mine in the van.

Like most of the Minnesota lakes in which I trained, Worster Lake contained a lot of algae, to which I am allergic. Even during this short swim, enough water entered my nose for it to drip the rest of the day. By evening, my nose had become plugged, but it reopened over the course of the next day.

In an attempt to avoid congestion from swimming in lakes containing algae, I tried a mask that covered my nose. I also tried a few types of nose plugs. I confirmed with USAT that I could use either of these in a triathlon. While the mask and plugs reduced the rate of water going into my nose, both leaked enough to never completely eliminate the annoyance of a plugged nose.

It amazed me that I only experienced congestion after swimming in Midwestern lakes. It was never an issue after swimming in lakes outside the Midwest.

The bike course led us from transition near Worster Lake to the Horsemen's Campground, then back. Since Joy and I had driven the bike course the previous day, I knew what to expect. Most sections of the course were flat, with few potholes or large cracks.

By now, a mist had replaced the earlier rain. Though the roads were now only damp, most bikers heeded the repeated warnings of the race director during the pre-race meeting to "slow down on corners."

Upon reaching transition, I appreciated the folded towel covering my running shoes. While the towel was dripping wet, saturated with rainwater, my running shoes were totally dry, as if I had only now removed them from the van.

The race director described the third leg as a trail run. While walking through the park the previous day, I was sure he had meant a paved trail, one used by walkers and runners. Once on the run, I realized I was mistaken. What he meant by "trail run" was running on a primitive trail, complete with tree roots, boulders, loose rock, mud puddles, splashes of grass, and many hills.

As I began the run, I noticed the rain had passed, though the sky remained overcast. My bike and run gear were dry owing to lessons from earlier races. Dry shoes, cloud cover, and cool air made for a comfortable finish.

As I rounded the last bend, the final hundred yards to the finish line became visible. Right about the same time, Joy, positioned near the finish line, spotted me. The next thing I heard was, "Push it! Finish strong!" It was Joy's voice, but with the force of my high school basketball coach. I had plenty of energy to sprint across the timing mat at the finish line. I finished first of the three in my age group and 28th of 85 Sprint triathlon competitors.

Before the start of the race, Joy and I had met Jim and Deb Panozzo from Michigan. For Jim, who would celebrate his 63rd birthday the following week, Tri the Creek was the second

Sprint triathlon. Joy and Deb then became better acquainted while Jim and I completed the sprint-distance race.

Afterward, we continued our conversation. I loved Jim's description of the run: "a cross-country course in the mud that took me back to my high school days." He also shared his feelings on this race and the sport of triathlon. "It was a lot of fun, but very humbling. It showed my weaknesses and the things I need to work on, but I am so grateful to God for the ability to take part in and finish a triathlon."

2017:
A FORK IN THE ROAD

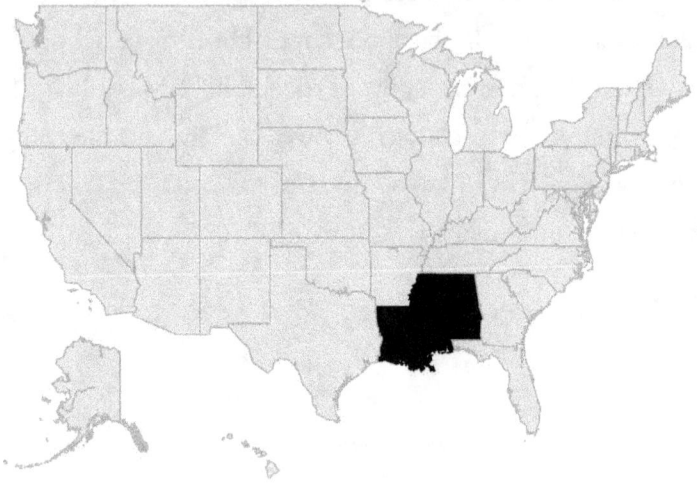

I have questioned my path in life a few times. The first major question, as I remember, came during my sophomore year in college when I realized that architecture, my original major, was not what I had expected, even though I convinced myself during the last years of high school I had found my dream career. I opted for a less-artsy form of engineering, and one I soon learned to love: metallurgy.

In early April 2017, having completed triathlons in almost two-thirds of the states and registered for races in two more, I second-guessed the knee-jerk decision Joy and I had made back in 2011 after my first triathlon.

Changes I'd put into place over the past year in the company I managed were not producing the results I expected. We needed change as the company grew. Employees and other managers were unhappy with some changes. The operational improvements I had promised my boss were not being realized. Was he right to question my commitment to the business, given my well-known pursuit of my triathlon goal?

I remembered the words of Jesus, recorded in Luke 14:28-30: "Is there anyone here who, planning to build a new house, doesn't first sit down and figure the cost so you'll know if you can complete it? If you only get the foundation laid and then run out of money, you're going to look pretty foolish. Everyone passing by will poke fun at you: 'He started something he couldn't finish'" *(Message Version).*

Jesus was speaking to some of His followers about counting the cost of the decision to follow Him. He did not want them to make the decision lightly, since He hoped they would stick with it. Following Him would not be easy. For some, it would be deadly.

I was having second thoughts. My job had become more demanding, and my training was suffering. I was tired of traveling. Still, what weighed on me the most was the concern that I may have begun this journey for selfish reasons, aiming to bring attention to myself or stroke my own ego rather than follow the Lord's plan. As I prayed one evening, I said, "Lord, I know I started on this journey without talking to You. If you want me to stop, I will."

Without a moment's delay, a soft-spoken voice within me replied, "Who says I wasn't part of it?" Joy and I needed to finish what we had started.

The challenges at work remained. Still, I planned to complete triathlons in four states that year, two in the spring and two in the fall. With these, I'd stay on track to complete a triathlon in each state by age 70.

Even though we made two trips to the South Central U.S., I would complete triathlons in only three states. Despite not feeling as fit as before, I still finished these triathlons as we explored new areas of the country.

• • • •

MISSISSIPPI: STATE #32

Mississippi Nickname:
The Magnolia State

The run course for the Tupelo Sprint Triathlon passed
Elvis Presley's childhood home.

Mississippi Triathlon Details

- Date: April 22, 2017
- Triathlon: 3rd Tupelo Sprint Triathlon
- Location: Tupelo Aquatic Center, Veterans Park,
  Tupelo, Mississippi

Published distances
- Swim: 300 meters (328 yards)
- Bike: 11 miles (17.7 kilometers)
- Run: 2 miles (3.2 kilometers)

Joy and I left our home in Maple Grove, Minnesota on a drizzling Thursday morning in the thick of rush hour. Later that day, on the opposite end of the rush-hour cycle, we crawled through St. Louis, Missouri. During our ten-day vacation, I planned to complete triathlons in Mississippi and Alabama on back-to-back weekends.

Continuing further south, we checked into our hotel in Festus, Missouri. Following the front desk clerk's advice, we made our way to the Main & Mill Brewing Company. For dinner, we ate their famous maple bacon burger, fries, and green beans that brought back memories of Joy's mom's cooking.

Back at the hotel after dinner, I read an e-mail from race director Aaron Ford. One statement made me wonder what might happen: "The race is still planned to go as scheduled due to the weather; however, there is a possibility of changing [the] start time or modifying the course. We will not know until that morning."

We arrived in Tupelo the next afternoon with plenty of time to rehearse the route from our hotel to the Tupelo Aquatic Center and tour the Elvis Presley Birthplace Visitor Center. While collecting the race packet, one of the race staff said they weren't concerned about rain as much as lightning.

Race morning brought the forecasted rain, which sometimes poured from the skies beyond what our van's wipers could remove. However, as the triathlon's start time approached, the dark clouds thinned. Small patches of blue sky appeared through wispy clouds in the west.

I finished setting up my transition space in a light drizzle, not feeling the need to cover my bike or bike shoes as I had done in my last triathlon. I left my shoes clipped into the bike pedals hanging downward, allowing gravity to keep water from collecting in them.

On days without rain, I normally looped a rubber band through a safety pin in the strap on the back of my right shoe before slipping the two ends of the rubber band over the rear-facing locking clamp on the back wheel's skewer. This held the right shoe horizontal, making it easier to begin pedaling before maneuvering my feet into the shoes. Today, however, a horizontally-placed shoe would have caught the rain.

Fifteen minutes before the triathlon began, we entered the Aquatic Center. Would it still be raining 30 or 40 minutes later when I finished the swim?

Following Aaron's prayer for the triathletes' safety and for the rain to stop, we lined up along the pool deck according to race-bib number. In the days before the triathlon, the event staff had assigned race numbers according to the estimated swim time each of us submitted during registration. They assigned the lowest race numbers to the fastest swimmers, so they would start first. They hoped to minimize congestion during the swim.

Once the first racer started their swim, another racer jumped into the pool every 10 seconds to begin their own. We swam to the opposite end, moved under the lane divider into the next lane, and swam back to the starting end. At the end of six laps, during which we repeated this sequence, we climbed out of the pool using metal handles and steps cast into the pool wall.

After completing my swim, I walked a few steps across the

pool deck to exit through the door of the Aquatic Center, happy to see it was no longer raining. A quick jog across a section of grass between the pool and parking lot brought me to transition.

After mounting my bike, I realized I had forgotten to loosen the Velcro straps on the tops of my shoes and spread the shoe openings. Putting on my shoes took longer because of this. After pedaling a few strokes, the bike was moving fast enough to coast. I used my left hand to steer and my right hand to spread open the right shoe. As a few bikes passed me, I maneuvered my right foot into its shoe, then repeated this sequence for the left foot.

By now, a few puddles dotted the damp roads. As I overtook a bike that had passed me moments earlier, I felt the spray of water from the bike's tire on my face—the only sign that the road was damp. Even the lenses of my glasses were clear, except for a few stubborn raindrops clinging to them.

The bike course featured two turnarounds. The first was past a modest hill—the only significant one on the course. We arrived at the hill (and the first turnaround) at the end of a street we reached after a right turn off North Veterans Memorial Boulevard.

On our ride to the second turnaround, further north on North Veterans Memorial Boulevard, we rode under Interstate 22. After passing the second turnaround, we returned to transition. A possum, which lay in the middle of the right lane after being struck by a passing vehicle, was the only obstacle.

The single-loop run course started on a trail that wove its

way south along the western edge of Veterans Park. At the south end of the park, we turned left onto Presley Parkway and ran past Elvis Presley's birthplace.

After a quarter-mile, we turned left to reenter Veterans Park on a paved trail. The trail cut through an open grassy space with small trees, continued between two large ponds, and went past a memorial before rejoining our earlier path. The finish line was just a stone's throw away.

At the end of the race, as we waited for the awards ceremony, John Vanderpluym, the first finisher in my age group, spoke of his Dutch ancestors—a heritage we share. We then found a second connection through his daughter. She and her husband had lived near our home northwest of Minneapolis before they retired. They now spent their summers in northern Minnesota.

As Aaron Ford called me to receive the award for my second place age-group finish, he presented me with a bag of coffee roasted and ground by High Point Roasters in New Albany, Mississippi. He also mentioned my home city and state, Maple Grove, Minnesota. Aaron added, "Believe it or not, I know where Terry's hometown is, having run around a lake in Maple Grove. My wife has family in Maple Grove." Afterward, Aaron shared the maps from his Garmin watch. They showed that he had run around Cedar Island Lake and Eagle Lake, both of which were within a couple of miles of our home.

Triathlon continued to show us how small the world was. Some years earlier, my cousin Jenny had compiled a booklet of small-world stories sent to her by family and friends. Our experiences through triathlon—and Jenny's accounts of unrelated people who shared a connection with the same person or place—proved to her (and to us) that "it's a small world after all."

● ● ● ●

ALABAMA: STATE #33

Alabama Nickname:
The Heart of Dixie

The start of this triathlon was from the Harriott II
paddleboat a quarter-mile upstream.

Alabama Triathlon Details

- Date: April 29, 2017
- Triathlon: 5th Baptist Health Capital of Dreams Tri
- Location: Riverfront Park, Montgomery, Alabama

Published distances
- Swim: 400 meters (437 yards)
- Bike: 20 kilometers (12.4 miles)
- Run: 5 kilometers (3.1 miles)

After the Tupelo Sprint Triathlon, Joy and I drove to the Gulf Shores region to explore a part of southeastern Alabama and the western panhandle of Florida we had never visited. With retirement on the horizon, we also wondered if this area could someday become a winter getaway or year-round home for us. While we did not meet any of them during this trip, we knew people from Minnesota (and from work) who had either relocated here or frequented it during the winter months.

We looked forward to watching the surf in the Gulf of Mexico, eating seafood, and walking the white sugar sand beaches of the coast. Our time coincided with a weekend beach volleyball tournament, a benefit we enjoyed on Saturday afternoon and Sunday.

The next Thursday afternoon, we headed north to Montgomery. Much of the trip followed roads lined by mile after mile of forest with clusters of flowering magnolias mixed in. On Friday, we visited a few historic sites in Montgomery before collecting the triathlon packet later in the afternoon.

The triathlon's name came from Montgomery's nickname, Capital of Dreams. Montgomery is the capital of the state of Alabama. Dr. Martin Luther King, Jr., leader of the 1960s Civil Rights movement and famous for his 1963 "I Have a Dream" speech, lived in Montgomery for ten years.

While picking up my race packet, I learned that transition would be held in the historic Union Train Shed at Riverfront Park. This was my first experience with transition set up both within a historic site and under a covered space.

This triathlon was the first and only one where we had a

problem related to our hotel. Before leaving for our tour of Montgomery, I had been using Joy's cell phone. I must have dropped it onto the bed before we left the hotel. Joy realized her phone was missing a few minutes after leaving, so we turned around to go back. We did not find the cell phone in our room, so we returned to rummage through our van, frantic to find it. We hoped someone in the hotel had come across it.

Later that day, we got Joy's phone back and learned why we hadn't found it in the hotel. In the few minutes after leaving, hotel staff had entered our room, grabbed the sheets (and phone), and loaded them into the washing machine.

We purchased a bag of rice and buried the phone within it, hoping to dry the device. Still, that was the end of this particular phone's life. It was also the last time I left her phone, or mine, lying on a hotel bed.

The next morning at around 7 a.m., we gathered on the dock in Riverfront Park. Here, Therese Bynum shared pre-race instructions and safety tips. She then asked everyone, spectators included, to sing the common birthday song for those celebrating their birthday today. We followed this by singing our national anthem.

We were ready to begin the triathlon. All triathletes boarded the Harriott II paddleboat for the quarter-mile ride up the Alabama River, from which point those of us in the Sprint triathlon would start the swim. Starting from a paddleboat was another first for me.

During the pre-race meeting, Therese reported that the water temperature was 72 degrees, making the race wetsuit-legal according to USAT rules. Since the air was humid and already approaching 80 degrees, I waited until we were riding upriver to put on my wetsuit. Today, I was wearing it for reasons other than warmth. With a wetsuit, a swimmer's legs float to the surface of the water without kicking. In addition, its slippery surface glides more freely through the water. Together, the added buoyancy and reduced drag work to save the leg muscles for the run. I started sweating inside my wetsuit from the instant I finished zipping it.

While the reasons listed above provided a valid impetus for wearing my wetsuit today, snakes made for an even stronger one. Before the race, I had overheard an area resident assuring another racer that there would be snakes in the river near the boat.

Once the Harriott II reached its destination a quarter-mile from the dock, it stopped. One by one, we jumped into the river with Therese shouting, "Go!!" When each swimmer surfaced and began toward the dock, Therese signaled the next racer to jump in.

The water was free of debris except for a couple of small branches floating near the surface, which caught between my fingers. Despite keeping my eyes open for one, I never saw a snake. Apparently, they had scattered with our splashing and kicking.

Three-quarters of the way into the swim, my cap came off. I stuffed it into the front of my wetsuit and finished without it. This was the second triathlon in which I had lost my swim cap. After the first time, in the Missouri River at the South

Dakota triathlon, I vowed to stuff it into my wetsuit rather than hold it while continuing to swim.

Upon reaching the dock, I followed other swimmers as we climbed out of the river using a metal ladder like those used in swimming pools. I reached the level of transition by jogging along a concrete walkway and up a few stairs.

With few hills, my bike computer was showing an average speed of around 21 miles per hour. It amazed me to see so many volunteers directing traffic—at least one at every intersection along the bike course. The courteous drivers with whom we shared the road made these volunteers' jobs easier. At one intersection, a female driver smiled as she waited, her car signaling a left turn to cross the bike lane. Her thoughtfulness was typical of what we found throughout our stay in Montgomery.

The run course took us past Dexter Avenue King Memorial Baptist Church, where Dr. Martin Luther King preached from 1954 to 1960, and around the Alabama State Capitol. This was also my first triathlon that featured a run around a state capitol.

I alternated running and walking, pausing at every aid station for a drink of Powerade or water. While drinking Powerade at an early aid station, a volunteer offered water to help cool me down. I nodded yes, expecting him to pour water over my head. To my surprise, the cold water hit my upper back and ran down the back of my triathlon suit, cooling me as gravity took the water to my feet. An immediate fan of this method, I asked a volunteer at an aid station later in the run to pour cold water down my back.

Two-thirds of the way into the course, I approached an

intersection. A patient driver was waiting for me to cross. From at least three car lengths from the intersection, I yelled to the woman directing traffic, "Let them go. I could use a break right now."

Without hesitation, the woman, who appeared near my age, responded in a distinct Southern accent, "I know you could, but I'm not going to be giving you one. C'mon through." I thanked her and crossed the intersection.

I couldn't help but smile. This exchange also reminded me of a quote from the Bible: "A cheerful heart is good medicine" (*Proverbs 17:22, New Living Translation*). Energized, I sprinted to the finish line. I finished second of four in my age group (men ages 60 through 64) and 99th of 119 finishers.

While I raced, Joy had been asking other older racers about their triathlon experiences. She met one man who had completed over 150 triathlons since the early days of the sport. Another man, who had started triathlon later in life, told her he had finished over 100 triathlons, including 27 races in a single year. A third described how he had completed his first triathlon after the death of his wife. Triathlon had given him a new focus and the opportunity to meet people.

• • • •

LOUISIANA: STATE #34

Louisiana Nickname:
The Pelican State

Finish line of the 2017 Sugarman Triathlon. The triathlon swim
was in the pond pictured in the background.

Louisiana Triathlon Details

- Date: October 1, 2017
- Triathlon: 8th Sugarman Triathlon
- Location: Sugar Mill Pond, Youngsville, Louisiana

Published distances

- Swim: 500 meters (547 yards)
- Bike: 15 miles (24.1 kilometers)
- Run: 3.1 miles (5 kilometers)

The Sugarman Triathlon suited our plan of driving to Florida to celebrate our wedding anniversary. Being in western Louisiana for the triathlon also gave us a chance to see Diana, our friend from Katy, Texas. We had last seen Diana when we stayed with her during the 2012 No Label Triathlon.

We learned that Diana's house in suburban Houston had filled with water up to the second floor in the flooding following Hurricane Harvey. For over a year, she had been commuting to Baton Rouge, Louisiana for work. Youngsville was the perfect meeting point for a face-to-face visit with her.

Joy and I left our Minnesota home a little before 6 a.m. on Friday morning to make it to the triathlon by Sunday. With a new audiobook playing on the radio, we set our GPS for Little Rock, Arkansas, where we would spend our first night. The overnight stop in Little Rock meant we were two-thirds of the way to the race venue in Youngsville, Louisiana, a southern suburb of Lafayette.

We finished the trip to Youngsville the next day, arriving in plenty of time for packet pickup. After a quick tour of the race venue around Sugar Mill Pond, we finished the evening with Diana, eating authentic Cajun cuisine at Poor Boy's Riverside Inn. Never before had we witnessed so-called pet raccoons begging for handouts near a restaurant's entrance.

Like many triathlons, Sugarman doubled as a fundraiser. This event supported two local causes, the Jacob Crouch Foundation for suicide prevention and TRAIL (Transportation Recreation Alternatives in Louisiana), an organization aimed at "building and maintaining opportunities for outdoor recreation."

Almost 200 racers competed in age groups, relays, or as Clydesdales or Athenas. Transition was set up on Waterview Street in front of the Sugar Mill Athletic Club.

We racked our bikes along one of the two edges of the street in the space marked with our race number. Along each rack, we alternated the direction our bikes were facing: toward the *Bike Out* or the *Run Out* end of transition. Alternating sides in this manner—a practice common to most triathlons—left space beside our bikes for other items in our transition spaces.

"You cannot win a triathlon in transition, but you can lose it." I don't remember if I read this quote somewhere or made it up myself from a similar adage...but it's true. Every second counts, whether in transition or any of the triathlon's three legs.

By now, I had learned that one key to a faster transition time in a Sprint triathlon was to minimize stuff in my transition space. At this triathlon, this included my bike (with biking shoes clipped into the pedals). My helmet sat top-down between the aero bars. My sunglasses nestled within the helmet, lenses down, bows open and pointing upward so I could slip them on and strap on my helmet within a few seconds during the swim-to-bike transition.

My faithful green and white striped beach towel, one of the two that had been with us at every triathlon, lay spread out in the space between my bike and my neighbor's. My running shoes with my race number belt, now rolled into a loose cylinder sitting upright in one shoe, were the only items on the towel. This was a far cry from my first triathlon, for which I had begun my swim-to-bike transition by sitting down to wash my feet using the wash basin in my transition space before putting on socks and eating a few gummy bears.

A few moments before the first swim wave began, the race director called all triathletes, volunteers, and spectators to the dock beside Sugar Mill Pond. Once gathered, we recited the Pledge of Allegiance. Next, a young woman sang a beautiful rendition of our national anthem. We then bowed as the race director offered an opening prayer.

I was part of the first wave, which comprised males ages 50 and older plus relay team participants. We began waist-deep in the bath-like lukewarm water of this manmade clay-bottom pond. The counterclockwise course included left turns around several buoys leading to the exit a hundred yards south of our starting location.

The flat out-and-back bike course followed local roads and neighborhood streets. Volunteers and members of the local police department made sure the course, which included my second racing encounter with roundabouts, had clear markings. At no time did I feel unsafe, even though we were riding with motor vehicles on the open course.

Still, sections of the course needed repair. Rough patches kept alert those who obeyed the call to stay to the right. Fortunately, other bikers forgave us when we chose not to obey. I found myself on the receiving end of forgiveness after I swerved in front of a guy to avoid a treacherous patch. He never said a thing.

The temperature of the humid air continued to rise through-out the triathlon, from the low 70s at the start to the mid-80s as I began the run. On the few Minnesota days that reached the upper 80s with high humidity, I would normally do my run training early in the morning while it was cooler or train indoors.

As a result, my run past the houses of this newer, gated neighborhood felt slow, with stops at each of the many aid stations. Despite drinking Powerade at each designated point, one of my hamstrings showed signs of cramping early in the last mile. As I continued running, the hints of cramping disappeared. I finished the last part of the run on the trail around the pond with a strong sprint through the dockside finish line.

I finished fourth of four in my age group, and 118th of 151 competitors in the individual Sprint triathlon.

Before we continued to The Villages, Florida, where we would be spending the next two weeks, we joined the 11 a.m. service at the Bayou Church, across the street from our hotel. This allowed us to experience a little more of French Louisiana, or Acadiana. Just as at home, we enjoyed singing together and talking with others after the service. To top off the visit, they invited us to celebrate the pastor's 33rd anniversary of leading this church.

We were no longer surprised that we were able to feel at home in a state so far south. Yes, there were some differences, such as the typical dinner meal or the most popular outdoor activities, as is typical across the country. Still, we always found people who welcomed us to their area.

2018:
RETIREMENT AND LOTS OF TRAVEL

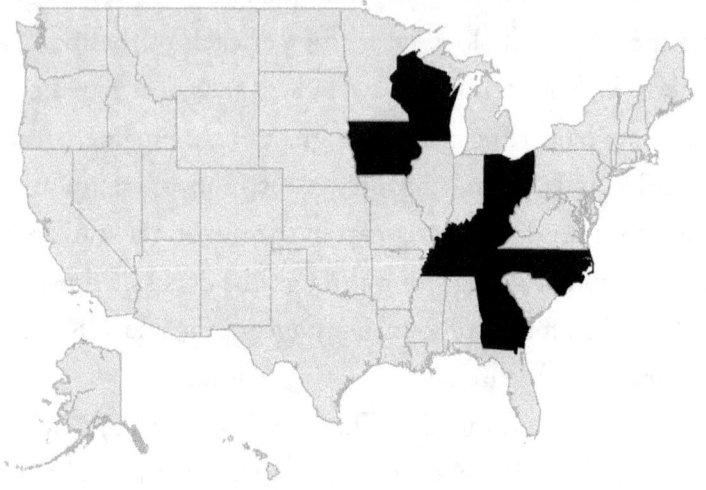

At the end of May 2018, before the second triathlon of this season, I retired from full-time employment after 43 years.

Certain family members I will not mention here had convinced themselves I would be bored in retirement; secretly, they hoped for an antidote in triathlon. These naysayers and worrywarts refused to listen when I said they should rest easy. I had many pent-up interests.

Within one month of retiring, I started consulting for two companies in industrial laser technology, my former professional career. One by one, those skeptical of my ability to stay busy in retirement relaxed. Perhaps they had been mistaken.

After continuing to train throughout the summer, Joy and I left Minnesota for a six-week tour in the southeastern part of the country. Triathlon would obviously be a big part of the itinerary.

Over the past three-plus decades, Joy and I had spent long periods apart because of my work-related travel. She made use of this time to develop a network of female friends through fitness, golf, card games, and Bible study. Now, within three months, Joy and I would be spending six continuous weeks together. While this was something we both looked forward to, we were also aware of the idiom "be careful what you wish for."

IOWA: STATE #35

Iowa Nickname:
The Hawkeye State

Packet pickup was at Thompson Shoes (left), across the street from the
Waverly Chamber of Commerce (upper right) and next door
to the East Bremer Diner (lower right).

Iowa Triathlon Details

- Date: May 5, 2018
- Triathlon: 7th TriByKnight Sprint Triathlon
- Location: Wartburg College, Waverly, Iowa

Published distances
- Swim: 300 yards (274 meters)
- Bike: 15 miles (24.1 kilometers)
- Run: 3.1 miles (5 kilometers)

With the extended 2017-2018 winter in Minnesota, my training in the first months of this year took place indoors—except while we were in Hawaii to visit my Aunt Nelda during the second half of January. Then, three weeks before the TriByKnight Sprint triathlon, 22 inches of snow fell at our Minnesota home.

While the weather warmed and the snow soon disappeared, the roads remained wet, their edges covered with salty sand and dirt from winter. My first ride outside occurred less than one week before the race.

On Friday, May 4th, we left home at around 1:30 p.m. for the three-hour drive to Waverly. By the time we arrived, my race packet was ready to be picked up at Thompson Shoes, one sponsor of this triathlon, which was managed by Wartburg College staff.

Stomachs rumbling, we went next door to the East Bremer Diner. The prime rib dinner, complete with the Diner's signature salad dressings, was exceptional. Before checking into our motel, we drove to the Wartburg College campus, where we explored the bike course for the following day's triathlon.

The next morning, with the start of the race approaching, all swimmers lined up around the six-lane, 25-yard pool of the Schuldt Natatorium according to our estimated swim time—fastest to slowest. After we sang the national anthem, a member of the race staff sent the first triathlete into the pool to begin his race. Another of the remaining 193 racers started every five seconds.

Upon entering the water, we swam down and back in each

of the pool's first five lanes. After each lane, we ducked under the divider to move to the one adjacent. After swimming down the sixth lane, we turned toward the starting end. Halfway back, we veered left to swim across a part of the pool designated for water sports, including volleyball and water polo, before walking up concrete steps to exit the pool. From here, we left the building and walked or jogged toward the pool parking lot, which served as transition for this triathlon, to grab our bikes.

Today was perfect for biking in the country. Clear skies. Light breeze. Mild temperature. During the ride, I looked down at my bike computer to see 77 degrees.

The bike course was a 15-mile loop north of Waverly on paved roads. Riding north out of town on a county highway, we passed between fields that were still black with soil, having been planted only days earlier. During this section featuring a continuous series of rolling hills, some bikers slowed as they came upon a mix of cars and trucks. While I never slowed behind a car or truck, the scene brought back memories of my Texas triathlon. Near the halfway mark of the bike course, we passed through the small town of Bremer, turning right at the center to begin our ride back to transition.

About a mile outside of Bremer, we passed a farm with three rusted threshing machines on display in a grassy field. As a young boy, I had watched these machines at work during oat and wheat harvests. From a distance, I observed as my dad and a few neighbor men tossed bundles of grain stalks into the machines, which worked to separate the grain and straw. Today, I did not see any sign that the owner was selling these farm implements; still, I noticed a *For Sale* sign for the acreage posted near the road.

We reached Waverly's streets after a few miles, with the longest hill of the course now conquered. The last section of the bike course crossed the Cedar River on a wooden pedestrian bridge—another triathlon first for me. A few blocks later, we arrived at the dismount line and returned to transition.

The 5k run leg was made up of three loops, all on streets within the Wartburg campus. During the last loop, we finished with a half-lap run on the asphalt track of Walston-Hoover Stadium, crossing the finish line at the 50-yard line of the football field. I finished third of four in my new age group, 65 through 69, and 153rd of 193 overall.

In early March, when I first learned of the TriByKnight triathlon in Waverly, Iowa, Joy called her high school classmate, Susan Doster, to see if she and her husband Paul would be available to get together during the weekend of the triathlon. Paul and Susan lived in Algona, Iowa, so it would be easy to visit them after the triathlon on our way home. While not the quickest route, passing through Algona only added 75 miles, a reasonable detour considering the total distance of the trip.

We had last seen Paul and Susan 27 years earlier, during the summer of 1991. They and their three children had traveled from Algona to join our family in Minnesota, and our two families had volunteered at the International Special Olympics in Minneapolis and St. Paul. That weekend had been full of memories. We met Kirstie Alley, Fred Savage, and Olympic gymnasts Nadia Comăneci and Bart Conner at the games. We also hosted the Irish basketball team for a backyard pool party at our home in Inver Grove Heights, Minnesota after one of their games.

After the triathlon, we traveled northwest from Waverly to our first stop: Clear Lake, Iowa, for lunch. Clear Lake is home to the Surf Ballroom, the venue hosting Buddy Holly's last performance with his band. The next day, February 3, 1959, their chartered airplane crashed north of Clear Lake, killing Holly, Richie Valens, and The Big Bopper.

While reading Loretta Ellsworth's novel *Stars Over Clear Lake* six months earlier, Joy had learned a bit of history about nearby Algona. During the Second World War, a camp outside Algona held German prisoners of war (POWs). Near the end of the book, Joy learned of a museum that memorialized the camp—and the residents who had served in this part of the war effort.

When we learned that Paul and Susan were members of the museum, we jumped on the opportunity to visit it with them. Glenn, docent of the POW Camp Museum, added to the various displays by sharing heartwarming stories from interviews with area residents, some of which he had conducted. *Common Valor* features at least one of Glenn's stories and contributions from Paul and Susan's daughter, Leah.

We finished the day of catching up on our families for hours around a home-cooked steak dinner at their house. It amazed me that despite the many years of not seeing Paul and Susan, we felt as if we had only been apart for a short time. While both families' children had grown, left home, and started their own journeys, we still shared a bond with our friends through our separate (but equivalent) joys, challenges, and experiences.

After attending church with Paul and Susan on Sunday morning, we resumed our drive home. Since U.S. 169 passes through Algona and within a few miles of our home, we returned using this route. Along the way, we detoured a few blocks as the road passed through Blue Earth, Minnesota, for a surprise visit to Joy's sister Sherryl and niece Penny.

WISCONSIN: STATE #36

Wisconsin Nickname:
The Badger State

Collage of views from the bike course of the Eau Claire Triathlon.

Wisconsin Triathlon Details

- Date: June 3, 2018
- Triathlon: 9th Mayo Clinic Health System Eau Claire Triathlon
- Location: Halfmoon Park, Eau Claire, Wisconsin

Published distances
- Swim: 500 meters (547 yards)
- Bike: 17 miles (27.4 kilometers)
- Run: 3.1 miles (5 kilometers)

Minnesota summers are notorious for being short: three months at the most. During the majority of weekends, our children and grandchildren occupied the extra bedrooms of our house, which sat on the edge of Fish Lake. We filled these days swimming, kayaking, strolling in our pontoon, or towing kids on a tube, skis, or wakeboard across the lake in our runabout.

Early on, I had imagined Wisconsin as being the last of the 50 states in which I would finish a triathlon. Secretly, I hoped that our children, their spouses, and our older grandchildren (or at least some of them) would complete it with me. I wanted to show them that this "old man" could do a triathlon—and they could, too. And, hopefully, they would experience triathlon's benefits and remain active.

With ice remaining on the lake later than usual this year, the water was too cold for water sports during the first weekend in June. Since Eau Claire was an easy two-hour drive east of our home, we decided this would be the year to check off the triathlon in Wisconsin.

We left our house a few minutes after 2 p.m. on Saturday for Sunday's triathlon and reached Eau Claire in time to check into our hotel before picking up the race packet. This Sprint triathlon included options for us to race as individuals in an age group, or as a Clydesdale or an Athena. We could also race as part of a relay team.

Earlier in the day, the organizer had held a kid's triathlon for children ages seven through fourteen. Kids competed either on their own or on a relay team. Seven- to 10-year-olds raced different distances from those ages 11 to fourteen.

The Eau Claire Triathlon raised funds for Friends of the Orphans and the Chippewa Valley Free Clinic. Friends of the Orphans provides a loving home for over 3,500 children in Latin America and the Caribbean; and, at the time of this writing, it has been doing so for over 40 years. The Chippewa Valley Free Clinic in western Wisconsin offers medical services to those without health insurance.

On the way to Peace Lutheran, one of the triathlon sponsors, for the Saturday evening worship service, we grabbed dinner: a couple of Culver's kids' meals. We arrived back at our hotel as the skies opened and rain poured down. Precipitation continued as we turned our lights off for the night.

I awakened Sunday morning to find that the rain had passed. It would not fall during the rest of our stay in Eau Claire. We arrived at Halfmoon Park under clouds, the air temperature just below 60 degrees with a light wind. As we waited for the triathlon to begin, I noticed the many volunteers by the wording on their T-shirts. Someone said there would be more than a hundred volunteers stationed at various locations along the racecourse.

The triathlon began with two men starting the swim. Each towed an inflatable boat connected to a cord wrapped around his waist. A disabled child sat in each boat. The man and child traveled together throughout the three legs of the triathlon. I know this because I passed both groups on the bike leg. Later, during the run, each pair passed me.

This was the third state in which I had experienced a triathlon beginning this way. What was it about triathlon and these demonstrations of love? Two of the races had also supported organizations dedicated to caring for children. Joy and I loved this about the sport.

Following a five-minute head start, the first wave—males under 40—began the counterclockwise swim from Halfmoon Lake's sandy beach, around two red buoys, and back to the beach. Waves with the rest of the 153 participants started at two-minute intervals, with relay team members comprising the last wave.

With the cool air this morning, my wetsuit made the wait tolerable. The faces and shivering bodies of those waiting for the swim without a wetsuit said they wished they had one.

The bike course took us on rolling hills, first through residential streets and a tunnel under the dense traffic of Claremont Road—a first for me in a triathlon. We continued through more neighborhoods, passing Sherman Elementary School, then into the country, past grain fields, beautiful patches of purple and white wildflowers in ditches, and farm homes. It surprised me to not see potholes on these northern roads so soon after the winter thaw.

As we rode away from the tree-lined byways of the residential areas, I noticed a gusty headwind, one strong enough to hold my attention. Even so, I passed a few of the other riders as I cut through the wind in the aero position. After the midpoint turnaround near Union Town Hall, we rode the tailwind back to the neighborhoods and to transition.

The run began on a paved trail, which led to a bridge across Halfmoon Lake. After crossing it, we joined a public road leading into Carson Park. Except for the hill near the park's entrance, the course was flat.

Soon after entering the park, I heard a clanging sound. It sounded like glass bottles clanking against each other. My first thought, odd as it seemed for a Sunday morning, was that someone was emptying glass recycling containers. Further into the run, I found the actual source. As I passed a stand of trees, I saw the horseshoe court with at least ten games in progress. I later read that Carson Park has 18 horseshoe courts with seating for a hundred competitors and spectators. I guess horseshoes is a serious sport in Eau Claire.

Later in the run, I spotted something ahead on the road. Initially, I pictured it as animal remains, maybe from a car collision. As I got closer, this object came into view. A huge snapping turtle, undisturbed by the many runners passing it, was taking its time feasting on a bunch of leaves it had found in the road. Running past a turtle in a triathlon was another first-time experience for me.

As we continued the loop through the park, we passed statues of Paul Bunyan and his blue ox, Babe, and the Chippewa Valley Museum. After exiting the park, we recrossed the bridge, then got onto the paved trail. This time, we left the trail to finish with a 200-yard jog along a narrow dirt trail, then across a grassy patch and short section of coarse gravel.

After crossing the finish line, I bent over to remove the strap holding the timing chip around my left ankle. As I stood up, a young volunteer handed me a bottle of ice-cold water. As I downed the water, Joy and I headed over to the refreshment tent, where we exchanged our meal and drink tickets for a grilled burger, some grilled onions, potato chips, and two root beers. My mouth still waters just reading this string of words.

I finished seventh of 10 in the 65 through 69 age group of men, and 91st of 153 finishers in the individual Sprint triathlon.

By the time we had finished the food and drinks, transition opened for me to remove my bike, wetsuit, and the others things I had left during the run. We swung by the hotel so I could shower, then made the short drive home. Tomorrow, I would begin my first full week of retirement.

• • • •

OHIO: STATE #37

Ohio Nickname:
The Buckeye State

Scenes from the Hocking Hills Sprint Triathlon bike course. Clockwise: water lilies at the north end of Lake Logan (upper right), near the top of the last hill before the turnaround (lower right), St. John's Church (lower left), and farm buildings (upper left).

Ohio Triathlon Details

- Date: September 8, 2018
- Triathlon: 15th Hocking Hills Sprint Triathlon
- Location: Lake Logan State Park and Lake Logan Beach, Logan, Ohio

Published distances
- Swim: 400 meters (437 yards)
- Bike: 20 kilometers (12.4 miles)
- Run: 5 kilometers (3.1 miles)

n August, Joy and I began planning an early October trip to The Villages, Florida, to celebrate our 45th wedding anniversary. Why not knock off the proverbial two birds with one stone? I began a search for triathlons in one or two states where I had yet to complete one.

As I looked for triathlons in two states along our route to Florida, I saw a pattern in the spreadsheet of dates and locations for fall triathlons in the southeast part of the U.S. I could complete triathlons in five different states on five successive weekends while making a loop through central Florida.

With me now retired, Joy and I had the flexibility to transform our original two-week vacation into a six-week one. These triathlons would bring us closer to meeting our goal. So, at the end of August, I registered for triathlons in Ohio, Tennessee, Georgia, North Carolina, and Kentucky.

The day before we began this trip, hoping to have space for everything we would need to bring for this trip, I stowed the second- and third-row seats into the floor of our Chrysler Pacifica. Next, I rolled my bike into the back end of the van, and, using two bungee cords, secured it upright against the edge behind the driver's seat. I then arranged the rest of the items for our road trip in a three-dimensional Tetris-like pattern.

I slid my triathlon case—an oversized green and black striped suitcase that held everything I would need for a triathlon, plus some things I hoped to never need—into the back end of the van. Joy had originally rescued this suitcase from a thrift store in Chicopee, Massachusetts. Beginning with the

Massachusetts triathlon, we had repurposed it into a triathlon case that traveled with us to every race.

At the bottom of my case I kept spare tubes, a package of CO_2 cartridges for inflating bike tubes during a ride, a tool for removing and tightening bike pedals, and a set of torque wrenches for adjustments to the bike's carbon fiber frame. On top of these lay a pair of socks, a bike jacket, several pairs of swim goggles, a wetsuit, and baggies filled with packages of sports drink powder and gels. I stuffed three water bottles into crevices between these. Near the top sat my biking and running shoes and the green and white striped towels. A one-piece triathlon suit I used in races and a spare suit joined these. The case was closed and zipped shut to keep everything together.

I stuffed my bike helmet and air pump into the empty spaces behind the bike's rear wheel. At the front of this compartment, behind the front passenger seat, we arranged our personal items for easy access. These included a roller bag, computer bag, and overnight bag for each of us. For most trips, these items, along with a case of bottled water, were all we needed for travel to a triathlon. However, for this trip, it was just the beginning.

While planning, Joy decided we should retry tent camping in an attempt to find a happy medium between rustic camping and a luxury hotel room. We had given up tent camping 30 years earlier because it had rained almost every time we set up a tent. For this trip, though, we were also taking camping gear. According to Joy, we needed a four-person Coleman tent designed to withstand wind and rain, two queen-sized blow-up airbeds with accompanying bedding and pillows, a tower fan, an electric frying pan, a coffee pot, electrical cords, and a multi-outlet power strip. I needed a hammer to set the tent stakes.

Rounding out our camping gear was Joy's homemade portable toilet, configured from a medium-sized white plastic garbage can lined with a heavy-duty plastic bag containing a few cups of cat litter. She topped the commode with a *Dora the Explorer* children's toilet seat.

Resting on top of the camping gear was Geno, a four-foot-tall 59-year-old stuffed giraffe, secured inside a large black plastic leaf bag. Joy's friend, Debby Peterson, had asked us to deliver it to Florida.

As I looked at the van filled with gear for this unexpected camping adventure, it reminded me of how little I knew about Joy, despite having been with her for over 45 years. Surprises like this made our marriage adventure occasionally frustrating, but overwhelmingly exciting. Joy is a mystery that I will never solve. Fortunately, I love a good mystery.

We left our Minnesota home at around 9 a.m. on the Wednesday before Saturday's triathlon in Logan, Ohio. By 4 p.m., we had arrived at our destination for the first leg of our trip: West Chicago, Illinois. We planned to stay with our friends, Jim and Kris Novak.

As we relaxed on their patio after dinner, classical guitarist Jim Perona unexpectedly dropped by. Jim's visit was a gift from our friends for our wedding anniversary, which would take place in a few weeks. For the next hour and a half, we sat mesmerized by the romantic Spanish and Latin music from Jim's guitar.

It rained throughout the following day, so we relaxed...
even catching an afternoon nap. The next morning, we left our
friends' home a little before 6 a.m. Our destination for tonight
was the Hocking Hills KOA campground outside Logan, Ohio,
where we would be staying through Saturday.

For more than half the trip from Chicago to Columbus,
Ohio, we drove through rain—compliments of Tropical Storm
Gordon. Finally, a little beyond Indianapolis, Indiana, we passed
the rain; however, we were sure it would stay on our trail. I
hoped aloud that one of the campground's cabins would be
available, but this ultimately proved not to be the case. For the
moment, the weather app on my phone was showing only a slight
chance of rain, and for a while, the forecast was correct. We
set up the tent and our campsite before precipitation eventually
arrived later that afternoon.

Packet pickup took place on the morning of the race. Still,
we visited Lake Logan Beach, hoping to preview the bike course.
We found the road to the park closed because of downed power
lines. With this part of the plan shot and hoping for the road
to be cleared overnight, we drove into Logan for barbeque at
Millstone BBQ. Later, with an early morning ahead, we crawled
into bed, serenaded by a symphony of raindrops on our tent
roof. Thankfully, the raindrops stayed off our heads (and away
from our bottoms).

The rain stopped during the night. However, the skies
remained overcast with a *not if, but when* threat of rain. Despite
this forecast, the 67-degree air temperature was a relief from the

temperatures in the 90s the area had seen in the days leading up to this race.

On race day, we reached Lake Logan a little before 7 a.m., just as transition was opening. Overnight, the power company had cleared the road leading into the park. After setting up my transition space, Joy and I chatted with other participants, many of whom were competing in their first triathlon. A female competitor introduced us to her two daughters, whom she hoped would become triathletes. With wide smiles, the two girls posed on each side of Geno, the stuffed giraffe. Joy sent the picture to Debby to confirm that her giraffe was still in one piece and undamaged, now over halfway to Florida.

The Hocking Hills Triathlon was part of the USA Triathlon's Women's Initiative (WIN) Series, a project that aimed to encourage women to take part in triathlon and other multisport activities.

About 15 minutes before the start of the race, the skies suddenly opened. With no wind to mitigate its descent, the rain fell straight down. The race director announced that the triathlon would start on schedule since there was no lightning.

I jogged to transition to cover my running shoes and safety glasses with the green and white striped towel lying beside the front wheel of my bike. With my bike shoes clipped into the pedals and hanging downward, they would stay dry inside.

All 72 racers started the race together. Walking into the 80-degree-plus water felt like crawling into a lukewarm bath. The swim course left Lake Logan Beach, heading straight out toward the first of two super-sized beach-ball-like blowups anchored to the lake bottom. After the initial chaos from this number of swimmers starting together, the group spread out, leaving plenty of space between us.

The water was shallow near the beach, so I used several dolphin dives to get into more depth before beginning a regular swim stroke. While swimming to and from the blow-ups, I often felt my hands or legs brush against plants...maybe milfoil, I thought.

With the heavy rain and wet roads, keeping everyone safe took priority over setting speed records. The out-and-back bike course first took us past a water-lily-covered pond, then small farmsteads. Flat roads soon gave way to small rolling hills, then to the steepest hills I had ever ridden in a triathlon. I would use the full range of gears during today's ride.

From the intersection of OH-180 and Pleasant Valley Road, I could see a farmstead ahead. At a distance, the largest building, which sported two cupolas and a massive covered porch, stood surrounded by a bright green lawn. From my vantage point, it looked like a small castle, dwarfing the property's other structures. Only as I passed in front of the building did I notice the telltale evidence of a barn: a top floor for storing hay plus a lower floor for feeding (and, most likely, milking) cattle. I saw a smaller building that looked like the farmer's house. Even though I had grown up on a farm, I never remembered seeing so spacious a barn.

The hill before the turnaround posed a new challenge. Halfway up the long, steep incline, I dismounted to walk my bike to the top. I could not ride all the way up. While it initially seemed that I was the first racer to resort to walking their bike, I noticed others walking their bikes up the hill as I rode down after passing the turnaround. Still, it surprised me that I had needed to walk the bike. What was happening? I often climbed similar hills during training rides.

The run took place on the first mile and a half of the bike course, which offered flat terrain as we passed the lily-covered pond followed by a couple of small rolling hills. After reaching the turnaround, we ran to the finish line, which was set up in the parking lot next to transition and Lake Logan Beach.

The rain was beginning to subside as the race ended, but it still persisted, and continued into the following day. During heavy rain the next morning, we disassembled and packed our tent and other camping gear. After a shower, taken mainly to dry off, we drove 45 minutes north toward Columbus to Canal Winchester. Here, we joined in Sunday worship at Peace Free Lutheran Church, a sister congregation of our Minnesota church.

Afterward, we started our journey toward Tennessee and the next race: the Dixie Triathlon in Huntingdon, Tennessee. With the exception of Geno the Giraffe, almost everything we had brought was now wet from the rain. Our first night's stop would be a hotel with laundry facilities north of Cincinnati, Ohio. We used the rest of the afternoon and the first part of the next morning to dry our clothes, triathlon gear, tent, and other camping supplies.

TENNESSEE: STATE #38

Tennessee Nickname:
The Volunteer State

Finisher medal and age-group award from the inaugural Dixie Triathlon.

Tennessee Triathlon Details

- Date: September 15, 2018
- Triathlon: 1st Dixie Triathlon
- Location: Carroll County 1000 Acre Recreation Area, Huntingdon, Tennessee

Published distances
- Swim: 500 meters (547 yards)
- Bike: 16 miles (25.8 kilometers)
- Run: 5 kilometers (3.1 miles)

Late Monday morning, we repacked our van and drove across the Ohio border into Kentucky for the next night's stay. Over the following two days, we spent one day each at the Creation Museum and Ark Encounter, both in northern Kentucky. On Tuesday and Wednesday nights, we again tried tent camping, this time in Big Bone Lick State Park in northern Kentucky under cool, clear, starlit skies, far from any city lights. With heat and humidity in the forecast for the next weekend near the triathlon venue, I continued searching for a hotel or motel room for Friday night. With all rooms booked, we accepted that we would need to camp.

We crossed into Tennessee on Thursday afternoon and pulled into the first visitors' center to search for a campsite. The staff pointed out our best option: Natchez Trace State Park, around 45 minutes south of Carroll County Recreation Area, where the triathlon would begin. While checking out campsites within Natchez Trace State Park, we stumbled upon Pin Oak Lodge. We couldn't resist a clean, air-conditioned room, especially given its affordable price. The lodge's restaurant and swimming pool, with a view of a small lake surrounded by tall stands of pine, were the icing on the cake.

The Dixie Triathlon was the dream of a local triathlete, Dr. Volker Winkler. Sadly, Dr. Winkler did not see his dream come true, as he had died unexpectedly earlier that same year. In his honor, Carroll County officials and residents poured their hearts into making the event a success. McKenzie Medical Center, the clinic Dr. Winkler helped found, served as the title sponsor of the race. The Dixie Carter Performing Arts Center in Huntingdon was the presenting sponsor.

Despite this being the first Dixie Triathlon, all 300 spots for the Sprint- and Olympic-distance triathlons were filled. In response, Huntingdon and Carroll County residents rolled out the red carpet for us. The number and enthusiasm of volunteers for this triathlon spoke of the community's commitment to the event. Huntingdon Middle School students placed personal handwritten notes in our race packets. Handmade signs offered inspiration. *The Laws of Triathlon–General Law #113: The Finish Line Is Just a Rest Stop* and other gems lined the bike and run courses.

Transition was set up in a grassy space between the park office and lake, next to the boat ramp and dock. Spaces were available on a first-come, first-served basis, with all Sprint racers on the lake side of the main aisle. Joy and I arrived before the official opening of transition at 5:45 a.m. Even though I wasn't among the first to set up their transition space, I found one just off the main aisle. Aiming for a quick transition, I set my helmet upside-down and centered between the aero bars of my bike. My clear safety glasses rested inside my helmet, lenses downward and bows spread upward. I planned to put my running shoes on the towel that lay on the grass beside my bike before transition closed.

Checking back a little later, I found my helmet lying on the ground, with my glasses in two pieces—the lenses and the frame. Without my reading glasses, I couldn't see well enough to reassemble the two pieces. Fortunately, Joy was able to do so.

I made a mental note to include a pair of readers in the small storage case behind my bike seat. I put the glasses back inside the helmet, but this time, I left them sitting on the ground next to the front bike tire. Just before transition closed, I put the helmet with glasses back on the aero bars.

Before kicking off the triathlon, Race Director Joe Fleenor reviewed the racecourse, promising "a surprise" for those on the Sprint triathlon course. Carroll County Mayor Joseph Butler followed up with a prayer. In it, he thanked God for the beauty of His creation and asked for everyone's safety. The pre-race ceremony concluded with Katie Hodges of the Miss Dixie Performing Arts Center singing our national anthem.

The swim for the Dixie Triathlon took place in the 1000 Acre Recreational Lake, a manmade lake with a clay bottom and cloudy gray water. We started in waves according to distance, age group, and gender. All Olympic-distance groups started first. As the first of the Olympic triathletes completed their swim, male Sprint-distance racers started according to age group. I started in the group of 26 males aged 50 and over.

About a minute and a half before the start of our wave, we walked onto the dock, faced the first yellow buoy, and jumped into the lake. The water was deep enough that I never touched the bottom when jumping in. At around 81 degrees, it felt comfortable. However, because of the temperature, we were not allowed to use a wetsuit according to USA Triathlon rules.

The Sprint-distance swim course included three left turns. Yellow buoys marked the first two. About 75 yards after the last left turn around the only orange buoy, I reached the exit.

With the steep drop-off, we swam within a few feet of shore before touching the uneven slippery clay bottom. Thankfully, volunteers stationed at the exit helped us with our footing as we left the water.

The bike-mount line was on a sloped section of the concrete boat launch. Since my initial focus was riding up the ramped surface, I placed my bare feet on top of my shoes and rode to the top of the launch. After reaching a flat section bordered by a pavilion and parking lot, I slipped my feet into the shoes.

The bike course continued out of the Carroll County 1000 Acre Recreation Area and up a small hill. A vacant barn at the top of the hill marked the beginning of our ride into Huntingdon. A country road took us northeast across several rolling hills into Huntingdon. The ride brought us through the city center, around the Carroll County Courthouse, and past the Dixie Carter Performing Arts Center. We left Huntingdon at its southern end, continuing on paved country roads past woods and alternating fields of soybeans and cotton.

As I came around a bend, I saw a long hill in front of me. Starting up, I downshifted, and my chain jumped off the front gearset. With the chain wedged between the frame and gearset, I dismounted. To free the chain, I flipped the bike upside down and pulled it from the frame before flipping the bike over and reinstalling the chain.

Only a short way up the hill, I thought it risky to try reclipping my shoes into the pedals while going uphill. I had never been fast at clipping in, and I needed to be moving while doing so. I turned my bike around and coasted downhill while clipping in my shoes. The moment I noticed a gap between bikers, I made a U-turn to climb the hill once again.

I wasted more time later in the course when I misread a sign with an arrow marking the bike course. Believing I had missed a turn for the Sprint-distance course and that I was, in fact, riding the course for the Olympic distance, I turned around. Seeing me make the turn while recognizing I was doing the Sprint triathlon, a volunteer yelled for me to turn back around, then turn right at the next intersection.

Near the end of the bike leg, I learned what Joe Fleenor had meant when he mentioned a "surprise" for the Sprint competitors. The surprise was a long, steep hill. As with the previous weekend's triathlon in Ohio, I walked my bike up the last half.

Another man around my age walked alongside me. He said he knew what was coming because he had ridden this course during training. We reminded each other that triathlon was our hobby, not our source of income. Still, I couldn't understand why I wasn't able to ride this hill. Steep? Yes, but not that long. This hill was so similar to the one on Marine Corps Base Kaneohe, which I'd had no trouble climbing during the triathlon in Hawaii. What was going on? Was age getting to me? Or was my training not preparing me?

During the short time required for this race, the temperature climbed from 72 degrees and a relative humidity of 89 percent at the start to the high 80s and humid as I entered the run course. The temperature, humidity, and hills all combined to make this an especially tough run. After we returned from this trip, I shared my experience with Jeanne Minder, senior triathlete, personal trainer, and gold medalist in triathlon at the 2015 National Senior Games. She said I had not trained enough in conditions of heat, humidity, and hills.

As we crossed the finish line, a volunteer placed a ceramic finisher medal, handcrafted in the Dixie Performing Art Center's Mudslingers Pottery Studio, over our heads. I finished third of four in my males 65 through 69 age group, and 122nd of 157 overall. Race Director Joe Fleenor presented the top three finishers in each age group with a handcrafted ceramic award produced by the same pottery studio.

While downing water and a slice of pizza, I overheard triathletes calling this bike course "one of the most hilly." I took comfort in their assessment. Still, I also overheard one guy say, "People from eastern Tennessee wouldn't even consider this course to be hilly."

Before departing on the next leg of our trip, we took one more picture of Geno, the stuffed giraffe, this time with an Elvis Presley impersonator. Debbie craved confirmation that her prized childhood companion was still in one piece and in good health.

We arrived in The Villages, Florida the following afternoon for a five-day stay with our friends Don and Sue. Geno the stuffed giraffe had completed his trip to Florida, taking up residence in nearby Eustis with his owner, Debby.

• • • •

GEORGIA: STATE #39

Georgia Nickname:
The Peach State

Entrance sign for Lake Lanier Islands Resort, where
my Georgia triathlon was held.

Georgia Triathlon Details

- Date: September 23, 2018
- Triathlon: 14th Lake Lanier Triathlon
- Location: Lake Lanier Islands Resort,
  Buford, Georgia

Published distances
- Swim: 400 yards (366 meters)
- Bike: 13 miles (21 kilometers)
- Run: 5 kilometers (3.1 miles)

I hated that my bike chain had come off during the Dixie Triathlon, especially since I'd replaced the front gearset of my bike and had it tuned before leaving on that trip. During one of the first days in The Villages, Florida, I took my bike to the Trek bike shop in Wildwood, Florida.

The technician put my bike on his stand, thinking maybe a minor adjustment would fix the problem with shifting. He saw no reason for the chain to come off. Still, he observed more than normal drag of the rear brake on the wheel. With the brake buried within the frame for aerodynamic reasons, the technician would need to disassemble the rear end of the bike to eliminate the drag. Our brief time in The Villages prevented him from fixing the problem.

On Friday morning, Joy and I began our drive to a suburb south of Atlanta to visit our nephew Joe Bents, his wife Alaina, and their daughter Ruby. We had a wonderful evening with this young family. Then, at brunch on Saturday morning, Alaina introduced us to New Orleans-style *beignets* at a quaint restaurant near their home. After bidding Alaina and Ruby farewell, we began our drive to the northeast side of greater Atlanta, to Lake Lanier Islands Resort for the triathlon.

We arrived at the resort for a light seafood lunch at a dockside restaurant in a marina. Having come from Minnesota, rightfully known for its many lakes, it surprised us to see Lake Lanier. The number of expensive boats was nothing we could have expected in the middle of Georgia. Pecan groves and peach orchards? Yes. Yachts? No.

While the race was to take place on Sunday, the race

director required us to leave our bikes in transition on Saturday afternoon. On Sunday morning, it became obvious why this was necessary. With limited parking near transition, getting approximately 550 triathletes and their bikes into transition, in the dark, on race morning would have been difficult—maybe impossible.

While walking my bike to transition on Saturday afternoon, I noticed an even greater drag of the rear wheel than I remembered. Joy suggested we have the bike mechanic who was onsite during packet pickup look at my bike. The young man assured us he could adjust the brake, though he found he did not have the correct socket. I went back to our van and grabbed the right one from the socket and torque wrench set I kept in my triathlon case. Even with the correct tool, the technician could not fix the problem. However, he thought adjusting the wheel might reduce the drag. After the first attempt made the drag worse, I asked him to give it another try. Imagining climbing hills along the course with the brake engaged, especially in heat and humidity, felt like a nightmare. His second attempt reduced the drag to a reasonable level. Still, I did not understand why it had worked.

Before the Ohio triathlon, I had adjusted the clamp on the wheel skewer. Maybe this had affected the alignment; yet I had never noticed this sensitivity during the previous seven years of riding this bike. Again, I chided myself for allowing this problem to surface now. Why hadn't I ridden the bike on hills near home after the tune-up? Maybe this problem would have surfaced during these rides before leaving to do five triathlons.

I remembered my recent struggles on the bike. Was the brake dragging on the rear wheel the reason I needed to walk the bike up the steepest hills in the triathlons in Ohio and Tennessee? I had many questions. Still, I had to finish three triathlons with this bike.

The Lake Lanier race today offered individual and relay options for the Sprint triathlon. Also available was an individual aquabike competition.

This was my first triathlon racing alongside college triathletes. Competing in the individual Sprint triathlon were male and female triathletes from eight universities: Auburn, Clemson, Emory, Georgia Institute of Technology, Oakwood, the University of Alabama, the University of South Carolina, and the University of Tennessee.

The morning started with a walk to transition in near-complete darkness. Once the sun rose, we were looking at clear, calm skies with an air temperature in the mid-60s. Near the start of the race, we gathered at the Margaritaville water park—the location for the swim leg—for the pre-race meeting. The race director reported the official water temperature at 81.7 degrees. According to USA Triathlon rules, anyone vying for prizes or awards could not use a wetsuit. The meeting concluded with the national anthem, during which one of the collegiate men held the American flag.

For the swim, the race director divided the field of competitors into 15 waves, starting with college men. Waves continued with groups of men from youngest to oldest. Mine, the last group of males, included 69 men aged 50 and over. Following us were the female collegiate swimmers. As with the males, females proceeded in groups from youngest to oldest. Starting from the sugar sand beach of the water park, swimmers within each wave walked into the water to just beyond the roped-off area and waited for the blast from a compressed air horn to start.

The swim course involved two right turns. After swimming away from the starting spot in the direction opposite the exit, we reached the first turn buoy. After a right turn, we swam parallel to the beach toward a second buoy, anchored less than 50 yards from the swim exit.

Exiting the water, I jogged to the dock that led to a steep concrete path up to the parking lot and transition. This was the longest distance and steepest climb between the exit of the swim and transition in any of my triathlons.

I mounted my bike on a flat section of the parking lot where transition was set up. Leaving transition, we rode the first few yards down a short, steep hill with brakes engaged. At the base of this hill, we turned right onto the parkway, a shared road within the resort. I used a block-long flat stretch to slip my feet into the bike shoes. The first hill now awaited us.

The picturesque ride flowed up and down a series of rolling hills past lots of water, a golf course, flocks of geese, and tall stands of pine trees. Though we shared the road with automobile and truck traffic, the many volunteers and police stationed along the course kept everyone safe.

The course continued outside the resort property onto a loop comprising more rolling hills on local roads in a mix of business and residential areas. The roads were smooth and free of potholes except for one small stretch under repair. The loop continued back to the main road, which led into the resort. Most of the congestion caused by mixed car and bike traffic occurred within the resort. It felt strange to pass a black sports car that slowed down while following another biker.

The run course was also within the resort, in the opposite direction from transition than the bike course. The road was flat for a little over half a mile; however, it became hillier as we proceeded along the course.

Late in the run, a young woman I recognized to be 35 years old from the number written in black marker on her left calf slapped me on the back. As she passed, she said with an ear-to-ear smile, "Way to go! You've got this!" As her hand hit my back, I noticed a sloppy, splashing sound from the sweat that now saturated my triathlon suit. Appreciating the encouragement yet feeling embarrassed, I yelled out, "Sorry for that."

As she turned her head slightly to reply, her face still lit with a smile, she said, "That's lake water, right?"

"Right," I said, now also smiling.

The support and encouragement shown by competitors like this young lady, especially toward those of us for whom triathlon is a hobby, is a common denominator in the sport.

I finished sixth of nine in my age group, and 401st of 531, including the college triathletes. Joy met me at the finish line with a bottle of cold water. After downing the water, a couple of banana halves, a slice of pizza, and a second bottle of water, I collected my gear from transition.

From there, we started our journey up the Atlantic Coast with Myrtle Beach, South Carolina, as our first destination. We wondered aloud what we would find in the wake of Hurricane Florence, which had passed through the southeast two weeks earlier.

NORTH CAROLINA: STATE #40

North Carolina Nickname:
The Tarheel State

While in Wilson for my North Carolina triathlon, we visited
the Vollis Simpson Whirligig Park.

North Carolina Triathlon Details

- Date: September 29, 2018
- Triathlon: 14th Battle at Buckhorn Triathlon
- Location: Buckhorn Reservoir, Wilson,
  North Carolina

Published distances

- Swim: 750 meters (820 yards)
- Bike: 17 miles (27.4 kilometers)
- Run: 5 kilometers (3.1 miles)

In the previous two weeks, Hurricane Florence had dumped over three feet—or nine-tenths of a meter—of rain in parts of the Carolinas. While some roads around Myrtle Beach, South Carolina remained closed from flooding, we were able to travel through this part of the state with only a few detours. Several houses still halfway underwater, along with many downed trees and twisted road signs, completed the picture of the hurricane's force.

After two days exploring Myrtle Beach, we drove northwest for a couple of days in and around Raleigh, North Carolina. We spent part of the time at an Apple store, hoping to resolve an issue with Joy's phone. I used this time to finish stories for my website about the recent triathlons in Ohio, Tennessee, and Georgia.

Around midday on Thursday, we made the short drive from Raleigh to Wilson. The route we chose took us through the countryside. Joy remarked how much she enjoyed seeing different parts of the states from country roads rather than only interstate highways.

Driving into Wilson reminded me of my first trip there in the mid-1980s. That quick in-and-out trip had been for a meeting with a potential customer for our company's laser welding technology. While I remember parts of the customer visit, the greatest memory came from dinner at a barbeque restaurant just outside Wilson. After being seated, the female server asked in her deeply Southern drawl what we wanted to drink. "Mountain Dew, please," I replied. Conversation at nearby tables stopped and all heads turned in my direction as the puzzled-looking waitress asked me to repeat my order. I guess my Minnesota "accent" sounded even more foreign to her than she had to me.

Since that time, I had worked with many people from the southeastern part of the country. It no longer surprised me to hear their various accents or ones from other regions of our country. I still heard them—just not as loudly.

On Friday morning at the Wilson Welcome Center, we met Drew Parker, who shared advice on what to see while in Wilson. Our first stop was Vollis Simpson Whirligig Park, a display of 30 "kinetic sculptures" designed and produced by the colorful and creative Vollis Simpson. Given the number of sculptures involving cyclists, I am sure Mr. Simpson must have loved biking. We followed up with a driving tour past Wilson's Southern-style mansions and through the historic business district.

During lunch, I noticed an email from the race director asking for volunteers. While waiting for the check, I read the email to Joy. Without batting an eye, she agreed to volunteer.

The sport of triathlon lives or dies by volunteers. They provide directions, water and sports drinks, and lots of encouragement. We need them to prevent collisions and other mishaps. Aspiring triathletes may want to watch, or, better yet, volunteer at a race. As a volunteer, you will see and feel what happens before, during, and after a triathlon, including the camaraderie and support among triathletes.

By now, Joy had earned veteran triathlon volunteer status as someone who added spirit to every race. Rather than waiting at the finish line for me to complete the race, she preferred to do almost anything except remove timing chips at the finish line. When not volunteering, she met other older triathletes or those accompanying them.

During packet pickup on Friday afternoon, Joy negotiated a place along the bike and run course. Positioned a few hundred yards from transition, her spot was a busy intersection for both the bike and the run. After the race, with a smile on her face and satisfaction in her voice, she said, "My job was busy and necessary. I prevented runners and bikers from colliding."

The temperature of the water in Buckhorn Reservoir today was a comfortable 78 degrees, putting it at the upper limit for a wetsuit-legal triathlon according to USAT rules. I used my wetsuit since I was expecting the extra buoyancy to give a faster swim time for this longer-than-average swim. The faster pace would more than offset the few extra seconds it would take to remove it in transition.

We started in three waves. All women started first, leaving from the ramp between two docks. Next to start were men aged 39 and under. The 57 males aged 40 and over began last. Those swimming for a relay team started according to their gender and age.

Our swim followed an equilateral triangle-shaped path with two left turns. We swam toward the first orange buoy, using a yellow sighting buoy halfway between the start and the turn as a guide. After the initial turn, we swam southeast into the sun, toward the dam on the reservoir's eastern edge. With the sun just a few degrees off the horizon, a round yellow sighting buoy between the two turn buoys became the key to reaching the second turn buoy in a straight line. Once we reached the second orange buoy, we made a left turn and headed to the exit, guided by another yellow buoy midway as well as a red inflatable waving pillar on the boat launch.

After the triathlon, I inspected the map in the Garmin app generated from data sent by my GPS watch. It encouraged me to see that straight lines connected the three legs of the triangle. I was getting better at sighting.

According to my bike computer, the temperature was in the high 60s as I left the park. The cool, still air felt refreshing—a welcome contrast to the last two triathlons.

As we left the boat launch and picnic area, the bike course passed a small herd of longhorn cattle. After turning right at the park entrance, we rode with automobile traffic, part of it on a state highway, until returning to the entrance near the end of the bike leg. Since all the turns were to the right, we never crossed traffic. During the pre-race meeting, the race director had warned, "If you take a left turn on this course, I don't know where you will end up."

Away from the reservoir, we rode a gentle roller-coaster series of hills described by one racer from Raleigh as "about as flat as it gets around here." We rode through rural residential areas and past small farms, a couple of country churches, and a few small businesses, including Triple J Produce near the end of the ride. In the more rural areas away from the state highway, we passed corn and soybean fields. We continued past pastures being cleared by more grazing cattle not of the longhorn variety. They seemed unfazed by the unusual amount of bike traffic.

Ironically, traffic during the bike leg was only a problem in the parking lot, near transition. As I approached, I rode up behind a white SUV crawling along. The driver, having no business driving this road during the race, couldn't decide where to park. Since I couldn't tell if he would turn left or right into a parking spot, I waited before riding past him. A moment later, he pulled off to the right.

The run course was made up of two loops, starting with the first half-mile on the same road as the bike course. We left transition, continuing on the road leading into and out of the Buckhorn Reservoir boat launch. As she had done earlier, Joy greeted me as I passed her volunteer station.

We turned right at the end of the road and went about 500 feet to the next intersection. Making a second right turn, we continued through a neighborhood of acre-sized lots with newer houses and young trees. In one yard, a young boy scurried behind the family's chickens, attempting to herd them into their cage.

Halfway to the dam, we reached the turnaround, then returned to the parking lot next to transition. Following a turn around a table holding cups of water and sports drinks for us to grab, we began the second loop.

On my second trip through the neighborhood, I found the boy still attempting to corral the chickens. I couldn't help but chuckle as I remembered the challenge of herding chickens from my younger days.

I finished third of three in my age group of men ages 65 through 69, and 122nd of 147.

During the awards ceremony, Joy and I met winners of two other age groups: Paul Bloom, age 71, and Sharon Roggenbuck, age 80. When called to receive her age-group award, Sharon cartwheeled her way to the podium.

We had over a week until the next triathlon, this one in Kentucky. We took advantage of these days to visit parts of western North Carolina we had never seen.

The first stop was at the Andy Griffith Museum in Mt. Airy. The hills in Andy's hometown surprised me, especially since the places around Andy's television home were flat. I learned that they had filmed the Andy Griffith show in Culver City, California.

Large patches of orange and yellow wildflowers in the median of the divided highways dominated the scenery as we continued south and west to our next stop, Asheville. We took a long day to tour the Biltmore Estate grounds and buildings. Movies set at the Biltmore have taken on new meaning since this visit.

From North Carolina, we continued into southwestern Tennessee. We began our three-day trip through the region by exploring Great Smoky Mountains National Park. During the park visit, we even ventured onto a section of the Appalachian Trail.

The next stops were Gatlinburg and Pigeon Forge, where Dolly Parton's Dollywood is located. We understood the region's appeal.

KENTUCKY: STATE #41

Kentucky Nickname:
The Bluegrass State

Transition for WinSprint 2018 was set up in front of the Winchester-Clark
County Recreation Center, which is housed in the former
site of Southeastern Christian College.

Kentucky Triathlon Details

- Date: October 6, 2018
- Triathlon: 3rd WinSprint 2018
- Location: Winchester-Clark County Recreation
  Center, Winchester, Kentucky

Published distances
- Swim: 400 meters (437 yards)
- Bike: 10 kilometers (6.2 miles)
- Run: 5 kilometers (3.1 miles)

From Tennessee, we continued into Kentucky, passing through the Daniel Boone National Forest on our way to Lexington, and, to its east, Winchester.

The WinSprint triathlon is another example of a triathlon organized and managed by a local recreation center to support a local cause. Funds from this triathlon purchase bikes for the Winchester–Clark County Recreation Center (WCCRC) annual Bicycle Rodeo. During registration, I read, "Last year, we purchased and gave away 26 bikes! We hope to give away even more during our 2018 event, and appreciate your support in helping make this a reality!!"

The staff at WCCRC coordinated and oversaw the day's event, which featured six race options. The choices were Sprint triathlon, with either road biking or stationary biking in the fitness center; Sprint triathlon relay, with either road or stationary biking; and duathlon, with either road or stationary biking.

On Friday afternoon, Joy and I visited the WCCRC to get acquainted with the venue. April, a Center staff member, mentioned the growing number of participants in the WinSprint Triathlon.

Starting with 40 participants in 2016, the race's first year, the number of racers had doubled to eighty by 2017. In this, the third year, registration exceeded the initial cap set by recreation center management of 100 participants. While Clark County was well represented among the participants, around 60 percent of us came from outside the county.

From the moment we arrived the next morning, we noticed an unusual number of children running around, laughing and sometimes screaming as they played with siblings or friends. To encourage families to attend the event, the Center was offering free daycare to parents who needed it while they raced. Another first for me in triathlon—and one I wholeheartedly endorse.

Another unique feature of this event, which I also like, was the lottery for the bike position within transition. During packet pickup on race morning, each of us selected a colored piece of paper with a number written on it. Mine was number twelve. The number on my paper corresponded to my number on the bike rack, where we were to set up our transition space.

This type of lottery, a different way of preassigning spaces, has two benefits. First, it limits the number of bikes on each rack; all racers have the same space for their gear. Second, it prevents a rush on race morning to get the best transition spaces. Additionally, in this triathlon, the *Bike Out* and *Run Out* used the same end of transition. This unusual arrangement gave a slight advantage to those whose transition space was at the exit end of transition.

The triathlon swim began with the first group of 10 swimmers, two in each of five lanes of the 25-meter pool. They would complete eight laps, or 16 lengths. A sixth lane remained open for swimmers requiring more than the allotted 15 minutes to complete the swim. A volunteer counted our laps, signaling us before we began our last lap and again when we completed the eighth lap.

After the swim, we either left the building for the outdoor transition area or, if taking part in the stationary bike event, left the pool for a nearby room within the fitness center to ride

10 kilometers on a stationary bike. This triathlon was my first that offered a stationary bike option, though I didn't choose it.

Naturally, the rider faced no hills or wind resistance on a stationary bike. This may explain why times on stationary bikes were much lower than on road bikes. The fastest bike split for an individual Sprint triathlete competing in the stationary bike event was 13:16, compared to the fastest bike split of 17:31 for the road bike event.

The temperature in the low 70s on the outdoor bike course felt comfortable. The course—the shortest bike ride of any of the triathlons I had completed to this point—left transition on streets leading south and a little west of Winchester. We turned left onto Boonesboro Avenue, a county highway leading out of town toward the turnaround at George Rogers Clark High School.

I saw plenty of volunteers as I turned right into the school's parking lot. Thinking I was following their instructions, I continued straight ahead, passing behind the school and around the end of the stadium and another volunteer, who was remarkably silent. It surprised me to not see another biker.

I continued counterclockwise around the school grounds and building. As I came around the last corner, I rode up a small hill, past the school's entrance and toward exit of the grounds as well as the highway on which I had ridden earlier.

During this section, I met other bikers going in the opposite direction. Should I have ridden clockwise around the building? The bike course map on the race website hadn't shown this detail. The volunteers said nothing. Either way, the distance was the same.

The run course took us through the Holiday Hills neighborhood west of the Center. During our conversation on Friday afternoon, April had warned me to expect lots of hills during the run. Her advice didn't disappoint. The course offered few flat sections, despite the hills not being long or steep. With many volunteers, we had plenty of moral support and encouragement.

Volunteers ensured we stayed hydrated through several water stops along the course. I still chuckle each time I recall the young girl, who looked to be around 10 years old, stationed with her mother midway through the run. As I approached her station, she grabbed a white paper cup filled with water from the table next to her and reached it out toward me. After I took the cup, she shouted, "Throw the cup on the ground when you're finished with it."

"Who is going to pick up the cup if I throw it on the ground?" I asked.

Without hesitating, she answered, "My mom will!"

Remembering my days as a parent of young children, I smiled as I folded the empty paper cup and stuffed it into the pocket on the back of my triathlon suit.

I finished fifth of seven in the men ages 60 and over age group, and 49th of 74 in the outdoor individual Sprint triathlon. After crossing the finish line and turning in my timing chip, I downed some more water and a banana. Securing my bike in the back of our van, I then reassembled the rest of the cargo. After a shower and breakfast at our hotel, Joy and I began our journey back to Minnesota. Today was our 45th wedding anniversary.

Despite this being a milestone anniversary, our travel for the triathlon meant there was no romantic candlelight dinner or trip to the movie theater. Still, just as Joy felt free to suggest tent camping, I was free to schedule a triathlon on our anniversary. This truly was our adventure together.

Back at home in Minnesota the next week, I took my Trek bike into Maple Grove Cycling, where I had purchased it, to have the brake serviced. A few days later, the technician phoned to report that the problem was more severe than a simple brake adjustment. A crack in the carbon fiber frame was causing the rear brake to drag on the wheel.

Replacing the frame was the only solution. Since the model I had ridden for the past seven years was no longer being produced, I would get an upgraded frame under Trek's warranty.

I didn't know when the crack had formed. Still, I was certain the rear brake had been dragging during the last five triathlons.

2019:
A REST YEAR

How could I know what retirement life would be like?
I was on target, even a little ahead of schedule, to reach
the goal of completing triathlons in all 50 states by the age of
seventy. However, my performance at the 2018 triathlons had
been mediocre, even after factoring in that I had completed
these races using a bike with a cracked frame and a rear brake
that had been always at least partly engaged.

I believed that with more consistent training, I would turn
in better performances in my upcoming triathlons. Now retired,
I had ample time for training. So, early in the year, at the time
I usually began planning the year's race schedule, I dedicated
2019 to improving my swimming, biking, and running strength
and endurance. I would not race this year.

Soon, I learned new things about myself. The regimen of
a daily and weekly schedule, even with heavy travel, had been
a help, not a hindrance, to consistent training.

My new flexibility reminded me of how much I enjoyed
learning. One of the funnest parts of taking part in triathlons
had been testing, then writing about, different training tech-
niques and training aids.

I tried a new run training program and Mark Allen's

strength training regimen. The extra time allowed me to interview and write stories of other triathletes over the age of 50, which I added to the SeniorTriathletes.com website.

I continued working with clients from my former professional career. Their projects were exciting and challenging. I learned about 3D metal printing, financial analysis, simulating manufacturing processes, and fabricating glass and ceramic optics.

My schedule, which was now loose and free, allowed me to study areas outside of triathlon and my former career. With Joy's encouragement, I became more familiar with our kitchen. I started brewing kombucha. I took up baking everything sourdough and began pressure-canning vegetables and meat.

Joy's fear that I would micro-manage her after my retirement never came true. Quite the opposite. Joy used her skill in delegating, honed through years of managing volunteers for political campaigns, to turn the tables. Before I realized it, I was baking thin sourdough crust pizza and cherry muffins for her and her girlfriends' card parties.

Joy and I used our new flexibility to take six grandchildren ages eight to fifteen on a week-long road trip. In July, Joy and I rented a 15-passenger van. Along with the grandchildren and my Aunt Nelda, who was visiting from Hawaii, we toured both the Creation Museum and the Ark Encounter in northern Kentucky. The visits we'd made during 2018, between the triathlons in Ohio and Tennessee, had impressed us.

Those who worried that I would be bored in retirement breathed a collective sigh of relief. Meanwhile, I wondered, *How did I find time for work?*

2020:
NAVIGATING COVID

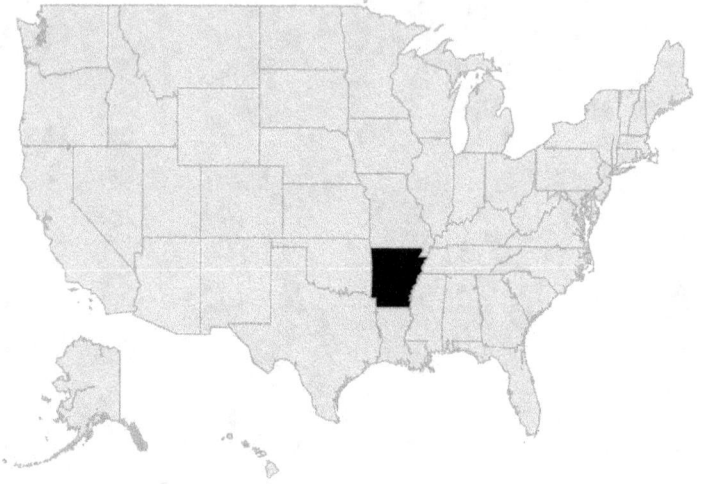

During our annual trip to Hawaii to visit my Aunt Nelda, we heard rumblings that a virus from China had landed in Washington State. In early March, Joy and I returned to Minnesota through Portland, Oregon, struck by the number of people in the airport now donning face masks.

Soon, authorities forced all of us to stay home, except to buy food. Training went on inside our homes and on our outdoor patios. Depending on where we lived, some trained in parks and on trails; yet experts advised us to wear a mask, even while biking and running outdoors.

I'll never forget the first time I ran with a mask. Within a half mile, condensation from my breath had saturated the mask, making it impossible to run—or, for that matter, breathe.

Rather than wear the mask with no one around, I slipped it over my mouth and nose only when meeting another person on the trail and for a few yards after passing them. This practice extended the time before my mask became saturated and unable to be used.

In the meantime, I started a consulting project to simulate a manufacturing process comprising five sub-processes. *Interesting,* I thought. *A triathlon has five steps: swimming, biking, running, and two transitions.* I called the race director for a triathlon that showed promise for taking place that year. We discussed using computer simulation to create a strategy for keeping racers separated. It was exciting to think of combining pieces of my former career with triathlon.

While government restrictions resulted in most races being canceled in 2020, a few states opened later in the year. Some allowed triathlons with restrictions and other changes. I completed only one triathlon that year.

ARKANSAS: STATE #42

Arkansas Nickname:
The Natural State

Masked triathletes awaiting packet pickup for the
2020 DeGray Lake Triathlon.

Arkansas Triathlon Details

- Date: September 13, 2020
- Triathlon: 22nd DeGray Lake Sprint Triathlon
- Location: DeGray Lake Spillway-Dam Recreation
  Area, Caddo Valley, Arkansas

Published distances
- Swim: 500 yards (457 meters)
- Bike: 13.5 miles (21.7 kilometers)
- Run: 3.1 miles (5 kilometers)

The DeGray Lake Triathlon was the only race in which I would take part during 2020. The government's response to the COVID-19 pandemic forced others in Kansas and Oklahoma, for which I had registered earlier in the year, to be canceled.

In December 2019, I had registered for a spring race in in Fayetteville, Arkansas: the Ozark Valley Triathlon. The organizer first delayed this triathlon until the fall, then later changed it to a virtual-only race.

I had no interest in a virtual race. This adventure's goal involved swimming, biking, and running in each state. Meanwhile, the DeGray Lake Triathlon, scheduled for later in the year, would continue as an in-person race when the State of Arkansas relaxed restrictions.

Our route to Arkansas first took us through central Iowa. Hundreds of acres of flattened corn stalks reminded us of the hurricane-level winds that had passed through the region in mid-August.

Three hours later, we were at our son Ben's home outside Omaha, Nebraska. For dinner, Joy and I prepared halibut I had caught in the Bay of Alaska a month earlier. We finished the evening watching *Frozen* for the umpteenth time with our granddaughters.

The next day, we continued to central Missouri and the home of our daughter-in-law Lindsey's mother. This was our second visit to John and Joan's home, where we had stayed before the Missouri triathlon. Before we left for Arkansas the next morning, John and Joan loaded us up with jars of salsa, relish, tomato sauce, and elderberry juice, all canned with produce from their garden.

By mid-afternoon, we arrived in Arkadelphia. After checking into our hotel, we drove the few miles to the boat launch at DeGray Lake for packet pickup. This was my first experience with a triathlon being run under COVID-19 restrictions.

To comply with state regulations, the race director encouraged us to set up our transition space during packet pickup. This meant leaving our bike in transition overnight. A group from Teen Challenge, a faith-based nonprofit organization, secured the area, including our bikes. Others from this group provided support throughout the race the next day.

Next, we drove the bike course...or most of it. Joy drove while I evaluated the road conditions and took a few pictures. A short distance from the park's exit was the Fish Net Family Restaurant, where we sampled the local Cajun cuisine.

COVID-19-related government restrictions meant spectators could not attend the race, which would include participants, volunteers, and race staff only. This would be my first triathlon without Joy watching or volunteering. Still, she never argued. I think she enjoyed sleeping in.

Another first for this triathlon involved applying my own body markings. Before leaving the hotel on race morning, I pressed on the tattoos with my race number from the race packet—another part of the COVID protocol for this race.

When I arrived for the triathlon, a volunteer handed me

a disposable mask. The race staff asked all triathletes to wear this mask until the start of their swim.

The weather on race morning was as near-perfect for a triathlon as one could imagine. A light breeze created a satiny feeling to the humid, 73-degree air. Even though the sun was shining, it did so through a thick haze caused by smoke from forest fires in California and the Pacific Northwest. The temperature of the DeGray Lake water was over 78 degrees. To comply with USAT rules, anyone competing for an award could not wear a wetsuit.

Before starting the swim, race director Bruce Dunn offered a prayer, one fitting for the unsettling time. After playing a recording of the national anthem, we were ready to begin the triathlon.

The COVID-19 protocol for this race included a time-trial start for the open water swim. Every five seconds, a new swimmer approached the timing mat, removed their mask, and tossed it into the nearby garbage can. They then crossed the timing mat to start the timer for their race and jogged into the water.

This swim reminded me of one benefit of a mass start and a wave start in an open-water swim. Despite the occasional contact with other swimmers, having them in visual contact reduced my need for sighting.

When swimmers spread out along a course, as in a time-trial swim start, choosing markers for the next turn and for the exit is crucial. We cannot rely on following the swimmer ahead of us. Every few strokes, I lift my head out of the water to look ahead at my marker. Am I swimming in a straight line? If not, I make a correction.

As we made the second and final turn of today's triangular course, we swam to the exit at the same boat ramp from which we had started. Now, I realized the one, and maybe only, benefit of the hazy, smoke-filled sky. Under a clear sky, I would have been looking into the sun while sighting for the swim exit. The haze made it easier to see the exit and stay on track.

As I was leaving transition for the bike mount line, I noticed a guy in front of me getting on his triathlon bike. It surprised me to see him slipping his shoes into a cage at the front end of a standard bike pedal. This seemed odd. I thought all triathletes who rode a triathlon bike clipped their shoes to the pedals.

Riding further from the mount line, I turned onto the road within the park that led to the dam. We would be using this road for the out and back portions of the course. As I rode up the first hill in the lowest gear, my heart rate soared. I caught my breath and shifted to a higher gear on a level section of road across the dam, preparing for the next hill.

As I reached the steepest part of the second hill, I downshifted to a lower gear. My bike came to an abrupt stop as the chain leapt off the front gear and lodged between the gearset and frame. Without enough time to unclip my shoes from the pedals, I tipped over, falling on my left side, scuffing my left knee and jamming the finger bearing my wedding ring. I felt my finger swell.

Typical of the camaraderie I had experienced in other triathlons, several bikers paused as they passed, asking how they could help. I thanked them for their offer but didn't need help as I reinstalled the chain.

Later, I wondered, *what is it about people who compete in triathlon that causes them to put their race on hold to help another triathlete?* I knew that podium positions could be lost by seconds. Still, several bikers slowed, while a couple even stopped beside me.

Since I was part way up the hill, I could not clip my shoes into the pedals. I still hadn't practiced this, and wasn't confident I could do it today. Instead, I walked, sometimes jogged, my bike up the hill to reach a section flat enough to mount my bike and clip in my shoes.

Once I was riding again, I could hear the chain jump back or ahead a gear every one to two revolutions of the pedal. Was there something I could do? Unable to find a solution, I continued riding past the thick woods that bordered the course. The incessant clicking sound rattled my thoughts, causing me to slow down as I imagined the chain slipping off once more. It stayed on.

As I started my run, the temperature was 10 degrees higher, now 81 degrees. The humidity persisted, similar to the conditions in which I had trained earlier this summer. I realized the lake was the only flat section of this triathlon course. As with the bike course, the run covered a continuous series of rolling hills. The T-shaped out-and-back course followed roads within the DeGray Lake Recreation Area. With the time-trial start to the swim, maintaining distance between racers remained easy.

We left transition toward AR-7, the highway along the

eastern edge of DeGray Lake. Before reaching the highway, we turned right. After going around the first turnaround, we crossed to the second turnaround, staying parallel to the highway. Once back at the road on which we had begun our run, we made another right turn to return to the finish line near transition.

I finished second of two in the men's 65 through 69 age group, and 76th of 86 overall.

After the race, I inspected my bike more carefully. I assumed that the crash had caused damage to both the chain and derailleur of my bike. A few days after returning home, a technician at Maple Grove Cycling repaired the derailleur and installed a new chain.

When we arrived in the area, we planned to spend a few days in a home within a retirement community outside historic Hot Springs. Joy and I were thinking of relocating to an area of the country with warmer winters, and especially without ice. Hot Springs was a candidate.

After Joy mentioned her struggle to breathe in the smoke-filled air, I called the realtor with whom I had arranged the stay. While he was not happy as I explained our need to cancel the reservation, he understood. I apologized for the inconvenience, and we started our drive back to Minnesota.

Early on in the trip, we followed the winding hills as we crossed the breathtaking Ozark Mountains. During the drive, I relived my most recent experience with my bike. Most of my bike training over the past year had involved using my bike on a trainer. I'd done interval training, speed drills, and long rides on the lower level of our house and the patio behind it. I hadn't ridden hills like these for a long while. Despite having my bike tuned before the triathlon, I hadn't proven it to be ready for racing. I scolded myself for not being better prepared.

2021:
A YEAR OF MORE CHANGE

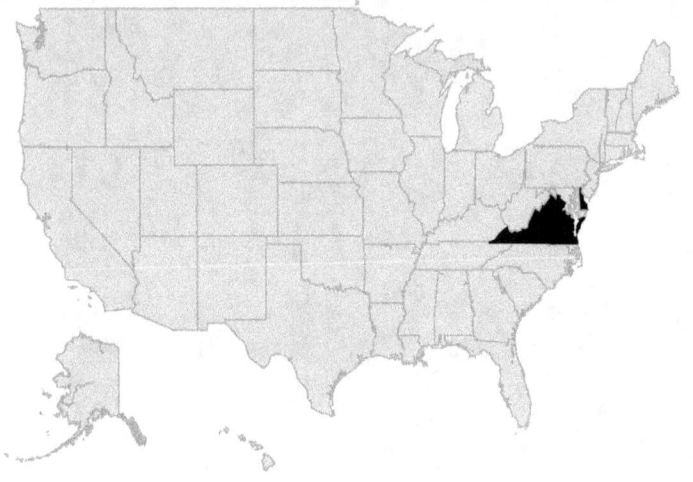

As the country continued to reopen early in the year, we resumed our adventure toward our goal. During our visit to Florida, we had surprised everyone, including ourselves, by buying a house in The Villages and putting our Minnesota house up for sale. The move from Minnesota to Florida dominated most of the year.

VIRGINIA: STATE #43

Virginia Nickname:
Old Dominion

The bike course passed curious grazing cattle.

Virginia Triathlon Details

- Date: May 9, 2021
- Triathlon: 16th Kinetic Lake Anna Triathlon
- Location: Lake Anna State Park, Spotsylvania Courthouse, Virginia

Published distances
- Swim: 750 meters (820 yards)
- Bike: 15.5 miles (25 kilometers)
- Run: 3.1 miles (5 kilometers)

Leading up to our trip to Virginia for the Lake Anna Triathlon, we stayed in The Villages, Florida for most of April. With the favorable Floridian weather, I swam, biked, or ran every day. I connected with The Villages Triathlon Club, sharing our triathlon adventure at a monthly meeting and joining one of their swim sessions.

While I was training during the first half of our visit, Joy was looking at houses. It surprised us to find one that met our strict requirements, so we made an offer to buy it. By the time we left The Villages in early May, we had signed the purchase agreement. We would be moving to Florida after two triathlons on the East Coast.

Our drive to Virginia took us to northeast Florida and along the Atlantic Coast through Georgia. The route then continued further inland, across South Carolina and North Carolina and into eastern Virginia. It surprised us to note the importance of corn, soybean, and cotton farming in these states—that is, when we weren't crossing marshland.

On Saturday afternoon, the day before Sunday's triathlon, Joy and I drove to Lake Anna State Park for packet pickup. En route, we detoured to visit the historic Spotsylvania Courthouse, also known as "the crossroads of the Civil War."

After collecting my race packet, which included a T-shirt, a pair of wicking socks, and race numbers for my bike, bike helmet, and the run, we drove the bike course to look for potholes or other obstacles I might find during the race. I made mental notes of the hills and turns along the way.

My phone said the temperature was 39 degrees as I crawled

out of bed the next morning. The forecast showed a chance of rain. Even though I was born and raised in Minnesota, which most people think makes me ready for cold weather, we'd spent the previous month in Florida with daily highs in the 80s and 90s. Today, I felt cold, and hoped it didn't rain.

Driving directions for Lake Anna State Park on my phone's navigation app showed me when I should leave to reach the park by 6 a.m. for the opening of transition. Under lingering COVID-19 restrictions, the race director discouraged spectators from attending the race, so Joy stayed in bed.

Though still pitch dark, the route looked familiar—at least most of it. Without Joy to watch the map on her phone, I obeyed the navigation's call to "turn left on Partlow Road." As I did so, I glimpsed a sign for Lake Anna State Park a little beyond the intersection. *Wonderful. A shortcut. I'll be there early,* I thought. After what felt like 10 minutes on winding roads I did not recognize, I noticed a small lumber mill I had passed moments earlier. My supposed shortcut was not a shortcut. I ended up back at the intersection on Partlow Road.

This time, I followed the Lake Anna State Park sign. Twenty minutes later, I arrived at the park—a few minutes later than planned, but with plenty of time to have my pick of spots in transition. Right before it closed, Jill Blankenburg, the race announcer, sang the national anthem. Following her beautiful performance, the race director requested that all swimmers congregate on the beach. He said that anyone who wanted to do a warm-up swim should go now.

I headed to Lake Anna to evaluate the condition of the

lake bottom. Would I run into water with sharp rocks, weeds, or muck? Would it be firm or slippery? Flat or irregular? My short swim in Lake Anna, one of Virginia's largest freshwater reservoirs, showed me I would swim in weed-free water with a bottom as beautiful as its beach: off-white sand with the consistency of sugar.

My elevated heart rate from the warm-up swim made it less likely that it would spike during the first minutes of the swim, when excitement often drove me to swim faster than I could maintain. For today, with the water at a cool 68 degrees, I appreciated getting the shock of cold water entering my wetsuit out of the way. By the time my swim began a few minutes later, water warmed by my body heat had filled my wetsuit.

After the practice swim, we gathered behind the *Swim Start* arch. It surprised me to see many brave triathletes swimming in sleeveless triathlon suits. Some men even swam without a shirt.

Once the air horn sounded and the first competitor had crossed the timing mat and entered the water, another swimmer started every five seconds. The time-trial start was a carryover from the 2020 COVID-19 restrictions. I had learned that this type of start has both pros and cons compared to the mass start: less contact between swimmers, but a greater need for sighting to stay on course.

Upon reaching the far-left buoy on the rectangular course, we made a right turn toward the second one. After swimming around this buoy, we swam to the beach. My swim leg ended as I crossed the timing mat.

The weather felt the same as it had when we departed the hotel. Since clouds filled the skies, I slipped on a light long-sleeved pullover for the ride. This was the first triathlon in which I rode my triathlon bike with running shoes and flat pedals with a toe cage rather than biking shoes and clip-in pedals. Once I began, my bike computer displayed an air temperature of 46 degrees.

After riding to the park entrance, we turned left, now heading northwest on the smooth, tree-lined Lawyer's Road. From its beginning, this bike course reminded me a lot of the course for the Ohio triathlon: plenty of hills through gorgeous stands of trees, with enough variety in the scenery to make the ride interesting.

At mile five, the course began an equilateral triangle-shaped loop covering another five miles of hills and turns that passed fields with grazing horses and cattle. On the stretch furthest away from the park, we rode past the Christmas tree farms of competitors Belmont and Ralph's.

In six months, cars would replace the bikes riding along this road today. Family vehicles sporting their prized Christmas tree would travel this road instead of the bikes that were heading back to the park today. After rejoining Lawyer's Road, we returned to transition on the same road we had ridden a few minutes earlier.

As the air continued to warm, the sun peeked through the clouds, and I transitioned to the run. Before heading out, I shed the long-sleeved shirt for a cool yet comfortable run, all of which took place within the park. As advertised, the run course included "an uphill coming out of transition." This hill continued for much of the first mile.

For the next mile and a half, we ran on a series of rolling hills. The last half-mile followed a paved walking trail that traveled downhill as it guided us toward the lake. The end of this trail broke out near the beach. We ran the final few hundred feet on grass to reach the finish line.

I finished sixth of seven in the men ages 65 through 69 group, and 187th of 225 participants.

This was the second triathlon that Joy had not attended due to COVID restrictions. I missed hearing her encouragement as I left transition and approached the finish line, then sharing a cold drink together before returning our gear to the van.

For the awards ceremony, the race director made use of the natural amphitheater created by the hill in front of the Lake Anna beach. To comply with COVID-19 restrictions, he asked attendees to spread out across the hill to stay distanced. With everyone separated, we celebrated the top overall and age-group finishers.

DELAWARE: STATE #44

Delaware Nickname:
The First State

The swim time included a hundred-yard jog to transition from the lake.

Delaware Triathlon Details

- Date: May 16, 2021
- Triathlon: 3rd Bear Triathlon
- Location: Lums Pond State Park, Bear, Delaware

Published distances
- Swim: 0.6 miles (966 meters)
- Bike: 10 miles (16 kilometers)
- Run: 3 miles (4.8 kilometers)

J oy and I began the week between the Virginia and Delaware triathlons with a few days in Williamsburg, Virginia. Since we had also brought Joy's new Trek Townie e-assist bike, we were able to bike a section of the Virginia Capital Trail, starting at Colonial Williamsburg. We then packed up and drove to Delaware's Atlantic Coast via the Chesapeake Bay Bridge and Delmarva Peninsula.

Upon crossing the bridge, views of grassy wetlands and water inlets replaced vistas of the bay. Further inland, we were surprised to see large, low poultry barns surrounded by wide open fields. We had not realized that the poultry industry was so important to this region. As we neared the Atlantic Coast, small towns transformed into commercial areas and beach-themed shops and motels.

Settling in at Bethany Beach, Delaware, we took the three days leading up to the Bear Triathlon to gaze at the Atlantic Ocean surf, stroll the boardwalks, inspect gift shop wares, and sample the seafood cuisine along the Atlantic coast between Ocean City, Maryland, and Rehoboth Beach, Delaware.

Late Saturday afternoon, Joy and I drove from Bethany Beach to Lums Pond State Park, outside Bear, Delaware, to get the triathlon race packet. It surprised us to see a line of cars stretching out of the park entrance and onto the road leading into the park. "Are all these people doing the triathlon?" I wondered.

Once in the park, we saw many reasons beyond the triathlon to visit here. Within Lums Pond State Park, the vast majority of visitors were kayaking, paddle boating, or picnicking. Some watched or competed in a cricket match being played in the field next to the transition location for tomorrow's triathlon.

After collecting my race packet, which included a T-shirt and race numbers for the bike and run, we drove the bike course. Near the end of the course, a mother deer and her fawn lay dead on the bike path. By the next morning, their remains had been removed.

I reached the park entrance a little before 5 a.m., anticipating a brief wait for the gate to open. During the drive, I imagined waiting behind a few vehicles with other triathletes who had arrived earlier than me. To my surprise, the park gate was already open, and I passed through without stopping. I was even more surprised when I reached the parking lot. Cars had already filled the first row of parking spaces next to transition, forcing me to park in the second row. Maybe because of the many race cancellations over the past year, the triathletes competing today seemed extra eager to race.

With the 48-degree air temperature during transition set up, it made me happy to be wearing a sweatshirt. However, as the sun rose and race time approached, the temperature climbed a few degrees. Meanwhile, the air remained still, with only a slight breeze. Clouds covered most of the sky.

The race director reported the water in Lums Pond to be 68 degrees, a temperature for which he encouraged us to wear a wetsuit. By the start of the swim, my full-sleeve wetsuit felt just right for the low-to-mid-50s air temperature.

Lums Pond is not open to the public for swimming. However, park officials had suspended the rule for this triathlon.

About 550 competitors in the Sprint and Olympic-distance triathlons combined started the swim in one of eight groups based on race distance, age, and gender. The first four waves included those in the Olympic triathlon.

The swim of six-tenths of a mile was longer than usual for a Sprint triathlon. After swimming diagonally away from the swim exit, we turned left at the first of three orange buoys on the counterclockwise course. After this turn, we swam straight toward the opposite shore. Reaching the second orange buoy, we again turned left and swam parallel to the beach toward the third turn buoy. We then swam back to the beach from there.

The swim leg was not yet complete, however, even though we were no longer in the water. To finish, we needed to jog or walk another hundred yards across a grassy path before crossing the timing mat. Only then was the swim leg over so we could enter T1.

We mounted our bikes just outside transition. The bike leg followed a course that headed toward the park's entrance following Bucks Jersey Road. The single-loop course exited and later reentered the park at the main entrance gate.

After exiting the park, we made four right turns following Howell School Road, Red Lion Road, and another state highway. From the time we left the park until we returned, we rode with local traffic. Thanks to volunteers and local police controlling traffic at intersections, we navigated the course without incident. The final of the four right turns brought us back onto Bucks Jersey Road, through the park's entrance, and back to transition.

The out-and-back run course took us on the grassy field used for the previous day's cricket match, tree-shaded dirt trails, and asphalt roads. Since the Olympic-distance triathletes were doing the Sprint run course twice, most participants of both triathlon distances were running at the same time. Much of the course was narrow, so we met many runners. The encouraging words that passed between racers as they met were on full display today. Almost everyone seemed happy.

After completing my race, I repacked my bike and the other gear in our van. As I sat outside transition on the edge of a picnic table waiting for the awards ceremony, John Dean and I struck up a conversation. John, an older triathlete like me, told me he planned to complete his one hundredth triathlon within the year.

I waited for the ceremony, but had to leave for hotel check-out. I finished second of five in the men 65 through 69 age group, and 107th of 163 overall in the Sprint triathlon. Though I missed the awards ceremony, the thoughtful race organizer mailed me my second-place award.

I returned to the hotel for a shower. After checking out, Joy and I began our journey back to Minnesota. The first part of our route took us through Amish country in Lancaster County, Pennsylvania. That evening, we arrived in West Chicago, Illinois for an evening with our friends Jim and Kris Novak.

We arrived home the next day, which marked the beginning of a three-month project of decluttering, donating, and packing for our move to Florida in September.

2022:
GOAL IN SIGHT

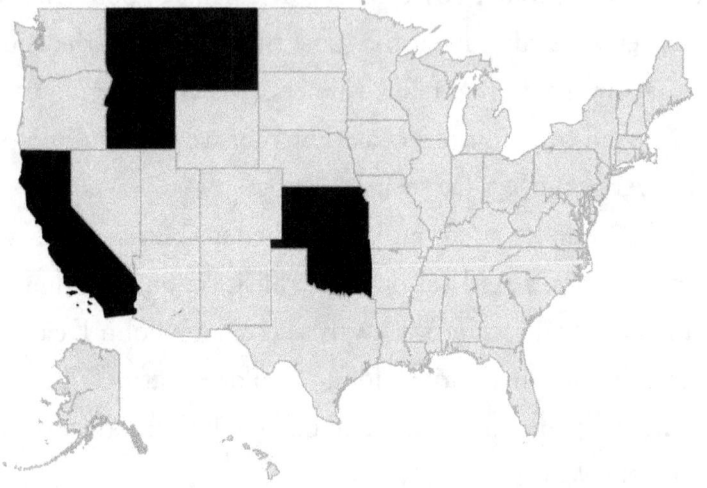

The date Joy and I had set for completing our Triathlon Across the USA goal was in sight and screaming toward us. Back in 2011, I had committed to reaching it before the end of 2023. I had six states in which to complete triathlons within the next two years.

This year, a wedding and a high school graduation would cause us to return to Minnesota for at least two weeks in late May. Other than those two events, the entire summer was open for travel to triathlons. We made the most of this time, again exploring the marriage of triathlon and camping.

• • • •

OKLAHOMA: STATE #45

Oklahoma Nickname:
The Sooner State

View of cattle grazing in a pasture along the bike
course of the Tulsa Triathlon.

Oklahoma Triathlon Details

■ Date: June 25, 2022

■ Triathlon: 8th Tulsa Sprint Triathlon

■ Location: Twin Coves Beach at Birch Lake,
Barnsdall, Oklahoma

Published distances

- Swim: 500 meters (547 yards)
- Bike: 12 miles (19.3 kilometers)
- Run: 5 kilometers (3.1 miles)

A few months after committing to the Oklahoma triathlon, we learned that our son Ben and his family would be moving from their home in Omaha, Nebraska to central Missouri. They planned to leave Nebraska on the day of the triathlon.

So, 10 days before we were to be in Oklahoma, Joy and I traveled from Minnesota to our son's home. During visits to a local fitness center, I continued to swim and cycle. I ran in our family's neighborhood, and we biked with our granddaughters, Mari and Anna.

We also helped pack for their move and load the U-Haul truck. Packing and loading used muscles never used as much in triathlon training. By the Thursday evening before the Oklahoma triathlon, we had finished packing the truck, except for a few last-minute items.

The next morning, we drove south from Omaha to Barnsdall, Oklahoma. Since the pre-race packet pickup location was 45 miles south of the race venue, I waited to pick it up until the morning of the triathlon. Instead, we stopped at Twin Coves Beach and Birch Lake, a mile and a half south of Barnsdall and the venue for tomorrow's race. I wanted to be certain I knew the route to the park the next morning.

From the beach, we saw the diverse varieties of hardwood trees, shrubs, prairie grasses, and wildflowers surrounding the lake, a reservoir formed by a dam on Birch Creek. We understood why Twin Coves Beach is a popular year-round destination for outdoor adventurists.

As we drove the bike course after visiting the park, the size of several hills impressed me—enough to show up in my dreams that night. The memories didn't lead to a nightmare, but they came close.

I knew the race would be sweaty the moment I stepped outside our hotel in Bartlesville the next morning. Even at 5 a.m., the temperature and humidity caused perspiration to run off my forehead and into my eyes while stowing our overnight luggage in the van.

Fifteen minutes later, we started the half-hour drive to Barnsdall and Twin Coves Beach. My goal was to reach Birch Lake to pick up my race packet at 6 a.m., set up my transition space, and get settled for the race, which was scheduled to begin at 7:10 a.m.

The water in Birch Lake that morning was 85 degrees. At this temperature, USA Triathlon rules prohibit the use of a wetsuit. Ten minutes before the start of the triathlon, I went for a short swim to check the lake bottom and jumpstart my heart rate. The lake's weed-free clay bottom was smooth, but not slippery. Even though the water was cloudy, it made for a comfortable swim.

The triathlon began when the first wave of 156 swimmers started on the triangular course marked by two orange buoys. After completing the swim and getting on my bike, I glanced down at my bike computer. The temperature was now 84 degrees.

This bike course set a new standard for "rolling hills" in a triathlon—something I hadn't expected in Oklahoma. Yes, the hills rolled like a sine wave. What made this different from normal rolling hills, however, was their height. Fortunately, my bike was in great condition.

At many triathlons, residents sit in lawn chairs along the bike course and cheer for triathletes as they pass. Today, the spectators were different. The gallery included two horses, which appeared puzzled by the many passing bikers. A small herd of cattle and flock of goats kept their eyes on us, though not as intently as the horses.

Near mile nine of the ride, as I was coming down a hill before a right-angle turn at its base, a small painted turtle scampered into the road. As it reached the middle, it saw me racing toward it and froze, pulling in its head and legs and laying still as I passed. A couple of volunteers at the base of the hill chuckled with me about the turtle.

As I approached transition at the end of the bike leg 53 minutes after beginning it, the temperature displayed on my bike computer was 99 degrees. The run course left transition near Birch Lake on a paved service road. Within the first mile, it joined the main road leading to the park entrance. My run alternated between running on flat and downhill sections and walking on the upside of the hills.

I reached the park entrance, took a water break, and followed the course to the right for a quarter-mile. After a second turnaround, I returned on the same course, this time making a short loop through one of the camping areas within the park. I crossed the finish line a few hundred yards downhill from the campground's exit.

As I did so, last among the five in my age group, I was a sweaty, dripping mess. While we were eager to get started on the next leg of this trip, I first took advantage of a generous supply of water, sports drinks, and fruit to begin rehydrating. I searched, but couldn't find a shower or a place to change clothes. Resigned to staying in my triathlon suit, I spread a towel on the van's passenger seat and crawled into the vehicle. Joy agreed to drive the three hours to Wichita, Kansas for tomorrow's triathlon. The drive took us on county and state highways through thousands of acres of prairie, much used for grazing cattle and horses. We also noticed a great number of oil derricks and wind turbines.

Dinner that evening was at Texas Roadhouse, a couple of blocks from our hotel in southwest Wichita. While waiting to be served, we called our eldest grandson, Alex, who was then working as a server at the Texas Roadhouse in Shakopee, Minnesota, near his home. Our excuse for the call (as if we needed one with Alex) was to ask for his recommendation for our orders. Once again, Joy had shown me how to create an opportunity to connect with our grandchildren.

KANSAS: STATE #46

Kansas Nickname:
The Sunflower State

The dam used to form Lake Afton, and the location for the triathlon swim.
I took this picture during packet pick-up the day before the race.

Kansas Triathlon Details

- Date: June 26, 2022
- Triathlon: 16th Mudwater Triathlon, Aquabike & Duathlon
- Location: Lake Afton Park, Goddard, Kansas

Published distances

- Swim: 750 meters (820 yards)
- Bike: 25 kilometers (15.5 miles)
- Run: 5 kilometers (3.1 miles)

W hat a difference a few hours and 150 miles made. As I woke the next morning in our hotel in southwest Wichita, Kansas, I heard rain hitting the hotel room window and light rumbles of thunder in the west. Joy and I decided she should rest at the hotel before our long drive after today's triathlon. Our hotel was on the route between Lake Afton and the interstate highway leading to tonight's stop: Joy's sister Sherryl's place in south central Minnesota.

The drizzle continued as I drove the 20 miles southwest of Wichita to Lake Afton Park. Lightning behind the clouds lit the western sky as the thunder grew louder. The outside temperature displayed on our van's instrument panel inched downward toward the mid-60s as I drove closer to the park, a route I had rehearsed after picking up my race packet yesterday.

I racked my bike during what was still a drizzle, taking advantage of the early arrival to secure a spot in transition with clear access to the exits. I waited, however, to set out my helmet, running shoes, and other gear. The rain intensified as the triathlon's start time came and went while I sat inside our van. Thirty to 45 minutes later, it seemed to stop. Not sure if the rain was over, I placed my shoes, socks, glasses, towel, and a biking jacket—items I needed to keep dry for the race—into two plastic grocery bags. A few minutes before transition closed and the pre-race meeting began, I placed the two bags next to my bike with the open ends facing the ground.

Today's event included four races: a Sprint triathlon, an Olympic triathlon, a duathlon based on the distances for the

Sprint triathlon, and an aquabike race using the same distances as the Olympic triathlon.

The swim for the two triathlon distances and the aquabike race took place in Lake Afton, a 258-acre manmade lake within the park. During packet pickup, I asked one of the race organizers to explain the triathlon's name. Why *Mudwater?* It didn't sound appealing. I wondered if this was the reason the registration form I completed back in March had included the question, "Do you think the event name should be changed?"

He said the race was first called the Lake Afton Triathlon & Duathlon. However, after a practice swim in the lake, one member of the local triathlon club told the organizers they should rename the event Mudwater because of the cloudiness of the water. The organizers agreed, and the name stuck. The water during that particular practice swim may have been especially muddy, but today, Lake Afton was not any cloudier or muddier than any of the other lakes in which I'd competed. This included Birch Lake, the site for yesterday's open water swim.

Once the rain stopped, it did not restart. All the gear I had left in the plastic bags stayed dry for the race. The water temperature, measured in the late afternoon the previous day, had been 86 degrees. Because of this high temperature, the organizers did not allow wetsuits.

A little before 8:15 a.m., one hour later than scheduled, the race director instructed us to proceed to the lake for the triathlon and aquabike races. According to my bike computer, the air temperature was 64 degrees. A wind from the northeast was whipping up waves on Lake Afton. I became chilled while standing around in a triathlon suit, waiting for the race to begin.

We walked into the lake behind the starting line until we stood in chest- to neck-deep water. Most did this to avoid becoming further chilled. While waiting for the race, I saw campers lining up by the lake. I'm certain I heard someone ask, "What are those crazy people doing?"

First to start were the competitors in the Olympic-distance triathlon and the aquabike. Five minutes later, the air horn sounded, signaling those of us in the Sprint triathlon to begin our swim. We swam parallel to the lake shore for this out-and-back course, returning to the starting line after we reached the halfway point.

As the precipitation continued to pass out of the region, the northeast winds grew stronger, creating even more choppiness. After passing the midpoint of the swim, we headed into the wind and waves. Under these conditions, more water than the usual went up my nose and into my mouth.

I swallowed even more water when, late in the swim, I smiled after glancing to my left. The smile came after seeing a triathlete who had decided to buck the waves by walking in knee-high water closer to shore rather than take them on by swimming in deeper water.

The air temperature, not counting the wind chill, was still around 65 degrees when I started the bike leg. Still chilled from the swim and by the cool, windy jog to transition, I pulled on and zipped up my bike jacket. The extra time to put on the snug-fitting jacket was worth sacrificing. The temperature was still 66 degrees at the end of the bike, with 30-mile-per-hour crosswinds.

Our route to the park on Saturday afternoon had taken us a mile west of Goddard, Kansas, then onto MacArthur Road, all east of the park. Most of the bike course for the Sprint triathlon followed MacArthur Road, though west of where we had driven to reach the Lake Afton Park.

The short drive on MacArthur Road yesterday gave me a sense of the course. This road, with rolling hills that fit my definition of *rolling*, was in excellent condition, even at several bridges crossing small creeks.

The wind was formidable for the duration of the out-and-back course, which took us past typical farms of southern Kansas. Because we were in farm country, it met little resistance as it blustered across the road. The only exceptions were stands of small trees lining the creeks that crossed under bridges. On another day, like the one in Oklahoma yesterday, this would have been a beautiful ride, given the flawless road and picturesque scenery.

While riding towards the turnaround, I overheard a racer coming from the turnaround warning someone traveling near me to "be careful on the way back."

I understood what he meant after turning around. Now, the crosswind's gusts seemed aggressive in their attempts to blow me off the road. Memories of the North Dakota triathlon flashed before me. Similarly, I could not work up the nerve to ride my lightweight carbon fiber frame bike in the aero position.

Flat as a pancake described the run course—a single loop

within the park. We passed the dam that forms Lake Afton, and a section of the course passed campsites, many of which were filled on this Sunday morning. With tall stands of deciduous trees surrounding the park, the wind we faced on the water and the open road during the bike leg was now only a cool, comfortable, gentle breeze.

I finished third of three in my age group of 65- through 69-year-old men, and 35th of 40 overall in the Sprint triathlon.

The contrast in weather between yesterday and today was striking. Saturday's race in Oklahoma had featured sunshine and high temperatures with lots of humidity. I should have prayed for a breeze. Today, overcast skies and gusting wind had followed a midwestern thunderstorm, complete with flashes of lightning, crashes of thunder, and a low-60s wind from the north that made for an interesting, though sometimes frightening, bike ride.

While waiting for the awards ceremony, the race staff treated us to hamburgers, hot dogs, chips, cookies, and drinks. As we ate and drank around one of the picnic tables inside the shelter house, I chatted with the race staff and other senior triathletes.

It surprised me to see Buck, a Wichita resident against whom I had raced in the Tulsa Triathlon yesterday. I also met the winner of the 70-and-over age group, a member of the Kansas River Valley Triathlon Club and Kona Ironman finisher.

A few days after the triathlon, I received an email from race director Alan Farrington recapping this race:

"Today's weather was unique, to say the least. In my 15 years of directing Mudwater, I haven't seen anything quite like it. We've

had a rain delay once before, had to cancel the swim once because of algae, and had to activate a heat contingency plan, but we haven't had the rain, followed by 30 mph winds, and temperatures as cool as they were for late June; all within the race time span. Everyone's gotta have one of those races to talk about for years to come. Maybe today was the one."

CALIFORNIA: STATE #47

California Nickname:
The Golden State

Our campsite for the Donner Lake Triathlon gave Joy a
view of the triathlon swim course.

California Triathlon Details

- Date: July 23, 2022
- Triathlon: 40th Donner Lake Triathlon
- Location: West End Beach, Donner Lake, Truckee, California

Published distances
- Swim: 0.25 miles (402 meters)
- Bike: 6 miles (9.7 kilometers)
- Run: 2 miles (3.2 kilometers)

I hadn't planned to do a triathlon in California this year, thinking I would choose one in Palm Springs, Los Angeles, or San Diego for the fiftieth state. However, after showing Joy where we would be for the Idaho and Montana triathlons, she encouraged me to look for a race in northern California. Checking off California during this trip would save a lot of time and travel next year.

While searching the Running in the USA website, I found the Donner Lake Triathlon near Truckee, California, scheduled one week before the triathlon I had registered for in Idaho. Truckee is in the region between Reno, Nevada and Lake Tahoe…places we had enjoyed visiting 30 years earlier.

Before signing up for this triathlon, we had already reserved a Class C motorhome for travel to the triathlons in Idaho and Montana. It would be best, we reasoned, to extend the motorhome rental to cover travel to the triathlon in California. By doing so, we could further test our feelings about RV camping.

After moving to Florida, Joy thought we should buy a motorhome for summer jaunts to cooler locales. I never agreed, nor thought she would enjoy camping. Renting was an economical way to test our thoughts.

After registering for this triathlon, I added another week to our RV reservation. Midday on Thursday, two days before Saturday's triathlon, we picked up the motorhome from its owner in Logan, Utah. That night, we had our first experience of motorhome camping at the Welcome Center RV Park outside Wells, Nevada.

Early during the drive, it became apparent that the

motorhome's sound system was not working. Neither of our phones would connect to it, so the Terri Blackstock mysteries we had planned to listen to sat closed. It was good to know that we were still able to hold long conversations, even over the road noise and my hyper-focus on keeping the motorhome in my lane.

The drive the next day to West End Beach on Donner Pass Road, a few miles west of downtown Truckee, doubled as a preview of the bike course. I would be riding a section of this road for the bike leg of the triathlon.

We arrived at West End Beach a little before 5 p.m., the earliest time I could pick up my race packet. With the beach and park filled with sun lovers and beachgoers this Friday afternoon, we found the parking lot full.

None of the open parking spaces were big enough for the motorhome. With further searching, we found a grassy patch at the far end of the parking lot, past the end of the pavement, large enough to park our rented camper.

We wondered out loud if we might be able to park at the beach overnight. That would be the most convenient option. However, by now, the Parks and Recreation department was closed. Still, we had our original plan.

Before we left Florida in May, I had searched for campgrounds around Donner Lake. The closest one was Donner Memorial State Park, three miles from West End Beach. Yet, even in May, there were no camping spaces available for tonight. The nearest commercial RV parks were 25 or more miles away.

Then, still during May, I found a website mentioning free overnight parking in downtown Truckee, near the train station.

I had verified the availability of parking with a person from the California Welcome Center in Truckee months earlier. So, we arrived in the area, planning to sleep in downtown Truckee overnight.

After picking up my race packet, we started for the free RV parking location. When we arrived at the appointed address, to my surprise, I did not see a single sign that suggested either free or overnight RV parking. Quite the opposite. Signs posted in alternating parking spaces stated NO PARKING BETWEEN 10 PM AND 5 AM.

The time was fast approaching 6 p.m. With the Welcome Center closed, no one could clarify the parking situation.

As we sat debating what to do, a train rumbled into town. As the engineer laid on the train's horn, I watched, from the corner of my eye, as Joy jumped a couple of inches off the seat. Making an executive decision, she declared, "We can't sleep here."

Before leaving the parking lot, she called the number for the local police department posted on the wall of the Welcome Center. A dispatcher took the call and within a few minutes, a police officer called.

"Could we park downtown, or maybe at West End Beach?" Joy asked.

The policeman was not sure if we could park at either location; however, he promised they would not ticket us, even at the beach. In the worst case, they would order us to leave the beach parking lot.

After being refused overnight parking by a couple of businesses on the road back to West End Beach, we took our chances and parked in the space we had occupied during packet pickup. This spot gave a clear view across Donner Lake, including the triathlon swim course, from the back window of the motorhome. We prayed, then settled in for what we hoped would be undisturbed rest before this triathlon. A peaceful night's sleep was the answer to our prayers.

At age 40, the Donner Lake Triathlon was tied for the longest-running of all my races. On Saturday, they held the Sprint triathlon and kids' triathlon. Adult triathletes could race in an age group, in Clydesdale or Athena categories, or as part of a relay team. Longer-distance triathlon, aquabike, and duathlon races would take place on Sunday. Racers chose either the Olympic or half-Ironman distance. Three distances of open-water swim races were also held.

My commute to set up my transition space the next morning was the shortest of all my triathlons: a five-minute walk from the end of the parking lot to the park's gated entrance. Transition was set up on a grassy space between the gate and the beach.

With a water temperature in the high 60s, the race was wetsuit-legal according to USA Triathlon rules. With a 41-degree air temperature, wearing a wetsuit became even more attractive.

As we lined up to start the triathlon, the beauty of this venue struck me. I never tire of looking across a large, calm lake with tree-covered mountains in the background. Today's clear blue skies only made the view that much more awe-inspiring.

We began the swim on a rectangular course in three waves, starting at five-minute intervals. The third and final wave included men over age 50 and women over age 40. I started near the back of the group, since I expected to have a slower swim pace at this elevation of around 6,000 feet.

After making the first of two left turns around orange buoys, my breathing became labored. I considered pausing to tread water, confident in my wetsuit to keep me afloat. Rather than stop, I slowed my pace, and my breathing returned to normal. I finished the second turn, now heading toward the bright yellow *Swim Out* arch, which was a short distance from the area where we had slept last night. After the race, Joy said she was sure she had watched me leave Donner Lake as she peered out the back window from a comfortable position on our bed in the motorhome.

From transition, all racers walked our bikes about 50 yards to the bike-mount spot outside the chain-link fence on the side of Donner Lake Road. I rode in the bike lane for a little over three miles to the Donner Lake Memorial Park entrance. A volunteer stationed here instructed us to make a 180-degree turn to loop around an orange traffic cone near the road's center. The bike course for this triathlon fit my definition of *flat and fast*. With gentle rolling hills on well-maintained roads in perfect weather, I would have enjoyed a longer ride.

The out-and-back run course left West End Beach, in the opposite direction from the bike course. Most of the run was on South Shore Drive, a neighborhood road with houses on one side of the street backing up to Donner Lake. Unlike the bike course, the run course included a series of short hills. Neighborhood residents lined both sides of the road to cheer on the runners. After turning around midway through the course, we ran on the opposite side of the street, the one closest to the lake, toward transition.

A short distance from the point at which we had entered the run course earlier, two volunteers directed us to cross through a narrow ditch. From here, we sprinted across a grassy section of the park to cross the finish line.

During the awards ceremony, I received a glass with the Donner Lake Triathlon logo etched into it for my third-place finish in my age group. Afterward, we began our journey toward Idaho and the next triathlon.

After a week of long days of driving, we could now follow a more leisurely timeline. We had five days to travel the distance we had covered in the previous day and a half.

IDAHO: STATE #48

Idaho Nickname:
The Gem State

The triathlon in Idaho had a unique swim format
because of this two-lane pool.

Idaho Triathlon Details

- Date: July 30, 2022
- Triathlon: 10th Preston Biathlon, Triathlon, and Fun Run
- Location: Preston Aquatic Center, Preston, Idaho

Published distances
- Swim: 500 meters (547 yards)
- Bike: 14 miles (22.5 kilometers)
- Run: 5 kilometers (3.1 miles)

L ater in the week following the Donner Lake Triathlon, Steve and Lori, our friends from Colorado Springs, Colorado, met us at the Cub River Campground outside Preston. For three nights, we camped next to them in our rented motorhome while they stayed in the one they owned.

On Friday afternoon, the day before the triathlon, we rode with Steve and Lori the 13 miles from the RV park into Preston using the Jeep Wrangler they usually towed behind their motorhome. While in Preston, I planned to pick up my race packet and complete the triathlon swim. Another new triathlon experience would be completing the swim the day before the bike and run.

Offering to complete the swim leg on Friday was necessary, since the Aquatic Center pool had only two lanes. If I couldn't have come on Friday, I could've done the swim on Saturday morning before the triathlon and biathlon. We were each asked to bring someone, in my case Steve, to count our laps, record our swim time, and report the time to an Aquatic Center staff member.

Between the swim and packet pickup, we walked along the main street of this farming community of just over 5,000 residents. With Preston buzzing with Rodeo Days and its nightly parades, we found the streets crowded with people perusing outdoor displays and sale racks of local shops while sampling treats from street vendors.

As we filled the time before packet pickup, we also shopped for groceries at Stokes Market, a family-owned grocery store. The range of products and competitive prices impressed us. The big corporate stores in larger cities had nothing on this one. It pleased us to know that some small towns similar to the one in which Joy and I had lived until high school graduation were still thriving.

During packet pickup, I spoke with Chris and Jeannine Groll, owners of the Groll Family Fitness Center in Preston and managers of this triathlon. In the event's early years, Preston did not have a swimming facility. A bike plus run event was the closest they could get to a triathlon. However, that had changed three years earlier, when the Preston Aquatic Center and its two-lane lap pool opened.

Today's event would include a Sprint triathlon, a biathlon with the same bike and run distances as the Sprint triathlon, and one-mile and five-kilometer so-called fun runs. Like many local triathlons and other multisport and running events, this one doubled as a fundraiser to support a local cause.

Proceeds from this race supported the Preston Aquatic Center and its "Every Child a Swimmer" scholarship. The fund still aims to support underprivileged children who want to learn to swim but whose parents cannot afford lessons.

One staff member of the Aquatic Center said, "I grew up in California, and learned to swim when I was old enough to walk. I want every child who wants to learn to swim to have the same opportunity."

My mother had taken me to swimming lessons during the summer in my earliest years of grade school. Today, as throughout my time in triathlon, I appreciated having learned to swim early in life.

Much later, while our youngest children were in swimming

lessons, their coach took me aside in an open lane of the pool to help me with my swim stroke. I had continued swimming in both pools and open water, comfortable in a wide range of water conditions. It surprised me to discover that many triathletes feared swimming, especially in open water.

The organizers had converted the parking lot behind the Preston Aquatic Center into transition for Saturday's bike and run legs of the triathlon and biathlon. Just before the race began, we mounted our bikes inside transition. Following a 10-second countdown, the race began as we rode across the timing mat.

This triathlon used a unique method for capturing our times. In most triathlons, we wrap a hook and loop fastener strap with a timing chip around our left ankle. The timing mat captures a signal from the chip as we cross it. I had completed some running races that use a race-number bib with the timing chip embedded in the bib. For this race, the organizer gave each of us two plastic-laminated metal foils. He instructed us to pin one foil on the left and the other on the right side of our race number belt or shorts.

The bike course left transition using the alley behind the aquatic center. Once we reached the street, a volunteer signaled us to turn left. Now on Oneida Street, we continued east out of Preston into the country with its rolling hills. As we left town, we passed a little over a mile south of a house popularized by the 2004 movie *Napolean Dynamite*.

Volunteers throughout the course made it easy for us to navigate its many turns while enjoying the sights and smells of fertile farmland. Most of the ride took place on roads passing between hayfields. This was interrupted by the occasional small farmstead and a mix of dairy and beef cows, goats, and horses. I saw hay in various stages, from the next crop being irrigated to encourage its growth to ones being raked to speed the drying process before baling. At one point, I passed through a cooling mist from the spray of an irrigation rig.

Throughout the bike leg, we rode in traffic: cars, trucks, and the occasional farming implement. This triathlon was the first in which I met a tractor pulling a hay rake—one wide enough to leave only six to eight feet for me to pass between it and the edge of the road. Despite the plentiful traffic, I always felt safe, thanks to the consideration shown by drivers.

After completing a rectangular loop near the midpoint of the course, we soon reconnected with Oneida Street. We now met a few apparent latecomers to the biathlon and triathlon. As we returned to Preston's city limits, we met racers taking part in the 5k fun run. They were running the course I would be on within a few minutes.

The flat run course followed the first part of the bike course on streets leading to the eastern edge of Preston. As with the bike course, we left transition through the alley onto Oneida Street. Near the edge of town, we turned left to follow a rectangular path that included three left turns. Upon returning to Oneida Street near the post office, we turned right and returned to the finish line.

After the Preston Triathlon, Joy and I caravaned with Steve and Lori in our two motorhomes toward Montana for next weekend's race. As we drove to our first stop—Dillon,

Montana—we passed more bright green alfalfa fields like the ones I had seen on the bike course. These soon gave way to fields covered with yellow petals of canola, also known as rapeseed, then to massive fields of potatoes with their vibrant purple flowers. A short stretch of lava fields reminiscent of the big island of Hawaii led to more potatoes and corn. Before long, grassy areas with grazing cattle replaced crop farms.

Our destination for the next two nights was Southside RV Park in Dillon. Our campsite, next to a small river, was the perfect spot from which to watch the comings, goings, and activities within the nest of an osprey family comprising dad, mom, and two young ones. The larger of the two siblings, now able to take short flights, was about twice the size of the other, who refused to leave the nest. During parts of two afternoons, we imagined aloud the conversation between the parents and their children.

MONTANA: STATE #49

Montana Nickname:
The Treasure State

The swim for the Montana triathlon was in Seeley Lake
at the Riverpoint Day Use Area.

Montana Triathlon Details

- Date: August 6, 2022
- Triathlon: 15th Youth for Christ (YFC) Seeley Lake Challenge Triathlon/Duathlon
- Location: Riverpoint Campground Day Use Area at Seeley Lake, Seeley Lake, Montana

Published distances
- Swim: 600 yards (549 meters)
- Bike: 10 miles (16 kilometers)
- Run: 3.4 miles (5.5 kilometers)

As our caravan continued north from Dillon toward Missoula, thick stands of evergreens appeared around us. The mountains brought additional streams and rivers. Wherever we saw water, we saw people engaged in watersports. We watched people fly-fishing (either standing in water or fishing from a boat), waterskiing, tubing, wakeboarding, kayaking, swimming... even lazily floating down a river on a tube. Others biked and hiked on trails, some along the water's edge.

As we approached our next campground outside Kalispell, we traveled along the east side of Flathead Lake. The smoke cloud and occasional flames of the Elmo wildfire were impossible to miss.

The next day, we made a day trip to Glacier National Park and Hungry Horse Dam. After our second night outside Kalispell, we moved south toward our last stop before the Montana triathlon: Salmon Lake State Park, a few miles south of Seeley Lake and 35 miles as the crow flies northeast of Missoula.

In 2006, the organizers had hosted their first race, which later became the YFC Seeley Lake Challenge Triathlon and Duathlon. The first triathlon here was the result of a senior project by Holly Friede. Holly's brother suffered from spinal muscular atrophy, and she was seeking a way to raise money for the disease's cure.

According to race director Cheryl Thompson, they kept the event going after the first year, using it to raise funds for the Greater Missoula chapter of Youth for Christ. Cheryl and her team have held the race every year except for 2007 and

2017, when the Jocko Lakes and Rice Ridge fires forced them to cancel it.

Today's event would include two Sprint triathlon options: one with a 300-yard swim and a second (my choice) with a swim of 600 yards. Those in the Sprint triathlon competed either as an individual or as part of a relay team. Another option was a Sprint-distance duathlon with a run, bike, run sequence. A kids' triathlon with 35 participants took place after the adult races.

On race morning, Joy and I packed up the motorhome and left the Salmon Lake State Park campground at 6:30 a.m. for the 9 o'clock start of the triathlon. Overnight, Cheryl and her team had transformed the parking lot of the Riverpoint Day Use Area into the triathlon's transition area. With this change, there were no longer parking spaces at the race site. Instead, vehicles could park at Pyramid Mountain Lumber, along Boy Scout Road, two miles southeast of the race's finish line.

Cheryl arranged for a shuttle bus to transport athletes and spectators to and from transition. A family member or friend could drop a racer, their bike, and other gear at Riverpoint Campground, a few hundred yards away. Then, the driver—in our case, Joy—would return to Pyramid Mountain Lumber. Steve and Lori arrived a little later, in time to wake Joy from her nap and travel with her by shuttle to attend the pre-race activities. This was their fourth time attending one of my triathlons as spectators. These friends were dedicated to being part of our adventure.

Forty-five minutes before the adult races began, the air temperature was 51 degrees. Choosing to wear a wetsuit with this temperature—and the venue's 4,000 foot elevation—was easy. About 20 minutes before the triathlon's start, I put on my wetsuit and went for a warm-up swim to loosen by muscles, raise my heart rate, and check the lake bottom and water.

As we waited for the race to start, Haley Yarborough, journalist for the *Seeley Lake Pathfinder* newspaper, approached me. She wanted to talk with me, then Joy, about our adventure with triathlon. Haley wrote an article based in part on this interview, which appeared on the paper's website on August 11, 2022.

The swim began with a time-trial start. Before the start of the race, all swimmers lined up single file within transition. Every five seconds, the person running the timing system shouted "Go" to the next racer. As one swimmer after another jogged or walked around 50 yards to reach the lake, I put on my goggles while waiting in line. Within seconds, my lenses fogged. Navigating the trail while dodging rocks and tree roots with fogged goggles would be dangerous. Instead, I removed my goggles until I reached the water's edge, then dipped them into the lake to clear the lenses. As I walked into water deep enough to swim a freestyle stroke, I slipped on my goggles, then swam toward the first turn buoy.

The trapezoidal swim course involved two left turns. To reach the first turn, I swam a little under 200 yards toward the southeast, away from the swim exit. After turning, I swam parallel to the beach a little beyond the swim exit before making the second turn. From here, I was about 220 yards from the beach. Once at the beach, I jogged along the dusty dirt trail to enter transition.

It took me longer than usual to get onto my bike. I needed to wipe the extra sand and silt from the trail off my feet before putting on my socks and shoes. By now, the temperature was approaching 60 degrees. The bright sun warmed my skin, especially with little to no breeze, so I left my bike jacket in transition.

The out-and-back bike course left the Riverpoint Campground area, turning right onto Boy Scout Road, away from the town of Seeley Lake. Evergreen trees lined our path for most of the ride. One exception came as we crossed over the river on Boy Scout Road. Another break in the dense stands of tall trees occurred near the bike turnaround, a section of road with marsh on both sides.

After turning around, I glanced left to spot a sleek dark brown horse running in the pasture beside the road. He seemed to be racing me. I kept pace with him, not sure if he was racing or just pacing me.

I often wondered what went through the minds of animals along the course as they seemed to watch the procession of racers.

Did they recognize us as people, like those who tended to them? Did they want to join us? Or were they content to merely watch while continuing to graze, or resume whatever they had been doing?

Apart from the first few hundred yards, the run course followed a narrow wooded trail interrupted by a short section of a gravel road through the woods of the Lolo National Forest. Not used to trail running, I found the run interesting. The terrain, with its winding path, tree roots, and dips and curves, forced me to stay focused.

Near the beginning of the third mile, I became distracted. As I passed through a small depression in front of a tree root, the toe of my right shoe caught on the root's leading edge. I stumbled forward, trying to regain my balance. However, before I knew it, I was diving, left arm first, into the ground.

The spongy surface covered by powdery silt in this section of the trail led to nothing more than a dime-sized scrape on my left knee and dirt on my legs, hands, and left forearm. While finishing the run, I must have wiped my hand across my face. Seeing dirt on my face, left arm, and legs as I crossed the finish line, Joy ran into transition to check for injuries. Without hesitating, Cheryl evicted her from transition after I assured Joy that I was fine...just dirty.

I finished first in my age group of men ages 65 through 69.

From here, we traveled with our friends, each using our motorhome, to Idaho Falls, Idaho, where we stayed two nights. The next Monday afternoon, we returned the motorhome to its owner in Logan, Utah. Steve and Lori continued to their home in Colorado Springs, Colorado.

While RV camping had its benefits, Joy learned she preferred staying in hotels. The investment in renting the motorhome saved us from purchasing one.

After transferring our bikes and personal items from the motorhome to our van, we started our drive back to Florida. The trip included a two-day stay with our son Ben and his family in their new home outside Jefferson City, Missouri.

2023:
THE FINAL STATE

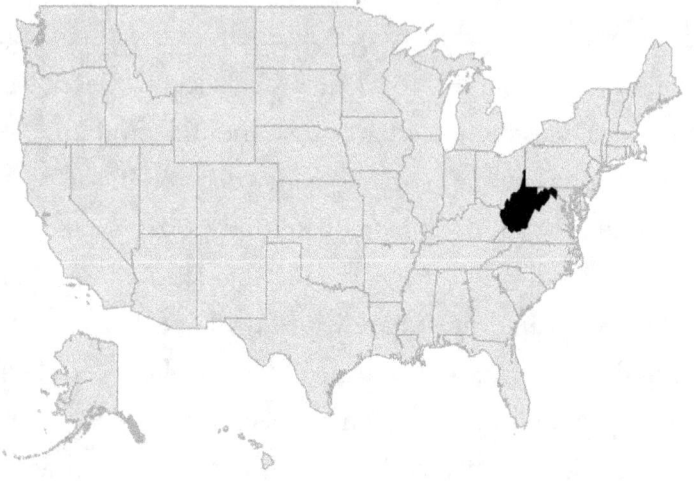

Thanks to the teaching of Peter Franz, our Minnesota pastor and friend, my focus on finishing well—and by that I mean both my life and the things I have started along the way—sharpened throughout the time of our triathlon adventure. His philosophy caused me to be more mindful of this verse from the Bible:

"Endings are better than beginnings. Sticking to it is better than standing out." — *Ecclesiastes 7:8, The Message*

While it took me longer than usual to find a triathlon in West Virginia because of the small number of races, I was happy to have found the one we did. This race was held at a time of year that was perfect for completing the 50th state's triathlon... and Joy's and my goal.

WEST VIRGINIA: STATE #50

West Virginia Nickname:
The Mountain State

Our three children joined Joy and me for the West Virginia triathlon. This picture captures our time together at Blackwater Falls State Park after the race.

West Virginia Triathlon Details

- Date: May 20, 2023
- Triathlon: 3rd Parsons Volunteer Fire Department Cheat River Triathlon
- Location: Mill Race Park, Parsons, West Virginia

Published distances
- Run: 3.9 miles (6.3 kilometers)
- Kayak: 3+ miles (4.8+ kilometers)
- Bike: 7 miles (11.3 kilometers)

T his triathlon stood out from races in any other state, since kayaking replaced the swim leg. The triathlon I had completed in Indiana offered racers the option to kayak instead of swim. However, I swam in that triathlon, believing that choice to be truer to the first triathlon in the USA in the early 1970s.

It surprised me to learn that an even earlier three-sport race, one held in France in 1902, had included running, cycling, and canoeing[1]. Today's triathlon, with kayaking instead of canoeing, was more like that race.

Joy and I departed The Villages, Florida two days before the triathlon at around 7 a.m. Inside our van, we packed luggage, golf clubs, and miscellaneous items for our two-month visit to the north-central part of the country. Three hybrid bikes hung on the bike rack secured to the hitch of our van. Our daughter Liza, son Ben, and I would ride the bikes on the mixed paved and gravel trail during the West Virginia triathlon.

We set our GPS to the address of our hotel that evening, near Charlotte International Airport. Ben's flight from St. Louis would arrive later in the evening. On Friday morning, our oldest son Jon and Liza planned to travel from Minneapolis to Charlotte.

All flights arrived on time. Friday morning's flight was 20 minutes early, allowing us to start our journey to West Virginia sooner than planned. By 11 a.m., we were on our way with the five of us, our luggage, and triathlon gear for three

---

[1]   "History Triathlon," CISM Europe, International Military Sports Council: https://www.cismeurope.org/ history-triathlon/

squeezed into our van. Our best recollection was the fact that this was our first road trip together as a family since 1985.

Our destination for this evening was Elkins, West Virginia, a 30-minute drive from Parsons, where the triathlon was being held. Along the way, we stopped at the New River Gorge Bridge. According to the U.S. National Park Service, this bridge was "the longest single-span steel arch bridge in the United States."

We finished the day by sharing a pizza and lounging between the hotel pool and hot tub. I did a few swim strokes in the pool so I could say I had been swimming in West Virginia. I hoped to avoid swimming during this triathlon.

The next morning, we left the hotel at around 8 a.m. This gave us plenty of time to pick up our race packets and set up our transition spaces before the 10 a.m. start. After a leisurely 30-minute drive, we arrived at Mill Race Park in Parsons, West Virginia, where the triathlon would begin and end.

Something felt odd as I walked to pick up my race packet. Those who had arrived before us whispered as they looked our way. A young man stood near a tripod-mounted video camera in front of a fire truck. *Maybe he is a reporter from a local TV station,* I thought. Then, as we arrived closer to the table with our race packets, I saw a banner recognizing our fiftieth-state milestone with pictures Liza had requested a few months earlier.

We picked up our timing chip, T-shirt, and mandatory whistle for the kayak leg. Later, we learned that according to West Virginia law, anyone on the water must carry a whistle. The fine for not having one was $50.

Since this triathlon was a fundraiser for the Parsons

Volunteer Fire Department (VFD), Fire Chief Kevin White served as race director. During the pre-race meeting, Kevin warned of the possibility of some loose material on the bike path, even though they had swept it the previous day. He also mentioned a couple of places on the Cheat River where we needed to be extra careful; in particular, he mentioned a downed tree. His advice was "keep left." The message stuck in my mind.

Chief White then welcomed a "celebrity," which, I learned, was me. He announced that finishing this triathlon meant having completed one in all 50 states. He called me to the front to present a special plaque prepared by the VFD to recognize the occasion.

Plaque commemorating my fiftieth state triathlon, presented to me by the Parsons, West Virginia Volunteer Fire Department.

After the pre-race meeting, the reporter, Tanner Gilmartin from WDTV, asked to record me answering a few questions. Sections of the interview appeared on the station's evening news.

As Kevin counted down to begin the triathlon, Liza, Ben, and I positioned ourselves at the back of the group. We crossed the starting line last and continued together at a pace I planned for the first mile. I wanted to avoid starting too fast, as I had done in the reverse triathlon in New Mexico.

It didn't take long to realize we were racing against fast runners. The distance between us and the last runner before us, a young woman, kept increasing. Upon reaching the end of the run course, all of the other runners were on their kayaks, or, for those taking part in a relay team, walking or jogging back to Mill Race Park.

Having lived on a lake in Minnesota for the past 20 years, I often kayaked, but I preferred peaceful waters, and seldom ventured onto the lake with anything higher than small waves. Today was my introduction to kayaking a river with rapids.

As I reached the riverbank, a volunteer directed me to "pick one of the green kayaks." According to her, the green kayaks weighed less than the others. I chose one close to the river and dragged it to the water's edge before putting on my helmet and life vest.

As I climbed onto the open kayak, I recalled a pre-race conversation with a couple of local guys that had centered upon today's kayak leg. Kayaking in this race concerned me. The last time I had kayaked was two years ago, and that had been in a calm lake. Hearing Kevin White warn of the area around the downed tree and "some rapids" added to my anxiety. I didn't relish becoming the triathlete who needed to be rescued. Besides, I wanted to finish this triathlon. During that conversation, I asked the guys if they were going to wear their running shoes in the kayak. While they were especially kind, the look in their eyes betrayed them. Of course, they would wear shoes. I'm sure they thought I was crazy.

As a result of their comments, we jettisoned the two-gallon clear plastic sealable storage bags Liza had packed for us to store our shoes in during the kayak leg. Still, I hesitated to get my shoes wet while getting into the kayak, just in case they would otherwise remain dry. I pushed the kayak into the water just enough to avoid stepping in and getting my shoes wet as I crawled inside.

In order to move the kayak into water deep enough to paddle, I used a thrusting motion. Sitting in the kayak, I lunged my upper body forward, and with each move, the kayak inched further. This worked, but it took far too long. By now, the young woman, the last runner before Liza, Ben, and me, was no longer visible.

As I passed through the first set of rapids, water surged over the front of my kayak with each wave, filling it to just below the level of my shoes. Once in calmer water, I laid the paddle across my lap, cupped my hands, and began throwing water out of the kayak. It didn't take long to realize this was futile, so resumed paddling.

At the next small rapids, I headed for a calmer area near the middle of the river to avoid taking on more water. The sinking feeling as the bottom of my kayak began scraping across rocks told me that seeking calmer water had been the wrong choice. When the kayak stopped on the rocks, I tried rocking, as I had done to move the kayak off the bank at the beginning. This time, the kayak did not budge. I was stuck. I rolled out of the kayak, tipped it to one side to empty the water out, and dragged it beyond this shallow spot, ever careful not to trip over or slip on a rock and fall.

As I neared the end of these rapids, two guys observing this fiasco from their lawn chairs on the left bank shouted, "Stay to the right." I also heard them say something about the current being stronger on the right side of the river.

What I had heard during the pre-race meeting was "stay left." It dawned on me that this only applied to the area where the tree lay in the river. I followed their advice…almost. The next time I got stuck was the next time I failed to follow it.

As I dragged my kayak off the rocks to the right, where the current was, indeed, stronger, Liza and Ben caught me. Ben said he had capsized while going through the first rapids, losing a hat Liza loaned him.

Liza, Ben, and I floated together from there to the kayak leg's exit. We tested our emerging skill for reading the water to find the strongest current and fastest route. Soon, we saw the downed tree lying on the right bank. Ripples and small waves grew into churning, two-foot-high waves as they passed the tree. Floating toward the most turbulent section, I told myself, "Keep paddling to keep the kayak straight." Despite

my heart's warning to head into the rapids with caution, I
started paddling.

Still not confident of my whitewater kayaking ability, I
approached the wildest water, thinking, *hold onto the kayak if
you capsize.* Finding myself safely on the other side and still
upright in my kayak, I relaxed, wondering how many more of
these tests I would have to go through. Moments later, I saw
two guys on the left shore motioning us to land. Since I thought
we had further to go, I had stayed in the middle of the river,
where the water was calmer, but faster-flowing. To reach the
exit, I tried, with minor success, to turn the kayak and paddle
perpendicular to the current.

Before long, the kayak caught on shallow rocks. I towed it
across large boulders, ever conscious that I was one slip from
falling and losing the kayak. As I approached the shore, I heard
Jon shout advice about safely getting there according to the
trials he had watched others go through.

With my kayak now on shore at the exit point, I removed
my helmet and life vest. Following Jon's coaching, I climbed the
last group of rocks before reaching *terra firma*, the flat grassy
space between the river and parking lot where our bikes waited.
After putting on my helmet and grabbing my bike, I walked
out of transition and onto the bike course, on the same trail we
had used for the run.

To turn around at the halfway mark of the bike leg, we rode
off the trail across a patch of thick, dark green grass where we
had left the trail for the river's edge to kayak. As the wet ground
gave way to my wider hybrid bike tires, I rejoiced in not having

my triathlon bike with me today. I'm not sure how well I could have navigated this patch with its narrower tires.

After rejoining the paved trail, I relived the time on the water and saw myself completing this triathlon, even if it meant walking the bike in case of a flat tire. I spent extra time appreciating my surroundings. I saw a patch of beautiful blue and white irises alongside one of several family homes, the river rapids, and many impressive natural rock sculptures. A couple of roosters in another yard crowed, and race volunteers stationed at each of the intersections shouted words of encouragement as we passed.

Liza, Ben, and I traveled more or less in a group, having decided we would finish together. I didn't want this race to be remembered for our competition. Neither did I relish being beaten by either or both of them.

"Never try something for the first time on race day." I had learned this wisdom early in my triathlon journey, and as far as I could remember, I had been faithful to it...except for today. For this race, I knew I was going to violate this rule. I had never kayaked in a river. Before today, I didn't even know the Cheat River *had* rapids. And without times for each leg, I'll never know how much time I lost in the kayak leg. However, my inexperience kayaking in water like that of the Cheat River cost a lot of time. Still, from the experience, I believe learning to kayak in rapids would be fun... outside of racing.

After enjoying snacks and drinks, we changed out of our wet clothing. My shoes, which I had worked so hard to keep from getting wet, would take four days to dry. We repacked the van, and said our thanks and farewells to the kind people of Parsons. Our next stop was Blackwater Falls State Park, where we walked to view the iconic falls and take a couple more family pictures. As we were returning to our van, the skies opened, so we cut short further sightseeing, instead resuming our family road trip. After overnight stops in Louisville, Kentucky and Wardsville, Missouri to deliver Ben back home, we arrived in Minnesota, where Jon and Liza lived.

We realized that our time together could be our last chance for the five of us to travel by ourselves. Each of our children had job and family responsibilities, two with school-aged children. Still, it pleased Joy and me to experience relaxed conversation between us, some light and humorous, some more serious given concerns about what we saw happening in our country. Every moment of the trip was enjoyable, and we hoped to be able to do another trip like this again.

The goal Joy and I had begun during the summer of 2011 was complete.

REFLECTING ON
THE ADVENTURE

—■————

Sitting on the overstuffed sofa in our daughter's lower-level family room, I watched Liza, Ben, and I crossing the finish line in West Virginia. As in most of my triathlons, Joy had been there to meet me.

A simple goal of losing weight had blossomed to yield unforeseen yet wonderful outcomes. I had learned a lot, and we had seen many people and places throughout America. It surprised us how often travel for a triathlon could become a conversation-starter with someone new to us simply because of our visit to their home state.

Reams of scientific reports show how important consistent physical activity, proper nutrition and hydration, quality sleep, and social contact are for healthy aging. The benefits extend throughout the body, including the brain.

I discovered that triathlon is an excellent sport for becoming and staying physically fit. Training for swimming, biking, and running engages different parts of the body. Balanced training helps prevent overuse injuries that can sideline us, especially as our bodies age.

I also saw exactly how triathlon mirrors life. I gained a new appreciation for the Bible's many references to racing, endurance, swimming, and running.

I was reminded that, as in life, having a person or persons with whom you can share the adventure is so valuable. I have often heard this same observation echoed by other triathletes. Having Joy, and, for some races, other family members and friends with me along the way made the experiences far more memorable and enjoyable.

As in everyday life, Joy and I understood our responsibilities, combined our strengths, stayed flexible, and sought to enjoy ourselves by focusing on good things. Joy still reminds me of the verse from the Bible on this last point:

"Fix your thoughts on what is true, and honorable, and right, and pure, and lovely, and admirable. Think about things that are excellent and worthy of praise" (*Philippians 4:8, New Living Translation*).

From a different perspective, triathlon taught me how to plan and deal with the sinking curveballs sometimes thrown our way. We had planned as we thought best, waited to see which parts of the plan worked and which ones didn't, then made adjustments to our next strategy. Still, sometimes I hadn't learned my lesson—just as in life.

Traveling to the triathlons often put us in places where we could be with family and friends. The extra time we spent with them was one of our greatest sources of enjoyment. Some even came to share our love for triathlon.

When we were in places new to us, we met wonderful, welcoming people. I found it encouraging to see the number of triathlons that doubled as fundraisers for people in need, including newborn babies, children who needed a bike or to learn to swim, and those at risk of suicide. It also gave me hope to see triathletes put their own race on hold to help another competitor.

While I have often seen triathlon called a "rich man's sport," I hope to have shown that it is possible to enjoy its benefits while on a budget. For many races, the registration fee is the same as for a 5k running race. Many triathletes I met raced with a bike they or a friend already owned.

Through the adventure, I also learned about aging. It feels foolish to admit this now, but on my fiftieth birthday, I went to our local community center and ran three miles on their indoor track. I needed to convince myself I wasn't old.

Ten years later, my goal was to complete triathlons in all 50 states by age 70. Why seventy?

Because I believed I wouldn't have the strength or endurance to continue training and racing in the sport after that age. I didn't know anyone in their 60s or 70s who had done a triathlon.

After more than a decade of competing in triathlon and witnessing older triathletes' accomplishments, I have abandoned the idea that age determines when we can no longer compete. Yes, we age—but the changes are individual. The point at which we stop competing should not be based on our number of birthdays, but on other factors, including our commitment to stay active. I find it interesting that people who hear about our travels often ask me, "Which place did you enjoy the most?" or "What was your favorite place to visit?" To my best recollection, no one has ever asked me about my fastest time or anything about my wetsuit, triathlon bike, or running shoes.

During the last few years of our triathlon adventure, a cousin Kathy and her husband Stuart Nesbit, both near our age, set out on their own adventure: visiting all 63 United States national parks. It turned out to be the perfect adventure for them.

What's your next adventure going to be like?

ACKNOWLEDGMENTS

THANKS TO OUR CHILDREN, JON, LIZA, AND BEN for supporting us on our adventure and for reading my draft. Thank you, Liza and Ben, for joining me in a few races and for encouraging your spouses, Scott and Lindsey, to join us in a triathlon.

Thank you, Nelda, for your encouragement, and for also reading and providing valuable feedback on my draft.

Thanks also to Mary Hollenkamp for proofreading and commenting on my draft, as you have been doing for so many years now with my website posts.

Finally, to the community of Senior Triathletes, thank you for encouraging me to write this book.

AUTHOR BIO

Terry VanderWert is an inspiring example of an everyday athlete with a commitment to aging actively. Alongside his wife Joy, Terry combines his passion for road trips, family visits, and exploring America through outdoor activities. Driven by a desire to support and encourage others, he founded SeniorTriathletes.com in 2016, a platform dedicated to promoting adventure through triathlons and other multisport endurance events. Today, Terry and Joy stay active in The Villages, Florida, continuing their journey of adventure and inspiring others to pursue their own.

Learn more at
SeniorTriathletes.com

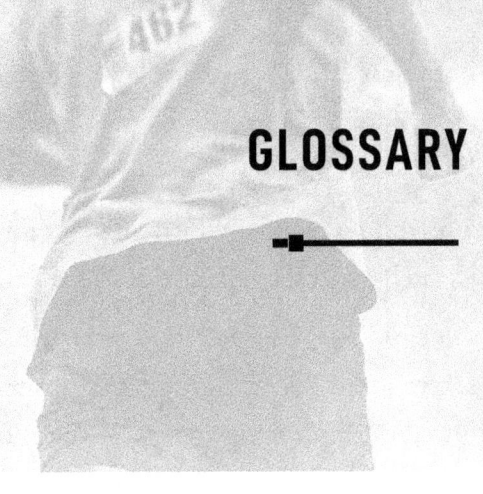

GLOSSARY

HERE ARE THE MOST common words and acronyms associated with triathlon, along with their definitions.

Aero bars: Extensions to the handlebars of a bike, designed to allow the rider to sit on the bike in an aerodynamic, or "aero" position. On a triathlon-specific bike (see *tri-bike*), two extensions often include shift levers at their ends. On a road bike (see *road bike*), the extension is often a single piece unit. The shift levers are on the ends of the handlebar for a road bike.

Aero position: A position while riding a bike in which the rider leans forward and down to reduce air resistance. Most triathlon bikes encourage riders into this position through their design, as it offers the most comfort.

Aerobic training: Exercises that use oxygen to produce energy, like walking, jogging, and easy swimming. Aerobic exercises raise the heart rate and breath rate moderately, yet still allow for normal conversation during the workout. Compare with *anaerobic training*.

Age group: A group of competitors of a similar age range and gender. An example of an age group is women ages 65 through 69.

Age grouper: A person who competes within an age group instead of other groups such as a relay team. See *Athena* and *Clydesdale*.

Anaerobic training: Exercise such as sprinting that leads to a heart rate greater than that of the aerobic zone. Conversation during anaerobic training is often difficult. Anaerobic training requires glucose stored in our muscles for energy besides oxygen. Compare with *aerobic training*.

Aquabike: A multisport race format comprising swim and bike legs. This format does not include a run leg.

Athena: A USA Triathlon (USAT) competition category for female athletes who weigh at least 165 pounds (75 kilograms), independent of their age. Still, a female of this weight may race in an age group if they choose.

Biathlon: A multisport race format comprising a single bike and run leg. A related format is the duathlon, which includes a run-bike-run sequence.

Bike leg: The second segment of a traditional triathlon, during which participants cycle a specified distance.

Body marking: A pre-race activity during which the participant's race number is written on one or several parts of their body, such as a hand, shoulder, or calf, using an indelible marker, or is applied using a temporary tattoo. These markings allow race officials and volunteers to identify a participant during the race. The location and number of marks varies among races. For some competitions, the participant's age is also printed on one leg, usually on the calf muscle.

Brick workout: A training session that combines two disciplines of a triathlon, most often bike and run.

Cadence: The rate at which a cyclist pedals, measured in revolutions per minute (RPM). It also refers to the number of steps per minute in running.

Clip-in pedals: Bike pedals that attach to special cycling shoes. Clipping the biking shoes to the pedals promotes greater cycling efficiency.

Clydesdale: A USA Triathlon (USAT) competition category for men who weigh over 220 pounds (100 kilograms), independent of their age. Alternatively, a male of this weight may choose to race in an age group.

DNF (Did Not Finish): A participant who started but did not complete the race.

DNS (Did Not Start): A participant who registered but did not start the race.

Dolphin dive: A technique used to enter shallow water more efficiently during the swim. This technique often involves a series of moves in which the swimmer pushes off the bottom of a lake or pond and reenters the water using a shallow dive. The swimmer repeats this as needed to reach water deep enough for a freestyle swim stroke.

Drafting: Riding close behind another cyclist to reduce wind resistance, or swimming behind another swimmer to reduce water resistance. For many triathlons, drafting during the bike leg is illegal, while drafting during the swim is allowed.

Duathlon: A multisport race format comprising a run-bike-run sequence. This competition does not include swimming or kayaking.

Fueling: Consuming sources of energy, such as gels, bars, and/or fluids during a training session or race.

Gels: Packets of semi-liquid (like a thick syrup or honey) or semi-solid sugary material designed for fast absorption to give a racer extra energy.

Half-IRONMAN® triathlon: A triathlon format comprising a 1.2 mile (1.9 km) swim, 56 mile (90 km) bike, and 13.1 mile (19.1 km) run. It is sometimes called a Half Iron distance, or IRONMAN 70.3, because the sum of the three distances is 70.3 miles.

® IRONMAN and IRONMAN 70.3 are registered trademarks of World Triathlon Corporation.

Hill repeats: A run training workout that involves several repetitions of a sprint up a hill, followed by walking or jogging back down.

Hybrid bike: A design that uses features of both road and mountain bikes, suitable for general-purpose riding over various types of terrain. The hybrid bike's flat handlebar allows for a more upright riding position, favoring comfort over speed.

In-water start: A format for the start of a triathlon or multisport competition that begins with a swim. Participants start from a position in the water. Race organizers often use this format when running into the water could lead to injury because the beach is rocky or the bottom is slippery. They also use this format in pool swims during which two people share a lane.

International triathlon: A triathlon format comprising a 1.5 km swim, 40 km bike, and 10 km run.

Interval training: Alternating periods of high and low-intensity training. This training format encompasses high intensity interval training, or HIIT, and Tabata.

IRONMAN® triathlon: A triathlon format comprising a 2.4 mile (3.8 km) swim, 112 mile (180 km) bike, and 26.2 mile (38.2 km) run. It is sometimes called a Full Iron distance or IRONMAN 140.6 because the sum of the three distances is 140.6 miles.

IRONMAN® 70.3: See *half-IRONMAN* definition.

Olympic triathlon: See *international triathlon* definition.

Open course: Bike or run course in which triathletes share the course with motor vehicles.

Open water swim: Swimming in large natural and man-made bodies of water, like lakes, ponds, reservoirs, rivers, and oceans.

Out-and-back: Course layout for a triathlon leg in which the path to the midpoint turnaround is the same or almost the same as from the turnaround to transition or finish.

Pacing: Managing speed and energy output to ensure endurance throughout the race.

Race belt: Elastic belt worn by a racer to display their race number bib.

Race official: Person on the racecourse tasked with ensuring that racers follow the rules.

Recovery: A process that helps athletes heal soon after training and competition. Activities include low-intensity exercise such as walking or easy swimming, sleep, massage, and/or eating and drinking anti-inflammatory foods and liquids.

Reverse triathlon: In this triathlon format, participants perform the three legs in reverse order: run, bike, swim.

Road bike: A design focused on speed and maneuverability for long distances on a wide variety of terrains. Bent or dropped handlebar ends promote a more aerodynamic position than sitting upright.

Repeats: A format of exercise or training that makes use of several (often five to ten) short periods of high-speed swimming, biking, or running followed by a period of recovery.

Run leg: The third segment of a triathlon, in which participants run a specified distance.

Sighting: A technique in open-water swimming to maintain a straight line toward a turn buoy or the exit. It involves periodically looking ahead at a marker on the swim course.

Splits: Times to complete each of the legs of a triathlon or other multisport race and each transition between the legs.

Sprint triathlon: A triathlon format often comprising a 0.25 to 0.5 mile (400 to 800 meter) swim, a 12 to 15 mile (19 to 24 km) bike, and a 3.1 mile (5 km) run.

Super Sprint triathlon: A triathlon format comprising shorter distances, often half of those employed for the Sprint triathlon.

Swim leg: The first segment of a traditional triathlon, in which participants swim a specified distance.

Swim wave: A group of participants who start the swim leg of a triathlon together.

SWOLF: A word formed from "swimming" and "golf" to provide a measure of swimming efficiency. As with golf, a lower *swolf* is better because it comes from a more efficient stroke.

Time-trial start: A format for starting a triathlon in which participants begin one at a time, often five to ten seconds apart.

Time-trial bike: Like the triathlon bike, this design focuses on aerodynamic efficiency. However, the triathlon bike sacrifices some efficiency in favor of comfort for rides of several hours required for longer triathlon distances.

T1: The transition from swim to bike in a triathlon performed in standard order.

T2: The transition from bike to run in a triathlon performed in standard order.

Transition: (noun) Sometimes called the *transition area*. A secured space in a triathlon where athletes switch between different legs of the race, such as swimming, biking, and running. They also keep items used in a triathlon there, such as their bike, running shoes, and swim equipment, when not being used in a race.

(verb) To add or change gear, clothing, and hydration between legs of a triathlon to prepare for the next stage of the race.

Transition area: see *transition (noun)*.

Transition mat: A small mat placed in a multisport athlete's transition space, often beside their bike, upon which athletes can stand while changing shoes.

Transition rack: The structure that holds triathletes' bikes in transition.

Transition time: The time to switch between legs in a triathlon or other multisport race.

Triathlon bike: A design aimed at placing the rider in an aerodynamic position to reduce air resistance. Triathlon bikes prioritize achieving speed in a straight line, but they can also corner and climb.

Tri-bike: See *triathlon bike*.

Tri-suit: A one-piece garment worn by triathletes. The suit is designed for use in all legs of a triathlon or multisport race.

Triathlete: An individual who competes in triathlons.

Triathlon: A multisport race comprising swimming, biking, and running segments or legs.

USA Triathlon: Abbreviation: USAT. This is the national governing body for triathlon, duathlon, Aquathlon, aquabike, winter triathlon, off-road triathlon, and paratriathlon in the

United States. USA Triathlon is a member federation of the U.S. Olympic & Paralympic Committee and the World Triathlon. Source: https://www.usatriathlon.org/about.

Wave: A group of triathletes who begin the swim (usually an open-water swim) at the same time.

Wetsuit: Neoprene garment that provides buoyancy and insulation to triathletes and other multisport athletes during the swim. To provide the full range of swimming motion, triathlon wetsuits are made of thinner material compared to those used for surfing or diving.

www.ingramcontent.com/pod-product-compliance
Lightning Source LLC
Chambersburg PA
CBHW071703120626
46550CB00001B/85